Praise for

THE ART OF ACTION

"Stephen Bungay has something genuinely interesting to tell us. His book is not one of those vacuous essays in 'leadership qualities' of the 'how would Napoleon/MacArthur/Alexander the Great have turned around General Motors' variety... What makes this book worth reading is the way in which Mr. Bungay calls time on an entire culture of gobbledygook. You don't succeed in warfare by having vague objectives and issuing ambiguous orders. And you shouldn't expect to succeed in business that way, either."

Laurence Eyton for *Wall Street Journal*

"What do you get if you cross a military historian with a management consultant? You get this fascinating book by Stephen Bungay... Bungay is as comfortable with management as he is with history and here cleverly draws on his knowledge of the latter to influence his thinking... A must-read for any would-be strategist."

Director Magazine

"At its most simple, executing strategy is about planning what to do in order to achieve certain outcomes. The challenge is often making sure that the actions we have planned are actually carried out until the desired outcomes are achieved. In his new book The Art of Action, author Stephen Bungay reveals all."

CEO Magazine

*The Prussian General Staff, under the elder von Moltke...
did not expect a plan of operations to survive beyond the
first contact with the enemy. They set only the broadest of
objectives and emphasized seizing unforeseen opportunities as they arose... Strategy was not a lengthy action plan.
It was the evolution of a central idea through continually
changing circumstances.*

Jack Welch, 1981

*Strategy is a system of heuristics. It is more than science,
it is the application of knowledge to practical life, the evolution of an original guiding idea under constantly changing circumstances, the art of taking action under the
pressure of the most difficult conditions.*

Helmuth von Moltke, 1871

THE ART OF ACTION

How Leaders Close the Gaps
between
Plans, Actions and Results

STEPHEN BUNGAY

NICHOLAS BREALEY
PUBLISHING

London • Boston

First published in Great Britain by Nicholas Brealey Publishing in 2011
An imprint of John Murray Press
A division of Hodder & Stoughton Ltd,
An Hachette UK company

This edition published in 2021

2

A CIP catalogue record for this title is available from the British Library

Hardback ISBN 978 1 529 37696 8
Ebook ISBN 978 1 529 38366 9

Printed and bound in Great Britain by Clays Ltd, Elcograf S.p.A.

John Murray Press policy is to use papers that are natural, renewable
and recyclable products and made from wood grown in sustainable
forests. The logging and manufacturing processes are expected to
conform to the environmental regulations of the country of origin.

John Murray Press   Nicholas Brealey Publishing
Carmelite House   Hachette Book Group
50 Victoria Embankment   Market Place, Center 53, State Street
London EC4Y 0DZ   Boston, MA 02109, USA

www.nicholasbrealey.com

CONTENTS

PREFACE TO THE FIRST EDITION

Most lives have threads running through them. Some start in childhood, some in later life. Some break off and resurface later. Some are continuous. Sometimes, a few threads come together. This book is the result of some disparate threads in my life doing just that.

As a boy, I was fascinated by military history. It began with playing with soldiers and making models of tanks and aircraft. As a teenager, I became more interested in how they were handled, and played wargames. The fascination shifted from machines and soldiers to strategy and tactics.

Life had more apparently serious demands to make on me, and the pressure of exams pushed models and wargames into the background. I studied Modern Languages at Oxford and wrote a doctoral thesis about the German philosopher Hegel. I realized how little people in England really understand about German intellectual and cultural history. Germany was still seen as the old foe. If you go back beyond the twentieth century though, Germany was England's old friend. I made my own friends there. Different as it was from my own motherland, Germany became a sort of intellectual fatherland for me.

As the demands of education were replaced by the demands of earning a living, I decided to join The Boston Consulting Group (BCG). I joined because working there seemed to be a very good way of learning about business and how an economy actually works. It was an unknown field for me, but I was drawn in by the reactivation of a thread: BCG were strategy consultants. Armies are not the only organizations which need strategies. Working as a business consultant was a way of understanding more about that curious business of strategy.

I stayed at BCG for nearly 20 years and, predictably, some of them were spent in Germany. I worked for clients in most sectors of the economy, which enabled me to discern patterns of success and failure which cut across all businesses. I became more and more interested in how organizations work, and was an early member of BCG's Organization Practice Group. Strategy was hard-nosed stuff, understood in terms of analysis and a calculator. Organization was "touchy-feely," soft stuff understood in terms of human behavior and judgment. However, in the back of my mind was the thought that the real hard men in the military took the soft stuff very seriously. They seemed to believe that success came from bringing the hard calculating and soft motivational sides together. They also seemed to believe that the soft stuff was more difficult than the hard stuff. They talked a lot about leadership; so did people in business. I wanted to go back and take a closer look.

In 1996, in a move between BCG's Munich and London offices, I took some time off to write a book about a battle which has long haunted my imagination, the Battle of Britain. With half a manuscript to show for my labors I went back to work, but when I left BCG in 1999, I took more time off to finish it before taking up a new job. I found a publisher and with the 60th anniversary of the battle coming up in 2000, I completed the book and *The Most Dangerous Enemy* duly appeared in September. In writing it, I went back to the fatherland and spent a week going through German archives, which helped me to develop a new perspective. I picked up an old thread.

My publishers commissioned me to write a book about the desert war of 1940–42, and *Alamein* appeared in 2002. They found my approach to military history refreshing because, with the habits of a consultant now being second nature, I saw battles not as clashes between nations – as the Battle of Britain is usually portrayed – nor as clashes between individual commanders – as Alamein is usually portrayed – but as clashes between organizations. I felt that examining things at this level offered better explanations of events and it seemed that many readers agreed.

The experience of a management consultant could add something to history. But I also felt that something could be gained the other way round: bringing the lessons of history to business.

I had become convinced that creating great organizations and devising great strategies is not a science but an art. In science our knowledge grows and builds on the past. There is progression. The sum of scientific understanding is greater today than in the past. In contrast in art, there are peaks and troughs over time. There is no progression. Artists today are not better than Leonardo or Michelangelo.

So it is with organizational development and strategy. Commanders today are not better than Julius Caesar or Napoleon. Things that have been mastered are forgotten. Each generation has to relearn old lessons and acquire old skills. They just apply the same principles to new situations. To learn the art of strategy and the art of creating organizations capable of executing strategy, we have to study the past and develop our skills through practice.

It was the writing of *Alamein* that prompted me to dive further into history in seeking some answers to problems my clients were grappling with.

In February 1941, General Erwin Rommel turned up in the North African desert with a modestly sized force called the Deutsches Afrika Korps and, despite intractable logistical problems, proceeded to give the British 8th Army a hard time for the next 18 months. With great consistency, the German army in North Africa was fast, flexible, and adaptive. They seized and exploited every opportunity their ponderous opponents gave them and yet always seemed to be working together to realize a cunning plan. At the time the British were baffled because Germans were supposed to be unimaginative, methodical, and slow, their national character shaped by "teutonic thoroughness." Explaining the campaign as a clash of nations did not seem to work very well. So the British came up with an alternative explanation: it was all about individuals.

Rommel was quickly dubbed the "Desert Fox" and lauded by his opponents as a military genius. By 1942, he was the general most admired within the ranks of the British Army and even Churchill paid him a compliment in the House of Commons. In 1950, a British officer, Desmond Young, published a biography containing a foreword by Field Marshal Auchinleck, one of Rommel's direct opponents. In it he wrote: "Germany produces many ruthlessly efficient generals: Rommel stood out amongst them because he had overcome the innate rigidity of the German military mind and was a master of improvisation." He was able to do so because he was not "a typical Junker officer, a product of the Prussian military machine... and it may well be that this accounts for his amazing – and it was amazing – success as a leader of men in battle."[1] In the body of the book, Young points out that Rommel was a Swabian from Württemberg, "the home of common sense in Germany," tucked away in the southwest of the country far away from the rigid Prussians in the northeast. Comparing him with a few young men he knew in the British Army, Young concludes that Rommel was a member of "this small company of exceptional young men, only on the wrong side."[2] So he was really British by nature, just born in the wrong place. National characteristics again, in a slightly more convoluted form than usual.

I have to confess that I did not find this very convincing.

If it is true, how did Rommel manage, overnight, to transform the 45,000 German soldiers under his command into fast, flexible improvisers? After all, there must have been quite a few rigid Prussians among them. And why did he not have the same effect on the 55,000 Italians he also commanded? If it all depended on him, why didn't things break down when he was not there? He was often away, out of touch with his headquarters, riding with a reconnaissance unit in the trackless desert. Yet decision making never faltered. Furthermore, the German Army showed the same characteristics in all theaters of the war, no matter who was in charge. When the Allies landed at Salerno in Italy in 1943, the Germans had them bottled up within hours and the same thing happened again at Anzio the following year. Rommel was long gone.

Within the German Army talent pool, Rommel was regarded as an exceptional small unit and divisional commander, bold and thrusting. He was a great operator. But he did not have the depth of intellect or the mental toughness of a Manstein or Guderian. His own subordinates regarded him as very hard driving but rather unimaginative. Rommel was a Picton, not a Wellington.

So what was going on in the desert all those years ago?

I began to work on the hypothesis that it was not nations or individuals that mattered, but the German Army as an organization. I looked at how it performed elsewhere, examined its equipment and organization, and then its approach to command and control. Here, some lights began to go on. I tracked things back in time, down increasingly obscure paths leading to officer selection and training and other good old-fashioned HR stuff, which in turn led to behavioral and cultural norms developed in the nineteenth century. The answer became clear: Rommel had inherited an intelligent organization in which the characteristics he displayed were inculcated in every officer. He was superb at running it – but it had been created by somebody else, many decades before. And that creator was a Prussian.

As I explored all this, I also began to realize that interesting though the desert war was, the implications went far beyond it. Back at work I was dealing every day with client organizations which were as ponderous and bogged down with plans as the 8th Army. The big issue was not strategy but *executing* strategy. There was plenty of activity, but not much action. The business environment had become fast moving and unpredictable, but business organizations had been designed for a slower, more predictable world. The word "chaos" was becoming fashionable in the management literature, but nobody seemed to have a simple way of dealing with it. The business environment was becoming more and more like the way war has been for about 200 years. The type of organization needed to survive and prosper in such an environment had already been developed and had built up practical experience of what it takes over the best part of 70 years – but nobody knew about it. What if its practices could be transferred to business organizations?

I had the conceptual framework and there were also tools and techniques. I adapted them for business use and tried them out in client work. At first I did not say where they had come from. Then I found that people were interested, so I let them have the whole story. Working with various colleagues, some of them ex-military, we refined and simplified the approaches and started to get results across a wide range of businesses. Although there are general principles and approaches, every situation is specific. Applying the principles is not a science but an art.

So the threads came together: military history, strategy and tactics, German culture, the nature of organizations, and leadership. It has been a very personal journey. It has taken me closer to the heart of what it takes to build great organizations, but I have not yet arrived at that destination. The road goes ever on and on. This book is a milestone along the route; the milestone is the point at which activity is turned into action.

PREFACE TO THE
TENTH ANNIVERSARY EDITION

At the beginning of 2021, my publisher got in touch to say that they had decided to mark the tenth anniversary of this book by re-issuing it, news which somewhat brightened the sombre skies of a January spent in lockdown.

The main reason they gave was its rather unusual sales history. Apparently, the sales of most business books peak soon after publication and then decline to a trickle. *The Art of Action*, however, has sold steadily year-on-year. This suggests that the main generator of sales is word of mouth. That, in turn, suggests that people who try to put the principles it describes into action find that they work. That is what matters most to me.

THE TEXT

We concluded that the main text was fit for purpose and should, therefore, remain unchanged but for one thing – the name given to the principles the book describes.

The principles have a long history. Organizations which have embraced them include the Roman Army and the eighteenth-century Royal Navy. They seem to have done so quite independently of each other. Both learned from failure, concluding that if they wanted to be successful, given the uncertainties of the environment they had to operate in and the limitations of the information and communication technologies of their day, they had to find a way of reconciling unity of effort and freedom of action. They remain among the most successful military organizations in history.

It was only in modern times that the principles were given a name. In Chapter 2 I outline the story of how they were developed, again quite independently, by the Prussian Army in the nineteenth century, and how the distinctive approach they represented was given a name for the first time: *Auftragstaktik*. That name was first coined by its opponents, but it stuck, and was inherited by the German Army of the twentieth century.

The Prussian case is particularly interesting because they had at their disposal technologies such as the telegraph, which could have been used to exercise tight control over large forces. In general, an increase in information processing and communications capacity leads to an increase in central control. The person generally regarded as the father of *Auftragstaktik*, Helmuth von Moltke, made the deliberate and controversial choice to resist temptation and give his people freedom of action, within bounds. Plenty of others then and since have taken the opposite path. It was a renunciation with far-reaching consequences.

After WWII, the effectiveness of *Auftragstaktik* was ruefully noted by those who had fought the German Army, and they deliberately copied it. Others followed. Its military incarnation is known today in the English-speaking world as "mission command".

The business world was clearly not going to get very far with "mission command", let alone *Auftragstaktik*, so I had to come up with something else. After a lot of agonizing, I let myself be inspired by Jack Welch's phrase "planful opportunism", and came up with "directed opportunism". I thought at the time that it was not very snappy, but it did accurately convey the core idea.

It never caught on.

So I decided to let others decide. Once *The Art of Action* came out, I spent a large part of my time talking about it in conferences and helping clients to embed the principles in their organizations. In doing so, they had to tell people what this approach was. Some of them simply called it "art of action", but others called it "leading through intent". The latter group became a majority, so I started using the term as well. It seems to make sense to people on the ground.

As a result, the main change to this text over the original is that all references to "directed opportunism" have been erased, and replaced with "leading through intent". I ought to have come up with that in the first place, but now it is there as the result of a democratic process.

THE RECEPTION

All writers publish their work because they want to be read. But the writers of business books also want to influence practice. Influence can be exerted indirectly through others propagating their ideas and directly through business leaders putting their ideas into action.

The basic principles of leading through intent have been picked up by others in various virtual media and a number of publications.[1] The website www.activeagileleadership.com offers a training course based on it.

One recent publication is especially gratifying because it does not simply take up the ideas, but actually develops them further. The author, Martin Samuels, is a senior manager in the UK civil service, but his book is a work of military history, *Piercing the Fog of War*, published by Helion in 2019. In it the author takes the "three gaps" model and derives from it eight different ways of exercising what the military call command and control, and what we might call directing and managing. He then illustrates these different permutations as they appear in British and German doctrine, and then in two in-depth case studies of actual engagements from the two world wars.

The "three gaps" model was designed to conceptualize the problem of execution, and hence the challenges any potential solution had to meet. As such, it is central to the book. However, the book also contains other models which offer ways of under-standing more specific issues and some of these have begun to take on a life of their own.

One of them is the "executives' trinity" which is explained in Chapter 7. It is based on military thinking about management, leadership and command. The idea of the trinity has its origins in a paper by Brian Howieson and Howard Kahn, which appeared in 2002 in an RAF publication called *Air Power Leadership: Theory and Practice.*[2] I have been asked to give a number of talks on the subject and, at one client, we structured a leadership development programme around it. It was the main theme of an international conference hosted by the Corporate Research Forum in Berlin in 2014 and, in 2021, the Berlin-based consulting firm Craft Agile launched a training programme based on it.

Another conceptual model, which is explained on only two pages of the book, has attracted a level of attention which was completely unexpected.

In Chapter 3 I argue that alignment and autonomy are not opposite ends of a spectrum but define two independent axes of a matrix. In order to explain von Moltke's solution to the problem of execution, I suggest that he demanded high alignment and high autonomy at the same time. This is really no more than common sense because the more alignment you have, the more autonomy you can afford to grant people. The trick is using the right alignment mechanisms. A lot of managers equate alignment with control. Instead, von Moltke formulated an intent and created a common shared understanding of its implications, up and down and across his organization. The techniques for doing so have been refined since his day, but it is the basic principle of achieving high alignment and high autonomy that seems to have struck a chord with many, as a Google search of "alignment and autonomy" will show.

One company which picked this up was Spotify. In 2014, Henrik Kniberg, now an Agile and Lean coach at Crisp in Stockholm, posted an engaging animated two-part presentation called "Spotify's Engineering Culture" which describes the "alignment–autonomy" matrix and some of the ways the company was trying to get into the "high-high" area. This short piece attracted a lot of attention and became something of a classic within the agile community. The role *The Art of Action* has played within that community is one of the consequences I least expected.

AGILE STRATEGY

In 2011, I was invited out of the blue to give a keynote speech at the Lean Kanban Central Europe Conference in Munich.

I had no idea why software developers would be interested in what I had to offer. It looked as if it would be a waste of time. My agent shared my skepticism. The speaking fee was very modest and I was tentatively holding the date they wanted for another client. Then the client changed the date. Because I had blocked the whole week, I was free on the few days following the conference, so I could stay over and visit friends in Munich I'd been wanting to see for a long time. And the Oktoberfest was on. So, in the end, I agreed to turn up.

I gave a talk which summarized the principles of the book. To my surprise, it generated a high level of interest. The organizer later told me it was given the highest rating of all the sessions in the conference. The interest grew rather than abated, and led to a series of further contacts with individuals and companies. Two years later, I gave another keynote speech about the executive's trinity at the Lean Kanban Central Europe Conference in Hamburg. What had happened?

What the audience at these talks heard was a set of principles similar to theirs but expressed in a different language and positioned, not at the level of processes, but at the level of operations and strategy. Their interest was excited, in particular, because they were facing the issue of how to scale agile practices and create an agile organization. Leading through intent offered a way of doing so that complemented agile processes.

This led to a range of enduring contacts with the agile community, including Mattias Skarin of Crisp in Stockholm. In 2019, after my business colleague Mark Bouch and I had run a workshop on leading through intent for agile coaches at Crisp, Mattias suggested that there was general demand to learn its techniques and that we should create a website dedicated to the theme of agile strategy. After delays caused by the pandemic in 2020, the website www.agilestrategy.co.uk went live in 2021.

Partly as a result of the experience of the pandemic, "agile" has become a business buzzword, so much so that fatigue, not to say cynicism, is setting in. This is a pity because, as a method for developing software, agile practices are superior in every way to the old "waterfall" approach. They have spread to processes beyond software development and many corporates are trying to become agile organizations by applying them at scale. There are now a range of methods for doing so and every major consulting firm has an "agile" practice area.

As usual when a new idea emerges in the business world, practice often falls short of aspiration, with old wine being poured into new bottles. In the case of agile, sometimes not even the bottles are new, just the labels on them. Meetings are dubbed "scrums", and the months separating them are re-named "sprints" but the change of name fails to produce the hoped-for miracle.

In parallel, consumption of the real new wine of agile practices has been rising, with overwhelmingly positive results. There is now a lot of talk about agile strategy. On this point I remain of the opinion that simply scaling up the number of agile teams will not, in and of itself, result in an agile organization, let alone an agile strategy.

I and two colleagues at the Strategic Management Centre in London, Rebecca Homkes and Anthony Freeling, began thinking about how to make strategy agile well before the term itself became popular. Agility is the ability to adapt rapidly and without disruption to changing circumstances. We approached the issue by thinking about the problem that agility addresses, which is the uncertainty and unpredictability of the environment, a problem commonly summarized by another buzzword, the acronym VUCA (volatility, uncertainty, complexity and ambiguity). We drew on a wide range of historical models such as systems thinking and Boyd's OODA loop (which stands for observe, orient, decide, act), as well as the thinking of Helmuth von Moltke (which is explored in this book), and married them with practices common in startups and innovative, high growth organizations. The result was a set of practices which we now describe collectively as "directional strategy".

Leading through intent, as described in this book, is an operating model which enables an organization to *execute* strategy in an unpredictable environment. Directional strategy is an approach designed to enable you to *develop* strategy in an uncertain environment. The two are complementary, and both can be complemented by agile processes which increase the speed and quality of innovation at the customer interface.

An organization can, therefore, become agile at three levels: at the level of processes by adopting agile methodologies, at the strategic level by adopting directional strategy, and at the operational level by adopting leading through intent. Leading through intent offers a link between strategy and processes and, in that way, is one element in achieving the Holy Grail of the day – organizational agility. To that extent, *The Art of Action* might be positioned today in that specific context, as well as the general context of how to execute strategy.

PRACTICE

Since publication, I have helped a wide range of companies to embed the principles of leading through intent, often in partnership with Mark Bouch. A few years ago, he and I, together with one of our first clients, David Roblin, published an article in *Pharmaceutical Executive Europe* which summarized what we had learned from these experiences. Our observations are not specific to the pharmaceutical industry, so it is worth summarizing them here:

1   Organizations used to high levels of autonomy will follow a different change path to ones used to high levels of centralized decision-making, but, in all cases, work on alignment comes first.

2   Most organizations have some form of matrix structure. Leading through intent requires clear roles and responsibilities and some matrix structures make accountability so diffuse that they have to be modified before progress can be made. This does not necessarily mean changing structure, but clarifying *how* the organization is intended to work.

3   The simplicity of the concepts and language enables people at all levels to relate to it. Creating a common language using simple concepts like "intent", "what and why" and "main effort" is of value in itself.

4   The role of the top management is to write a statement of intent themselves and request backbriefs, and to constantly reinforce the principles. Unsurprisingly, a lot depends on how far they "walk the talk", as the common saying goes. Nevertheless, the most important work is that done below the C-suite at the level of distributed leaders, who are running operations. They are typically one or two levels below the ExCo. Sometimes it is even possible to start at that level if there is sufficient sense of direction from above, and then build back up. The briefing-backbriefing cycle looks like a cascade but is, in fact, a process of sense-making, unpacking the meaning of the higher intent to translate it into sets of actions, so, given a modicum of high level guidance, it can start almost anywhere.

5   Making focused choices at all levels is critical to success. Projects not directly supporting the overall intent should be dropped. People often have to decide not to pursue some options in order to make sure that others are a success. We all know that resources are limited. We should also recognize that fact and turn down the volume of noise about stretch goals, BHAGs and the like.

6   We have experimented with e-learning programmes but concluded – for now at least – that although they can provide some reinforcement, the workshops at the heart of the process have to be conducted between the people involved, either face-to-face or virtually. Bringing together multiple functions is particularly valuable. It has also become clear that single workshops are not enough. Strong follow-up is needed and objective setting and budgeting processes, as well as performance management and reward systems, must be aligned to create an integrated operating rhythm of reviews.

7   Internal facilitators and champions play an important role, the former as support to the line and the latter as sponsors. The ultimate aim is full internal ownership, and the most successful cases follow a journey from a "new initiative" to "the way we do things round here" so that leading through intent becomes part of the culture.

8   In companies with a history of central control, there is likely to be resistance from those who perceive a loss of influence or authority. We are not alone in observing that a top-down control culture is also "demand driven" – over time people may become groomed to prefer to receive detailed direction. In most cases this is a learned behaviour, which can be unlearned. Leaders have to actively encourage initiative and resist the temptation to solve people's problems for them. They need to learn instead how to "bound" people's problems and provide them with coaching, support and encouragement. Some

people will struggle with this and a few will find it impossible to give up control. They remain a minority and, for the majority, the risks are low and the rewards are high.

9   In order to really take root, leading through intent cannot be pushed, but must be pulled in. There is only so much central functions can do and, at some point, the line must take the initiative. The first impulse often comes from HR and a leadership development programme, but the best results are achieved when an operational leader decides that they are going to make it happen and leading through intent is positioned simply as the way operations are going to be run, day to day.

10 Getting first results takes longer than most people expect, and they will fade unless there is persistence. Distractions are constant. The most common mistake is to declare victory too early, assume it has been embedded and to launch a new initiative. History shows that what has been gained can also be lost. Never give up.

I am not naïve enough to claim that leading through intent solves all your problems and I refuse to make facile claims about its effects on results. Success is dependent on many things, including luck. However, there are some patterns. The following benefits are fairly consistently evident:

❑ Increased speed of decision-making and shorter cycle times;

❑ An improvement in productivity because of greater clarity and focus;

❑ More creative problem solving and innovation throughout the organization;

❑ Faster learning and improved ability to deal with complexity and uncertainty;

❑ Higher employee engagement, with a majority of people – often over 90% – reporting greater clarity about how to deliver strategic goals and a greater sense of personal responsibility.

Common sense suggests that these factors will help to improve the bottom line. Quantified proof of that will have to wait, maybe forever.

Lacking the numbers they would need to make a business case, more cautious practitioners might like some other reasons to embrace leading through intent. I would cite three.

The first is that I adopt the medical principle found in the Hippocratic Oath: "first do no harm". I apply it to strategy development. Strategy builds on a company's strengths, so it is as well to find out what they are before changing direction. But it applies equally to operations, and in introducing a new operating model like leading through intent, one needs to be on the look-out for side-effects. The methods of the Total Quality movement of the 1980s tended to suppress innovation. The wave of Business Process Reengineering of the 1990s proved to be disruptive and was often just another name for downsizing, with negative effects on employee engagement.

So far, we have not noticed any negative side-effects from leading through intent, but one needs to be mindful. It would be possible to use the strategy briefing process as a mechanism for tight control rather than as intended, which is to set direction, define everybody's area of freedom, and keep your finger on the pulse. The whole approach assumes a high level of competence and a willingness to accept accountability for outcomes on the part of those given freedom of action. Although we have not directly encountered any cases in which middle and junior management was generally not up to the demands, they must exist. Every management team will need to build the skills needed to create alignment but, if they lack competence in doing their basic job, leading through intent will founder.

A mitigating factor here is the second reason worth citing: awareness of limits. There are cases in which individual autonomy has little value and tight central control is called for. Von Moltke himself documented one example when the passage of two armies through difficult terrain required tight co-ordination from the center, and he and his headquarters staff took over direct control of operations until that passage was completed (see Chapter 7).

Equally, this case shows the advantage of using leading through intent as the default operating model. It is flexible. It is always possible to tighten it up if circumstances require, and then relax it again. However, if tight central control is the default and it is then loosened without the requisite alignment disciplines in place, the result will either be chaos or paralysis – because nobody knows what to do – or indeed some combination of the two. That is not a happy prospect. Leading through intent is a safer default option.

The third reason for having confidence in the efficacy of leading through intent is that behind the specific practices developed in modern times by military organizations lie much older principles, which have proved themselves again and again and, when brought together, offer the reassurance of intellectual coherence.

TIME AND CHANCE

A lot of the research which went into the writing of this book was a form of intellectual archaeology. Digging into the past revealed the equivalent of robust architectural structures as well as skillfully crafted artefacts. My task was not to transport them carefully into a museum for display, but to translate them into terms we can understand so that they can be recovered for the present in the only form that matters, which is practical adoption. In that sense, my role was simply to be a vessel for the message and to distort it as little as possible.

I thought I knew what the message was and who needed to hear it. In fact, I was not entirely right about either.

The first decade of the life of *The Art of Action* has been characterized by serendipity, and I expect this to continue. There was no concerted marketing effort and I had no grand plan. Some of the effects were expected, many were not. To me, the matrix showing alignment and autonomy as two independent variables was just a step in an argument explaining von Moltke's solution to the problems posed by the three gaps. I did not expect it to grab people's attention in the way it has. I only gave a talk at the Lean Kanban Central Europe Conference in 2011 because I wanted to see some friends in Munich. The agile community turned out to be an important audience and their reaction has taken me down new paths I had not foreseen.

I have slowly realized that serendipity is the way the world works. Client relationships have been driven by it as well. I had written a business book. Yet it has infiltrated the world of motor-sport.

Long before the book was published, a former Surgeon Commander in the Royal Navy called David Slavin discovered, by googling, that I was working on how to apply mission command to business. He knew all about mission command from the Navy, so he invited me to introduce it to Pfizer in Sandwich. Some time later, he visited McLaren to discuss their expertise in telemetry, which he thought could play a role in conducting clinical trials. He mentioned me to them, so they invited me to give a talk. I ended up running some workshops for Paddy Lowe, who later left McLaren to become Technical Director of the newly formed Mercedes F1 team. They had just signed up Lewis Hamilton. Paddy invited me to give an evening talk at the team's first offsite in January 2014 and introduced me to Toto Wolff. Toto liked what he heard, so I ran some workshops for the leadership team, all of whom got the book. Things developed from there. My colleague Rebecca Homkes got involved. The rest is Formula One history.

Von Moltke, of course, would not have been surprised by any of this. I like to imagine that he would have smiled and given me a nod of approval for not planning beyond the circumstances I could foresee and adapting to each newly created situation.

THE ART OF ACTION

When authors are writing, the text that results is theirs. When they publish, the work is given a life of its own and it begins to belong to its readers as well. Texts are interpreted. What their authors meant is one factor in their meaning. What their readers are searching for is another. The result is like a tune with variations.

In sounding the opening theme, I hope I have done so in a way that encourages you to join the other players who have turned the message from the past into living practice today.

Stephen Bungay
London, May 2021

CHAPTER ONE

THE PROBLEM

What Do You Want Me to Do?

*The intelligence of an organization is never equal to the
sum of the intelligence of the people within it*

AN UNANSWERED QUESTION

While the gray December rain drizzled down outside, the ground
floor of the hotel had all the lights, sounds, and colors of a stage
show. A well-known global technology company was holding its
annual senior executive conference. The hundred or so top people in the company were listening to their bright, dynamic chief
executive give his "state-of-the-nation" address, to be followed
by an open question-and-answer session.

The CEO's message was hard, but he was engaging and convincing. The markets were tougher than they had been in decades,
new competitors had established themselves, customers were
making higher demands, and technological change would
require massive expenditure. Nevertheless, there was reason for
cautious optimism. A new strategy was in place: a new emphasis
on customer service, exploiting leading-edge technology to create a new generation of products, and a series of initiatives
around people and culture. The organizational structure had
already been changed. The company had a great brand and great
people. But – and here he paused – not a lot was happening.

He made his appeal. The company needed pace. Things were
changing too slowly. The markets would only wait so long. The
strategy had been debated and formulated twelve months before,
signed off six months before, communicated internally and

externally – but it was not happening. Sure, there were still open questions; there always would be. Nevertheless, the people in the room could not all meet again in a year's time and be saying the same things. The time for debate was over. It was time for action, to get on and do it. The future was in their hands.

The CEO was impressive. He spoke without notes. He was in command of the issues; his words were fluent, but not facile. He was open about the difficulties and made it clear he was confident but concerned. The applause was genuine. He sipped from his glass of water and moved on to the Q&A session. Be open, please. No holding back, tell it like it is, challenge anything and everything. Let's put things on the table today, not tomorrow.

There were a few questions about what was going to be done about this or that. Then over on the left a woman took the wandering microphone. She was responsible for a sizeable chunk of the business. "I understand the strategy," she said. "I agree with it. I think it's a good one, perhaps the only possible one. We have talked about it a lot and communicated it down the line. There are lots of initiatives. But…" – here she paused slightly – "what do you want me to *do*?"

The question was precisely placed at the intersection point between naïvety and sophistication and intoned with a note of plaintive frustration. The smiling nods and approving murmurs from the audience suggested that it would have been unwise to interpret it as naïve; that indeed, she had had the courage to ask the risky question that everyone wanted answered.

The reply was measured, but evinced frustration of its own. As I said, the CEO observed, we do not have all the answers. But surely you don't expect me to tell all of you what to do? This is not a command-and-control organization. You are big boys and girls. I am not running this company, we all are. We have a strategy, we have long-term objectives, we all have budgets. We are running a business and we have a direction. It is for each of us to decide what we have to do in our own area and to get on with it.

This response was not unreasonable. That, surely, is what a modern, devolved structure is all about. The question had not sounded like a request for direction; there seemed to be plenty of that already. Nevertheless, her question remained unanswered. What was missing? In the hotel lobby, in the coffee breaks, over the buffet lunch, and in the bar in the evening I tried to find out. People were more than happy to talk.

The organization was lethargic but also full of frantic activity. People were working so hard that the HR people were seriously worried about issues of work–life balance and potential burnout. However, all this activity was having no discernable effect on the company's performance.

Revenues were falling, margins were eroding, service standards were deteriorating, and, most worrying of all, they were losing share of the already declining market to a confident new competitor. The sagging top line was rendering the burden of fixed costs insupportable. Everybody knew that and everybody knew what it meant: they would not all be there next year. Those who were there would have to work even harder. During the conference they had been canvassed for their views about the issues which needed to be addressed. As a result, more initiatives had been added to the already substantial list of long-term goals, medium-term objectives, and short-term priorities. Someone told me there were 11 of those. In the afternoon it became 17. There was much talk about "having a day job as well as all this."

The situation seemed to be very complex. There was uncertainty about the causal relationships between the mutually reinforcing elements of the doom loop they seemed to be in and therefore what to do about them. Should they cut costs or invest in revenue growth? Or both? There was uncertainty about what really mattered. Was it service or price or was the product suite too old? They needed to improve revenue, margins, and service, but how to do all three at once? Where should they start? Every time they discussed their problems people came up with new things to do and these were added to the lists.

To resolve the uncertainty, people held meetings to define and analyze what was wrong. The most common outcome of such meetings was the discovery of more problems, which extended the uncertainty. People started their conversations with "the reason this is a problem is…" In pondering the current state and what should be done, all sorts of subproblems emerged, along with reasons not to do things and why they would not work. Everything they could do would cost too much. There were things they might do but couldn't because they lacked information, be it about external markets or competitors, or internal information such as when a new product would be available. All agreed that they needed to find out more. Doing so took time.

The provocative and risky question from the floor had many echoes. They were all familiar with the strategy – or at least with the themes of the strategy. But nobody knew what they themselves should do. So everyone discussed the generalities of the overall situation and what "the company" ought to do. The most senior people were beginning to lose patience. There was a history of entrepreneurialism, but it was getting them nowhere. In fact, it was making things worse. They needed to leverage their scale globally, but as long as country managers were calling the shots and demanding scarce technical resources from the center to fix trivial local problems, the fundamental need for a new technology platform could never be addressed. To hell with entrepreneurialism; it was just an excuse for selfishness and waste. The center wanted to take charge. "We have to tell people *exactly* what we want them to do," one senior executive told me. "We must spell it out *in painful detail*," gritting his teeth as he uttered the words. He meant them.

Yet what were those actions he wanted to spell out so exactly? And if they were carried out, would they work? How, indeed, would the organization know if they worked? People in the operating units were skeptical, anxious that the center would indeed take control without knowing what it was doing. Country managers all had their stories about what disasters ensued when central initiatives were imposed. "They just don't understand that markets are different," I was told. "We're a global company. You can't do the same thing in Thailand as you do in Germany. Some of this stuff is just crazy, so we ignore it. They come up with something new every month anyway, so in a few weeks it will all go away and they will be on to something else... like the balanced scorecard."

As people failed to do what was wanted – either because they did not understand what was wanted in the first place or because they understood only too well and thought it was wrong – the resulting frustration and suspicion led in turn to a call for tighter control. As the initiatives specifying actions increased in number, so did the metrics specifying targets. These gradually gave way to metrics about actions. Input measures dominated output measures, and in plan reviews questions about what was being achieved were replaced with questions about how things were being done. Senior management spent much of their meeting time creating, discussing, and reviewing measures and numbers. The numbers themselves became very detailed, yet divorced from overall goals. Behavior became driven by targets rather than performance. A sales group spent substantial meeting time discussing the need to build a long-term relationship with a key customer, based on service. In the next session they focused on how to "push" product into that same customer in order to meet their targets.

Trust was eroding between the top and the bottom and across the market and technology functions. For all the metrics, accountability was very diffuse. In the complex matrix, few people were uniquely accountable for anything. However, in the quest to increase motivation and commitment, performance bonuses were being linked more tightly to specific measures. People objected that they were not in control of what they were being measured on. They were told to work more closely with their colleagues and get on with it. As distrust grew, so did resentment, and it turned into a sense of helplessness.

I was told that a member of the executive board had addressed a management team with a very clear mandate to make recommendations for the business that he would support at the board. When he left the room, the group said, "This will never happen – and what's the point anyway?" It was not that they did not trust him as an individual. They did not trust the organization, in part because of its poor track record in pushing things through and making them stick, and in part because they did not believe the board members were united. Stories about disagreements abounded. Differences in opinion, even differences of emphasis, were magnified in the tales that were told outside the boardroom door.

Things did not look good. Maybe the markets would turn. They must turn some time, although nobody knew when. To stand and wait would serve no one. What was the cause of the problems?

AN UNDIAGNOSED DISEASE

The following year, I was invited to do some work for the research and development arm of a global pharmaceutical company. The history and culture of this organization were very different.

The technology company had had a long history of devolved responsibility, with powerful country heads taking many important decisions. This worked well, but over time gave rise to duplication of effort and turned into an undisciplined failure to exploit scale through standardization. In contrast, the pharmaceutical company had a strong center, drug development was highly disciplined to meet the requirements of regulators, and there were a lot of standardized processes. That would surely enable the organization to get things done.

But not much was happening there either. In fact, it looked very much as if the whole industry was in a long-drawn-out crisis, trapped like a frog in a saucepan of water which was beginning to approach boiling point.

It is still in the saucepan. The world pharmaceutical industry is spending more and more to produce the same or less than it has done in the past. The length of time taken to bring a potential drug to market is 11–15 years. The trend is lengthening. The chance of a potential drug making it through the clinical trials process and being approved for use is about 1 in 20. The trend is declining. The average cost of a drug reaching approval has been estimated at about $800m. The trend is rising. People working in the vast R&D organizations of the industry are working harder and harder and achieving less and less. It is not unusual for someone to spend their whole career in drug development and never be part of a team which successfully brings a drug to market.

Something had to be done. That was already clear when I turned up for the first time at an R&D site of my new client on a bright summer afternoon.

Once again, there was a lot of activity. There was also a great deal of thinking. Strategies had been developed for exploiting scale, developing technology, managing risk, growing the pipeline, building trust, developing people, and much else besides. The talent and resources available were staggering. Every other employee in the R&D organization had a PhD in science or medicine or both, and the company was sitting on a cash pile with which it could acquire new expertise, invest in technology, or buy the rights to new drug compounds. Most of the world's leading consulting firms were employed on a regular basis, analyzing trends and future scenarios, developing new IT systems, and introducing new ideas to improve efficiency. There were impassioned internal debates about the virtues of focusing on big-ticket "blockbuster" drugs against smaller, targeted drugs, about a strategy based on precision medicine, about the role of new bio-markers and the deciphering of the human genome. All were being explored, but nothing much was being achieved.

While there were a lot of clever people who were very well informed, taking decisions was difficult. In fact, the greater the volume of information, the harder it was to decide what to do. Developing drugs is, by definition, pushing forward the boundaries of knowledge and entering areas of high uncertainty. So most decision-making bodies were committees of experts covering all the various disciplines which could have something to say. Because of the high risks inherent in the business and the serious potential consequences of making mistakes, decisions taken in one committee were reviewed in other, higher ones to ensure proper control. Approving decisions took months. By the time they had been approved, the situation had usually changed, new information was available, and the decision had to be reviewed again. Sometimes decisions were deliberately postponed in order to get more data, for there was always more to know. There was a quest to find the sort of certainty offered by science. It was never fulfilled.

Given the large number of specializations, the organization was very complex. The project teams actually running the drug trials cut across a matrix of country-based sites and global functions. This rendered it difficult to make accountability clear, especially as over the long life of a drug under development the makeup of the team would change. People's hard reporting line was to their functional line heads, who had prime responsibility for their evaluations. So the functional heads tended to have most sway over how people spent their time. All the functions had their own plans, objectives, and targets, and these ran into conflict with the projects. For example, the person leading the regulatory sub-team on a project just six weeks away from filing a new drug with the FDA was told by his functional head to attend a week-long meeting abroad about the latest developments in global regulatory affairs. He felt helplessly torn. Had he gone, the project would have missed its filing date, costing millions of dollars in lost revenue. In the end he stayed. The projects were the sole source of actual value creation, but the teams working on them often felt they were engaged in a peripheral activity.

Every member of a project team thus faced the daily problem of working out what they should do. They spent a lot of time in meetings and exchanging emails. Most emails were CCed out of fear of the consequences of leaving someone out or failing to syndicate a decision. Given the complexity of the issues involved, meetings went into a lot of detail in order to try to work out what mattered and what didn't. Given all the noise, some genuinely important things were passed over, for if someone had something to communicate it was very difficult for it to be heard. It was not uncommon for people in a meeting to ask for information which had already been circulated well in advance. They had not noticed it – and there was little time to read it anyway.

Things got bogged down. People spent all their working days in meetings or reading emails, but still had their own work to do for at least two bosses. In the end, frustration would drive some of them simply to do something, whether it made sense or not. Real decisions were made in informal encounters in the corridors and then announced later. They were not always good ones, but at least they moved the debate on. As no one was quite certain who was responsible for what, internal hierarchy dominated.

A submission was once radically altered at the last minute by a senior executive. The regulators rejected it, as the team had expected. This led to a long delay and a loss of credibility. The team could have dealt with the intervention had it come earlier, since they had the best information about the matter. In practice, seniority conferred the right to overrule any decision at any point, although it was not clear that the organization intended this to be the case.

So people became cynical about all the meetings, just turned up to be seen and deferred to the most senior person present. Many people stopped taking any decisions at all and delegated upwards. One senior executive responsible for a budget of $2bn told me that the last straw was when he had been asked by a refurbishment committee to decide on the color to paint the walls of a meeting room on the floor below. The people on the refurbishment committee either did not know what decision-making authority they had or were not prepared to use it. Few people knew what their freedoms were or where their boundaries lay. Because boundaries were so unclear, the only safe course of action was not to explore them, but to keep your head down and play safe. Stepping over them could result in punishment.

Stories did the rounds, like the one about the person who noticed that there was a lack of coordination between the US and European parts of her global study team and wrote to the leaders of both parts to suggest that they get together, copying in a senior representative of the line. She had no direct reply, but the senior person copied in complained to her boss that she was interfering in an area which was none of her concern. The leaders of the US and European parts of the team did indeed hold a global meeting, which did prove to be necessary.

Things had reached the point at which showing initiative or trying to put in an outstanding performance to achieve project team goals was felt to be positively dangerous. On one project, the leader of the regulatory work put in a massive effort to get the filing in on time and to a very high standard. In doing so, he put senior management under a lot of pressure to sign off quickly. He was subsequently passed over for further jobs and left the company. The project leader who supported him had to wait for a long time to get another assignment and also left. The reasons for this were unclear, but the word in the corridors was that he was punished for putting in an extraordinary effort. The organization appeared to reward compliance rather than initiative or creativity. The result was passivity and fear.

The desired outcome – an increase in the number of new drugs – was still missing from the picture, so controls were tightened. It was appreciated that "what gets measured gets done," so after a long IT project, a new balanced scorecard system was finally signed off. It contained 64 individual metrics for each site. No one was quite sure which ones to use and there were some theological arguments about how many each person or function should have in each of the four main categories. The process for setting budgets and business targets was run by Finance, and the process for personal targets was run by HR. Both had their own methods. The result was two sets of targets which were overlapping but different. No one was quite sure what the organization really wanted of them.

The pharmaceutical industry is strictly regulated. There has to be an audit trail to show exactly how each step in a trial has been conducted. So the trials are run against a set of Standard Operating Procedures, or SOPs, which are agreed with the regulators. They act as a control on how things are done. No one was quite sure exactly how many there were – some rumors went as high as 2,500 – because nobody knew them all, and they were in any case continually being changed and updated. To make sure that it achieved the highest standards of excellence and compliance, the company put enormous effort into SOP training, but people inevitably tried to avoid it. This raised the specter of potential litigation, so participation was more rigorously enforced. The amount of training was specified and if people failed to put in the required number of days, they would lose points from their bonus entitlement.

One woman with 15 years' experience was informed in an email from corporate headquarters that she had to complete her SOP training by the end of the month or lose some points. This occurred one week before the drug she was working on was due to be filed. She was leading a subteam which had managed two unusually complex trials in record time. Nobody seemed to care about that. It certainly had no effect on her bonus, which was now under threat of being cut. She managed to squeeze in the training in the end. Some of the new SOPs had been written by people she had herself trained some years before.

***

There is something systemic to these examples. They show large organizations, rich in resources and full of talented people, trying to execute strategy and failing. One organization gave its managers a high level of autonomy; the other was highly centralized and aligned all its operations around tightly defined processes. Both ended up exhibiting similar behavior. The malaise transcends business sectors and nationalities. It is an organizational disease which threatens to be an international pandemic, although the disease is undiagnosed.

These two examples describe a set of symptoms which are all around us. We see organizations operating in a complex, uncertain environment. In an attempt to cope with the complexity the organization grows complex as well. It becomes opaque, which creates internal uncertainty to add to the uncertainty outside. Different parts of the organization are concerned with different things and seek to do a good job by optimizing them. The results clash. Faced with uncertainty, people search for more information; faced with complexity, they do more analysis. Meetings proliferate and decisions are delayed. People in the front line become frustrated at the lack of the decisions they need someone to make to let them get on with their job, and people at the top become frustrated at the apparent lack of action, although the level of activity is high. More initiatives are launched, increasing the level of activity. The psychological effect is to increase confusion. There is lots to do, but what will have the greatest effect and who should do it? Accountability becomes more diffuse, so controls proliferate. This slows things down and restricts the scope for front-line decision making. In an attempt to increase clarity, actions are specified in more detail. The emotional effect is an increase in cynicism and frustration. Trust erodes. The cycle is toxic.

The causal nexus is also unclear. Are people searching for more information and avoiding decisions because of the complexity of the environment? Or is the search for information creating complexity and rendering decision making more difficult? Or is the difficulty of taking decisions leading to the search for more information and creating more complexity? In any of the situations described, any or all of these may be the case, and probably are. At a fundamental level, every problem relates to every other and exacerbates it. There is no hierarchy of cause and effect but a set of reciprocal relations within a system: every cause is also an effect and vice versa.

We should not confuse the set of symptoms with the disease. If the observed effects are systemic, then the underlying causes must also be systemic and must be understood as a whole. It is a truism that in a complex system like the human body, an observed effect, like a yellowing of the skin, may indicate a problem in an internal organ such as the liver. It is no good sending the patient to a dermatologist. We have to understand a little, at least, of how the causal system works, and then choose the point or points at which to intervene to alter the system as a whole.

Answering that simple question "What do you want me to do?" is quite a problem.

GETTING THINGS DONE

Generating activity is not a problem; in fact it is easy. The fact that it is easy makes the real problem harder to solve. The problem is getting the *right things* done – the things that matter, the things that will have an impact, the things a company is trying to achieve to ensure success. A high volume of activity often disguises a lack of effective action. We can mistake quantity for quality and then add to it, which merely makes things worse.

The problem is well documented and it is widespread. In a recent survey, conducted over a period of five years, a leading consulting firm collected responses from 125,000 managers from over 1,000 companies in over 50 countries. Employees in three out of five companies rated their organization "weak" at execution. As the consultants laconically observed: 'When asked if they agree with the statement 'Important strategic and operational decisions are quickly translated into action', the majority answered no."[1] The organizations found it difficult to do what they regarded as important.

This is odd. Why can companies do things that don't matter very much but can't do things that do?

The problem is also enduring. One of the most experienced teachers of courses on strategy implementation in the US laments that conversations he holds with managers on the subject of execution have hardly changed in 20 years.[2]

This is odder still. When we know we have an important problem which is not new, why can't we solve it?

If a problem is widespread and enduring, its origins are likely to be deep-seated. The solution is therefore unlikely to be a quick fix or something new to add to what we do already. It is likely to be something fundamental, which involves *changing* what we do already.

It is the contention of this book that this old problem has an old solution. The solution is not only old, but also fairly simple to understand. Indeed, once understood, it feels like little more than common sense. Unfortunately, being common sense does not make something common practice.

This naturally prompts the question: "If this solution has been around for a long time and is simple to understand, why *isn't* it common practice?"

There are two main reasons. The first is that the history of management thinking has built up barriers to adopting the solution. Management thinking has its origins in nineteenth-century science. It saw business organizations as machines, and the management model it adopted was grounded in engineering. While this view has been disavowed by modern management thinkers, its legacy is insidious.

The second reason is that although the failings of the legacy model are clear, it is not clear what it should be replaced with. Lacking an alternative, practicing managers fall back on the engineering model as a default. They often do so without knowing it, because it is so fundamental. They end up with deep-seated problems they cannot address because they are as unaware of the origins of those problems as of the alternative on offer.

To challenge our insidious legacy we need to become aware of it.

LEGACY THINKING

In the decades following the Industrial Revolution, many businesses were built up around factories which were essentially machines, and the people needed to operate them were integrated into them like the proverbial cogs. The machine became the model for business as a whole. Machines are designed to carry out a set of definable tasks and they do so if properly controlled by their operators. Machines are mindless, they just do what their designers want. If something goes wrong it is because a part has malfunctioned and needs to be repaired or replaced.

In 1911, Frederick Winslow Taylor's classic *The Principles of Scientific Management* enshrined the machine model for several generations. This approach to management rests on three premises:

1   In principle it is possible to know all you need to know to be able to plan what to do.
2   Planners and doers should be separated.
3   "There is but one right way."

15

A manager was a programmer of robot workers. The essence of management was to create perfect plans and tell people precisely what to do and how to do it.

Taylor and his followers had a tremendous impact and helped to professionalize management in ways we now take for granted. Their methods resulted in great improvements in efficiency. Taylor studied repetitive, menial tasks (like shifting pig iron onto railcars) in great detail and worked out how to perform them optimally, as a machine would. Just about every business involves tasks with similar characteristics, and today a lot of those tasks are indeed performed by robots, or have been standardized in computer programs.

Yet Taylor did not believe that his methods should be applied only to a particular set of tasks. Scientific management was to replace the old approach entirely. This old approach dated from the pre-industrial era of tradesmen. Then, Taylor writes, managers sought to induce each workman "to use his best endeavours, his hardest work, all his traditional knowledge, his skill, his ingenuity, and his goodwill – in a word, his 'initiative', so as to yield the largest possible return to his employer."[3] He wanted to consign that to history.

However, businesses also involve tasks which are not menial or repetitive, but where knowledge of particular circumstances is critical. The less stable and the more dynamic the environment is, the more they matter. One of them is developing strategy. In the case of tasks such as these, all three of Taylor's premises are false.

In 1955, those premises were explicitly challenged by Peter Drucker in his classic *The Practice of Management*. Describing scientific management as "our most widely practiced personnel-management concept," Drucker praised the brilliance of its early insights, but added that "its insight is only half an insight."[4] He argued that simply because you *can* analyze work into its component parts, it does not follow that it *should* be organized that way.

16

He also argued that planning and doing are not separate jobs, but separate parts of the same job. Scientific management, he claimed, can only work at all if jobs remain "unchanged in all eternity." However, it is a major function of enterprise to bring change about.[5]

The assumptions about human behavior accepted by Taylor and pervading business practice at the time were also being challenged by psychologists including Douglas McGregor, whom Drucker mentioned with approval. In *The Human Side of Enterprise*, which appeared in 1960, McGregor called the traditional view that human beings dislike work, fear responsibility, and therefore need to be tightly controlled "Theory X." He suggested the alternative view that "man will exercise self-control and self-direction in the service of objectives to which he is committed," which he called "Theory Y."[6] Theory Y was the missing half of Taylor's insight. It was the initiative baby he had thrown out with the pre-industrial bathwater.

The assumptions about human knowledge underlying the ideal of the perfect plan have proven to be more stubborn. They were given a jolt by the oil price shocks of the 1970s, when the world revealed itself to be less stable than everyone had thought. They provided clear evidence that planners could not know everything they needed to know, and that the business environment had an element of unpredictability. Ironically, it was just at that time that Taylorian principles were extending themselves well beyond routine tasks into strategic planning and control systems.[7]

Strategic planning rose and fell. Its hubris was perfect knowledge, its fatal flaw the increasing rate of unpredictable changes in the environment. Between inception and execution, every plan could be derailed by something unexpected, and most plans were. So what was the point of planning? Surely a company needs some sort of direction? In 1994, the nemesis of strategic planners, Henry Mintzberg, could write that "we are now ready to extract the planning baby from all that strategic planning bathwater."[8]

So we have ditched the bathwater in Taylor's assumptions about human behavior and human knowledge. We are left with two babies: the understanding that people can indeed regulate themselves if they are committed to some objectives; and the understanding that objectives do need to be set in some way or other.

At least since the time of *In Search of Excellence* in 1980, its first blockbuster bestseller, management literature has rejected the model of a business organization as a machine and its people as robots. Managers are exhorted to stop managing and start leading, to empower people, and to master something called "change management." The volume of the volumes has become cacophonous. However, many managers remain rather confused, as there is little consensus about how empowerment is actually supposed to work.

Most of the systems in large organizations which determine how people carry out planning and budgeting, target setting and performance management, are still based on engineering principles. Globalization leads to standardization, pressure for increased compliance and fear of litigation impose further constraints, and, despite our avowed rejection of the consequences of scientific management, we may in fact be moving closer to turning not only workers but managers into robots.

Maybe, deep in our hearts, that is what we would like. Certainly, the problems of executing strategy are often expressed as a frustration with people. The authors of one of the most widely read recent books on the subject report that business leaders frequently say that the problem is that "people aren't doing what they're supposed to do in the plan."[9] If only everybody would do as they are told, everything would be fine. Maybe. Or maybe not.

This brings us to the second reason the problem of executing strategy is so enduring. There is no accepted set of management disciplines for achieving the outcomes we want in the dynamic, uncertain environment we are faced with today. While it is fairly clear what we should *not* do, there is so much advice about what we *should* do that it is not clear what matters. What are the things which really make a difference?

THE DISCIPLINE OF EXECUTION

At its most simple, executing strategy is about planning what to do in order to achieve certain outcomes and making sure that the actions we have planned are actually carried out until the desired outcomes are achieved.

In a stable, predictable environment it is possible to make quite good plans by gathering and analyzing information. We can learn enough about the outside world and our position in it to set some objectives. We know enough about the effects any actions will have to be able to work out what to do to achieve the objectives. We can then use a mixture of supervision, controls, and incentives to coerce, persuade, or cajole people into doing what we want. We can measure the results until the outcomes we want are achieved. We can make plans, take actions, and achieve outcomes in a linear sequence with some reliability. If we are assiduous enough, pay attention to detail, and exercise rigorous control, the sequence will be seamless.

In an unpredictable environment, this approach quickly falters. The longer and more rigorously we persist with it, the more quickly and completely things will break down. The environment we are in creates gaps between plans, actions, and outcomes:

❑ The gap between plans and outcomes concerns *knowledge*: It is the difference between what we would like to know and what we actually know. It means that we cannot create perfect plans.

❑ The gap between plans and actions concerns *alignment*: It is the difference between what we would like people to do and what they actually do. It means that even if we encourage them to switch off their brains, we cannot know enough about them to program them perfectly.

❑ The gap between actions and outcomes concerns *effects*: It is the difference between what we hope our actions will achieve and what they actually achieve. We can never fully predict how the environment will react to what we do. It means that we cannot know in advance exactly what outcomes the actions of our organization are going to create.

Although it is not common to talk about these three gaps, it is common enough to confront them. It is also common enough to react in ways that make intuitive sense. Faced with a lack of knowledge, it seems logical to seek more detailed information. Faced with a problem of alignment, it feels natural to issue more detailed instructions. And faced with disappointment in the effects being achieved, it is quite understandable to impose more detailed controls. Unfortunately, these reactions do not solve the problem. In fact, they make it worse.

There is a model for creating a link between strategy and operations and bridging the three gaps. It involves applying a few general principles in continually changing specific circumstances. They are not difficult to understand, but their implications are profound. The model recognizes that our knowledge is always limited and seeks to do more with the knowledge we have. It unsentimentally places people and human nature at its core and seeks to direct people rather than control them. In this way, it casts off our legacy thinking while rescuing both babies from the bathwater.

Each of the principles addresses one of the three gaps, but all of them reinforce and are dependent on each other.

1 DECIDE WHAT REALLY MATTERS

You cannot create perfect plans, so do not attempt to do so. Do not plan beyond the circumstances you can foresee. Instead, use the knowledge which is accessible to you to work out *the outcomes you really want* the organization to achieve. Formulate your strategy as an intent rather than a plan.

2 GET THE MESSAGE ACROSS

Having worked out what matters most now, pass the message on to others and give them responsibility for carrying out their part in the plan. Keep it simple. Don't tell people what to do and how to do it. Instead, be as clear as you can about your *intentions*. Say what you want people to achieve and, above all, tell them why. Then ask them to tell you what they are going to do as a result.

3 GIVE PEOPLE SPACE AND SUPPORT

Do not try to predict the effects your actions will have, because you can't. Instead, encourage people to *adapt their actions* to realize the overall intention as they observe what is actually happening. Give them boundaries which are broad enough to take decisions for themselves and act on them.

The purpose of this book is to describe how this alternative model evolved, the practices on which it was built, and how they can be applied in business today. The principles are probably no surprise, although it may be surprising how much of a difference they make. You probably know something about them already, but you may not know how to make them work well in practice. Doing so is not as easy as you might think.

However, you can get some help. Others have been here before – a surprisingly long time ago. And they are the last people you would expect to have followed this path.

This book covers a story going back some 200 years.[10] The solution had been put into practice before Taylor created the problem. It is the story of an organization, although the organization is not a business, but an army. The army was not one most people would think of as being progressive, either. It was the Prussian Army. It followed precisely the evolution trajectory we are on, but with a head start of about 150 years.

In the eighteenth century, the Prussian King Frederick the Great had come closer than anyone has ever done to creating an army of robots. It was highly successful. In the early nineteenth century it met with disaster, and embarked on a program of fundamental change to enable it to cope with an altered environment. The changes it embraced were based on insights into the limits of human knowledge and a view of organizations as organisms rather than machines. Far from throwing out Taylor's initiative baby and Mintzberg's planning baby, the Prussians embraced them both and helped them to grow up. The methods they adopted evolved from practical experience and experimentation, so they work. They have since been copied by many modern armies, including the British and American.

One benefit of moving far away in time and looking at the military rather than the business domain is to make it easier to spot the essentials. If we can identify some principles we can then apply them in our own specific context. The environment faced by the military made the problem of strategy execution acute in the nineteenth century. In business the problem has only recently become similarly severe. As a result, the military has built up more experience of how to deal with the issues than we have in business. That experience is well documented and accessible. It is ours for the taking. We may find that the farther back we look, the farther forward we can see.

The word "strategy" comes from the Greek *strategos* – στρατηγός – a military commander.[11] But of course, business is not war. In order to learn from military experience we have to adopt the right perspective. We are seeking to define the principles which enable large organizations to realize their goals and gain competitive advantage in a complex, uncertain, and fast-changing environment.

The following is a description of the nature of combat from an academic thesis about the nature of military thought:

> *Combat is an interaction between human organisations. It is adversarial, highly dynamic, complex and lethal. It is grounded in individual and collective human behaviour, and conducted between organisations that are themselves complex. It is not determined, hence uncertain, and evolutionary. Critically, and to an extent in a way which we currently overlook, combat is* fundamentally *a human activity.*[12]

Compare that passage with this one:

> *Business is an interaction between human organisations. It is* **competitive***, highly dynamic, complex and* **risky***. It is grounded in individual and collective human behaviour, and conducted between organisations that are themselves complex. It is not determined, hence uncertain, and evolutionary. Critically, and to an extent in a way which we currently overlook, business is* fundamentally *a human activity.*

The only words I have changed are the two in bold. If the result seems a plausible description of business, the story that follows may offer some valuable lessons.

A ROUTE MAP

In the next chapter I tap into the help on offer in order to understand causation and outline the theory on which the solution is based. I find it in the concept of "friction," the defining characteristic of the environment of war, which I argue is also the defining characteristic of contemporary business which makes executing strategy so difficult. Friction creates the three gaps. The concept of friction is entirely consistent with systems thinking and chaos theory, but it is more useful to managers because it describes how working in a complex adaptive system is experienced. Its elements can be seen and felt, so we can more easily work out how to deal with them.

Each gap raises specific issues and requires us to take different steps in order to close it. However, ultimately all three are aspects of a single issue: how to get the outcomes we desire. The steps we take to address all three gaps are therefore merely elements of an integrated approach to running an organization.

In Chapter 3 I give an overview of that approach by telling the story of how it evolved into its present form in its military context. I do so not only for interest, but because the long change process described holds lessons for us if we seek to adopt it today. If Chapter 2 describes theory, Chapter 3 describes a set of practices developed in order to meet the challenges of the theory. Those practices are in many ways counter-intuitive. Their legitimacy rests on the logic with which they proceed from the theory, but also their demonstrated efficacy in practice. In the light of that logic and their efficacy, the practices begin to look less counter-intuitive and more like common sense. By the end of Chapter 3 you will have an overview of the approach. The parts will make more sense if you have first understood the whole. I need some shorthand to refer to the approach, so I have called it "leading through intent."

The question then becomes how to make the solution work. The practices began as experiments by individuals, turned into general habits, and have spread to others through the use of specific techniques. This makes them transferable and scaleable. Chapters 4, 5, and 6 take each of the gaps in turn and explore the techniques which can be used to close them, drawing mainly on current business experience.

The final chapter steps back to examine the limits of the approach, and also to look at what it can achieve. It is not appropriate everywhere all of the time within any organization. I believe that it is appropriate in most places most of the time, but its limits must be understood in order to apply it effectively.

None of what follows is new – simply neglected. I have not invented it. I have merely applied it to a domain which uses bits of it from time to time but rarely draws it all together. The insight offered is into the power of getting it right. The value offered is about *how* to get it right. The practices have been developed through experimentation over a long period, by different organizations in different countries. While they constitute a way of working which was developed to deal with the chaos of battle, they are precisely attuned to the needs of the business environment at the beginning of the twenty-first century. Taken together, they constitute a way for an organization to consistently provide cogent answers to the basic question which should be posed by every one of its members: "What do you want me to do?"

CHAPTER TWO

THE CAUSE

The Three Gaps

Friction makes doing simple things difficult and difficult things impossible

CLAUSEWITZ AND FRICTION

In 1832, the wife of a recently deceased Prussian general published a work containing 125 chapters divided into eight books and running to over 1,000 pages, which her late husband had labored over for some 25 years. He was only fully satisfied with the first chapter, which describes the nature of his subject: contemporary warfare. In these pages he tried to convey what warfare was really like. At their heart is an account of the problem of execution. War is an environment, he argued, in which getting simple things to happen is very difficult and getting difficult things to happen is impossible.

The work was called *Vom Kriege* (*On War*) and its author was Carl von Clausewitz. In struggling to give an accurate account of the amorphous and confusing reality he observed and experienced on the battlefield 200 years ago, he unwittingly provided us with a telling account of the environment of business today and a description of the causal system behind the problem of turning activity into action.

Carl von Clausewitz was born in 1780 and, having joined the Prussian Army at the age of 12, had his first direct experience of war only a year later. That experience was added to frequently over the next 20 years as the conservative powers of Europe struggled to contain the unprecedented forces unleashed by revolution in France and intensified by the genius of Napoleon. Clausewitz was on the field on the catastrophic October day in 1806 when two French forces, acting almost as one, destroyed the Prussian Army in the twin battles of Jena and Auerstedt. He was caught up in the retreat from Auerstedt, captured, and held in France. Released in 1808, he joined a circle of Prussian military and social reformers, acting as personal assistant to their leader, von Scharnhorst. When in 1812 Napoleon forced Prussia to join an alliance against Russia, Clausewitz put his conscience before his king and joined the Russian army as a staff officer.[1] In 1813, he was allowed to officially rejoin the Prussian Army. His active service came to end with his participation in the Hundred Day campaign of 1815, in which the Napoleonic meteor finally burned out on the field of Waterloo.[2]

Clausewitz had experience in line and staff roles and knew first hand what it was like both to plan an action and to conduct one. He had also been at the heart of a group grappling with the technical, political, and organizational problems of reinventing the Prussian Army in the wake of the defeat at Jena–Auerstedt. He was by nature an intellectual who felt driven to reflect on and understand his experiences. He began writing as early as 1803 and, after being given a position in the War College in Berlin in 1813, he started producing drafts for a major treatise to be called *On War*. He never finished it. In 1831, having been sent to organize the containment of an outbreak of cholera in Poland, he contracted the disease himself and it swiftly killed him. The following year, his devoted wife Marie published what he had always intended to be a tombstone.[3]

On War is not only very long, but has a reputation as an abstract, difficult text. As a result, Clausewitz is in good company among his remarkable generation of Germans in being more cited than read. The real peculiarity of his writing is the combination of abstract conceptualization and description of experience, and the span of the subject matter, from technical military matters to psychology. This both creates the difficulties of the text and has ensured the enduring hold it has had over its genuine readers up to and including the present day. It is the result of a manful effort to confront and grasp the reality of war in a way never previously attempted.[4]

Clausewitz felt the need to confront this reality early on. His first article, published in 1805, was a critique of the most widely read theorist of the day, Heinrich Dietrich von Bülow, who believed that the essence of war could be captured mathematically, through such things as the geometric relationship between the location of an army's objective and its base.[5] Clausewitz castigated von Bülow for distorting the nature of his object. He was trying to turn war into a science because that would make it understandable and tractable. That attempt, Clausewitz believed, created a dangerous delusion.

The first of the eight books making up *On War* is entitled "On the Nature of War" and consists of an attempt, spanning eight chapters, to characterize it so as to understand what a theory of war could be, even in principle. The second book, "On the Theory of War," then considers the implications for a theory. Clausewitz thus describes what it is that he has to account for before developing a theory. That description has remained one of the most enduring elements of his entire work.[6]

If Clausewitz's undertaking were to have any value at all, it had to account for the true nature of war. You have to have experienced war, he wrote, in order to understand wherein its true difficulties lie. From the outside it looks very simple, its intellectual demands seem shallow, yet the real difficulty is hard to convey.[7] There is a gap between appearance and reality.

The nature of that gap is the main theme of the first book. The gap is described as the difference between what we know and what we can do, as the gulf between planning and execution.[8] In a later section about strategy, Clausewitz gives an account of Frederick the Great's campaign of 1760, which, he observes, has often been cited as an example of strategic mastery. What was truly remarkable about it, however, were not the marches and maneuvers in themselves, but the way they were carried out – "it is these miracles of execution," Clausewitz writes, "that we should really admire."[9] The fact is that in war "things do not happen of their own accord like a well-oiled machine, indeed the machine itself starts to create resistance, and overcoming it demands enormous willpower on the part of the leader."[10] In war, "everything is very simple, but the simplest thing is difficult... taking action in war is movement in a resistant medium."[11]

This experience, well known to every practitioner, was ignored by theorists like von Bülow. The reality needed to be conceptualized, but there was not even a word for it. Clausewitz needed one. The image of the resisting machine gives a clue. He uses an image from mechanics, and in so doing chose an English word – rendered as *Friktion* in German – to show that he is using it in a special sense. "Friction," he wrote, "is the only concept which covers in fairly general terms what it is that makes the difference between real war and war on paper."[12] One leading Clausewitz scholar has summarized the concept of friction as referring to the totality of "uncertainties, errors, accidents, technical difficulties, the unforeseen and their effect on decisions, morale and actions."[13]

It is important here to understand the nature of Clausewitz's disagreement with von Bülow, and others of the school of scientific generalship.[14] They too recognized that chance and uncertainty played a role in war. The difference was that they believed these factors could be eliminated by a more scientific approach to planning. Certainty of outcomes could be achieved by anyone who could gather and correctly process data about topological and geographical distances, march tables, supply needs, and the geometrical relationship between armies and their bases. They believed that in many cases this would render fighting unnecessary.[15]

Clausewitz disagreed on two counts. First, he believed that friction was as inherent to war as it is to mechanical engineering and could therefore never be eliminated but only mitigated. Secondly, he believed that studying march tables and the like was not a fruitful means of mitigation. In fact, he came to think that friction had to be worked with. It actually provided opportunities, and could be used by a general just as much as it could be used by an engineer. The first thing was to recognize its existence. The second thing was to understand its nature. That was and remains more difficult.

Interestingly, when illustrating what he means by friction, Clausewitz does not use a military example at all, but chooses instead to describe a man setting out on a journey:

> Imagine a traveler who decides toward the evening to cover a further two stages on his day's journey, some four or five hours' ride with post-horses along the main highway; nothing very much. Then when he comes to the first stage he discovers that there are no horses, or only poor ones; then a mountainous area and ruined tracks; it gets dark, and after all his trials he is mightily pleased to reach the final stage and get some miserable roof over his head. So it is that in war, through an accumulation of innumerable petty circumstances which could never be taken into account on paper, everything deteriorates and you find that you are far from achieving your goal.[16]

This homely example shows the effects on the traveler of *external* circumstances he could not predict. He could perhaps have alleviated his troubles by gathering more information before he set out, making enquiries from others about the route and the facilities on the way, but doing so would have delayed him. He had a limited amount of time to make a decision based on partial information. We all do the same when planning future actions, like going on holiday. Travel agents notwithstanding, we arrive at departure to find we have to check our hand luggage, the flight is delayed, there are no taxis at the destination airport, the hotel is at the top of a dirt track, there is a building site next door, the room does not have a sea view after all, and the shower runs cold. The plan is imperfect, and the actual outcome falls short of the desired one.

Clausewitz goes on to describe further sources of friction from *internal* circumstances and to claim that all of them are heightened in war:

> *The military machine, the army and all that goes along with it, is basically very simple and therefore looks easy to manage. Consider, however, that no part of it consists of just one element, that all of it is made up of individuals, that every element produces friction of its own at every turn. Everything sounds fine in theory; the commander of a battalion is responsible for carrying out a given order, and as the battalion is welded together by discipline into a single unit and the commander is known to be a man of zeal, the block will pivot around its trunnion with hardly any friction. In reality that does not happen, for war instantly exposes the exaggerations and half truths of the plan. The battalion is still made up of individual men, any one of whom, if chance dictates it, is in a position to impose a delay or make things go awry. The dangers inherent in war, the physical demands it makes, aggravate the problem to the extent that they can be regarded as its main cause.*
>
> *This appalling friction, which unlike mechanical friction is not concentrated at just a limited number of points, is everywhere in contact with chance, and produces unpredictable effects precisely because they are in the main the product of chance.*[17]

The very business of getting an organization made up of individuals, no matter how disciplined, to pursue a collective goal produces friction just as surely as applying the brakes of a car. Because of the role of chance, actual outcomes are inherently unpredictable. Furthermore, in war physical and psychological stress heightens friction still further. In this case we find that we cannot do what we planned, so once again our desired outcome is not achieved. There is a gap between the actions we planned and the actions actually taken. Of course, we might not have achieved our desired outcome even if we had done what we planned, because our plan may well have been flawed, as in the case of the traveler. We cannot tell.

Superficially, Clausewitz could be considered to have done nothing more than discover Murphy's law rather earlier than its eponymous formulator. At another level, he could be considered to be the first person in history to have had real insight into a fundamental factor governing organizational endeavor of any kind. No engineer would dream of designing an engine without taking into account the effects of mechanical friction. If Clausewitz is right, no one should develop a strategy without taking into account the effects of organizational friction. Yet we continue to be surprised and frustrated when it manifests itself. We tend to think everything has gone wrong when in fact everything has gone normally. The existence of friction is why armies need officers and businesses need managers. Anticipating and dealing with it form the core of managerial work. Recognizing that is liberating in itself.

Clausewitz's account contains another insight: that organizations are made up of people. If this should seem obvious, the implications of acknowledging it are not. In contrast to those of the scientific school like von Bülow, Clausewitz includes psychological factors in his basic account of war, and regards them as an inherent source of friction. Not only is an army not a "well-oiled machine," the machine generates resistance of its own, because the parts it is made of are human. Although Clausewitz's metaphors are all taken from mechanics rather than biology, he clearly sees where the metaphor itself begins to break down. He is reaching toward the idea of the organization as an organism. While the scientific school sought to eliminate human factors to make the organization as machine-like as possible, Clausewitz sought to exploit them.

If we are to deal with friction, we need to tease out its fundamental elements to distinguish them from specific examples, and do so in such a way that we can then work out how to address them in practice.

To help us to do this, we are fortunate in being able to follow Clausewitz's thought processes over time, thanks to scholars who have examined the genesis of his concept of friction. This enables us to think along with him.

FRICTION AND NONLINEARITY

Clausewitz first used the term "friction" in a letter to his future wife written on 29 September 1806, just a fortnight before the Battle of Jena–Auerstedt. The assembling Prussian Army had three commanders-in-chief and two chiefs-of-staff, one of whom was von Scharnhorst. They all disagreed about what to do, and Clausewitz laments the difficulties von Scharnhorst had in arriving at a single coherent plan of deployment "when he is paralyzed by constant friction with the opinions of others."[18] The word is used to describe the effect of a clash of views between individuals which slowed down decision making. The source is internal, confined in this case to the top leadership.

The image clearly stayed in his mind and expanded. Five years later, in 1811, during a lecture he gave at the Berlin War College, Clausewitz referred to "the friction of the whole machinery," which he divided into two elements: "the numerous chance events, which touch everything"; and "the numerous difficulties which inhibit the accurate execution of the precise plans which theory tends to formulate."[19] Friction has now become much more than disagreements between senior officers. It encompasses numerous obstacles to execution within the organization as well as chance events in the external environment.

In April 1812, Clausewitz wrote a letter to his pupil, the Crown Prince, listing eight sources of friction:

1   Insufficient knowledge of the enemy.
2   Rumors (information gained by remote observation or spies).
3   Uncertainty about one's own strength and position.
4   The uncertainties that cause friendly troops to exaggerate their own difficulties.
5   Differences between expectations and reality.
6   The fact that one's own army is never as strong as it appears on paper.
7   The difficulties in keeping an army supplied.
8   The tendency to change or abandon well-thought-out plans when confronted with the vivid physical images and perceptions of the battlefield.[20]

At first glance, this list looks quite heterogeneous. A closer look reveals more unity. A prominent source (items 1, 2, 3, and 6) is poor information, of both one's own forces and the enemy. Others are to do with the interpretation of information and the psychological reactions to it (items 4, 5, and 8). Item 7, difficulties in supply, is the only factor not clearly to do with the gathering and interpretation of data; though it may play a role there as well. We have partial information, imperfectly processed by people under stress.

If we turn again to Clausewitz's most mature account of friction in Book One of *On War*, some patterns emerge from the disparity of the elements he enumerates. The following table is derived from a reading of it:

GENERIC SOURCE OF FRICTION	SPECIFIC SOURCE FROM *ON WAR*
Imperfect information	Uncertainties False information Rumors
Imperfect transmitting and processing of information	Making judgments based on probabilities Stress caused by emotions, including fear Stress caused by physical exertion The number of people in an organization who can cause a misunderstanding or delay Differences of views, especially between leaders
External factors	Chance (e.g., the weather) Complexity reducing the chances of success through an accumulation of risk

We experience friction because of our cognitive limits as human beings.[21] We have limited knowledge about the present and the future is fundamentally unknowable. Because war involves a struggle between two opposed wills, the outcome of any action taken by one party is at least in part dependent on the actions of the other. The amount of information each needs in order to take decisions is therefore in principle infinite, and is also in principle only partially accessible, as it involves an independent agent: the enemy. Even if near-perfect information were accessible, it would be open to different interpretations, affected by the psychological states of those interpreting it, their interests and emotions, and all heightened by the exposure to danger, the resulting stress, and the physical exertion inherent in war. The more protagonists there are, the more interpretations are likely, and the harder it is to create a uniform view.

Hence complexity itself exacerbates other sources of friction. If information is imperfect, judgments must be based on probabilities, for much is simply unknowable. The story of the journey, each stage of which involved factors unknown in advance (such as the state of the road, the availability of horses), illustrates how complexity can reduce the chances of overall success. There is only one way the plan can go right, but any number of ways in which it can go wrong. Again, if one had perfect information in advance, one might be able to do something about it. The classic external factor which is unknowable is the weather. If it were known, it would not be a problem. If you knew it was going to rain, you could plan accordingly – it will slow down the enemy's march as much as your own – but such knowledge is unavailable.

Clausewitz draws all these apparently disparate elements together into a single concept because all the elements interact with each other and their effects are not additive but multiplicative. There is an inherent tendency to exacerbation. While individual elements can be mitigated, the general phenomenon cannot be completely eradicated. The reason for this is the external environment, the situation created by the state of war itself, which renders the information needed fundamentally inaccessible. Clausewitz's remarkably modern account of this environment is found in his first chapter.

In it, he lays out what it is that a possible theory of war has to account for. He draws together the threads of his argument in a final section, declaring war to be a "remarkable trinity" consisting of:

> *the primordial violence of its element, hatred and enmity, which can be considered to be* blind instinct; *the interplay of probabilities and chance, which make it a* creative inner activity; *and its secondary nature as a tool of politics, which renders it a matter of* intellectual calculation.[22]

Human passions, will, and reason all play a role, the importance of which varies from case to case. A theory of war must account for all of them. To describe how it can do so, Clausewitz uses an image from contemporary science. Once again, it is from mechanics:

> *The task for theory, then, is to maintain itself suspended between these three tendencies as if they were three magnets.*

Clausewitz is referring to a real phenomenon, and may indeed have seen it demonstrated. A pendulum released over a single magnet will quickly come to rest perpendicularly above it, as anyone can predict. Released over two equally powerful ones it will swing to one, then the other, losing velocity. It will eventually come to rest within the orbit of one or the other, depending on which one's orbit it is in at the point at which it no longer has sufficient energy to break free. The chance is 50:50. A pendulum suspended over three equally powerful magnets behaves quite differently. What it does has been well described by the scientific historian Alan D. Beyerchen:

> it moves irresolutely to and fro as it darts among the competing points of attraction, sometimes kicking out high to acquire added momentum that allows it to keep gyrating in a startlingly long and intricate pattern. Eventually, the energy dissipates under the influence of friction in the suspension mounting and the air, bringing the pendulum's movement asymptotically to rest. The probability is vanishingly small that an attempt to repeat the process would produce exactly the same pattern. Even such a simple system is complex enough for the details of the trajectory of any actual 'run' to be, effectively, irreproducible.[23]

The outcome is unpredictable because tiny differences in the starting conditions or in the environment of each run can produce a significantly different pattern. Concerned to challenge the assumption that there could be a science of war, Clausewitz used a scientific experiment to demonstrate its true nature. Scientists of his day could not explain the pendulum's behavior. Newton had struggled to account for the motion of the moon orbiting the earth orbiting the sun – the "three-body problem" – and failed.[24] The reason is that the science of the day was linear. A linear system has two characteristics. It is proportional, in other words a small input produces a small output and a large input a large output; and it is additive, in other words the whole is the sum of the parts. A nonlinear system is neither.[25] Clausewitz understood at the time that war is nonlinear, but could not conceptualize it other than by reference to friction, chance, and unpredictability.

Today, there is a whole realm of scientific endeavor called nonlinear dynamics with mathematical foundations. It has been known since 1975, rather misleadingly, as "chaos theory." Systems are nonlinear when the state they are in at a given point in time provides the input to a feedback mechanism which determines the new state of the system. Some such systems are sensitively dependent on the starting state. If so, future states are unpredictable. Such systems are called "chaotic." The term is misleading because their states are not random, merely unknowable.[26] Only recent increases in computing power have enabled scientists and mathematicians to grasp their behavior.

If Clausewitz had been familiar with late twentieth-century science, he would probably have described war as chaotic in the sense of nonlinear. He opens his work by describing war as a duel and likens it to wrestling.[27] It is therefore a clash of two independent forces, with the actions of each depending on the actions of the other. In wrestling, each opponent uses the other's weight and force. Clausewitz repeatedly refers to phenomena not as cause and effect but as reciprocal; that is, as co-determining because of mutual feedback. The violence involved in war, the aims of the opponents, and their will and forces are all described in these terms.[28] He stresses that war is not an isolated act but is embedded in political processes which are not strictly part of it but nevertheless influence it.[29] The means of war have an effect on its ends, which are in constant interplay.[30] These observations culminate in the image of the three magnets. Today, we can understand what he meant better than his contemporaries were able to.

We experience friction even as individuals when trying to get anything done. When we work on a collective enterprise as part of an organization, the experience becomes acute. Imperfect information is imperfectly transmitted and imperfectly processed. For an organization to act rationally and coherently on the information it possesses is infinitely more difficult than for an individual, because an organization consists of individuals who are not only themselves finite but have independent wills with brains and desires which are not interlocked. Organizations are engaged in collective enterprises which are far more complex than individual ones. The information available is imperfect not simply because we do not know what we need to know, but because we know things that are irrelevant. There is not only a lack but a surfeit and the surfeit becomes noise, drowning out what we need and making it ever harder to detect it. Add to uncertain and noisy multiple sources of information the vagaries of transmission and high variation in processing, and we can begin to see why friction should be an inherent feature of any organization, be it an army or a business.

There is an increasing body of literature seeking to understand economics in terms of chaos theory.[31] The practical results, based on the hope that the complex mathematical models of chaos theory may allow us to understand the actual behavior of markets, have been mixed. However, a comparison of market economies with the features of nonlinear systems would lead one to expect that the economy is a nonlinear system; and phenomena characteristic of nonlinear systems can readily be observed not only in the economy as a whole but within specific markets.[32]

Managers need not concern themselves too much for now with whether or not mathematicians will succeed in modeling the economy by using chaos theory. The question for managers is what to do. For that, Clausewitz may be more useful.

Clausewitz was able to characterize war as chaotic 200 years ago. It was by no means clear at the time that business, which in its modern sense was in its infancy, shared these characteristics. That was about the time that battles had grown so big that no single individual was in a position to control them directly. Wellington was one of the last to do so at Waterloo. Even a few decades ago, there were many businesses in which the key strategic decisions could be taken by a few people. A committee could decide whether or not to invest in a large new low-cost plant, where it should be, how big it should be, what technology it should use, and so on. That decision could well determine the company's competitive position for years. Today, such decisions are only part of the story. Critical information is held at the periphery, strategy has to be developed and adopted by large numbers of people, and the half-life of a viable strategy has shrunk. Change is now the norm. The syndication of decision making and the ubiquity of change have dramatically increased friction in businesses. It rises with the number of decision makers and it is higher in a changing environment than in a steady state.[33]

Friction is a function of the *finitude of the human condition* – the fact that our *knowledge is limited* and the fact that we are *independent agents*.[34] It matters when we work together in organizations because we are then trying to overcome our limitations as individuals by pooling our knowledge in order to achieve a collective purpose. Our limited knowledge is due to things we could know in principle but happen not to – that is, *lack of information* – and things we could not know even in principle – that is, *unpredictable events*. And the fact that we are independent agents with

40

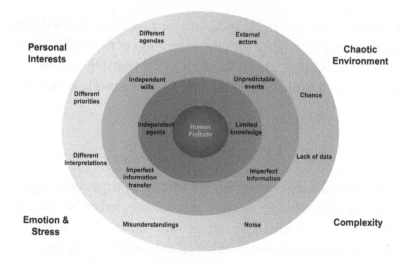

Figure 1 The overall concept of friction

wills of our own means that there is further information loss in *transmitting and processing information* between each other, and we can react differently to that information – even if it is perfectly transferred – because we have *independent wills*.

Figure 1 displays the concept visually. At the center is the fact of human finitude. It will never change. The implications of it spread out in concentric circles. While friction is a fact of life, the farther away from the center its consequences are, the more tractable they become. The circles could be extended almost *ad infinitum* to encompass myriad particular circumstances and individual instances. As one moves from the center toward the left, the consequences are more internal to the organization; as one moves right, the consequences are more to do with the external environment. The organization and the environment interact. Outside the rings are internal, psychological, and real, external factors which further exacerbate friction.

This framework is grounded in everyday experience, and has some rigor because it simply charts the logical consequences of what is it to be a human being. We can now use it to analyze our

41

problem so as to lay the foundations for a solution. That solution will have to help us deal with the outer rings of the circle: how to cope with limited information, how to transfer among one another the information we do have, and, as a result, how to act.

THE THREE GAPS

Clausewitz describes the effects of friction in terms of two gaps. One gap, caused by our trying to act on an unpredictable external environment of which we are always somewhat ignorant, is between *desired outcomes* and *actual outcomes* (as in the example of the simple journey of the overoptimistic traveler). Another gap, caused by internal friction, is the gap between the *plans* and the *actions* of an organization. It comes from the problem of information access, transfer, and processing in which many independent agents are involved (as in his example of a battalion being made up of many individuals, any one of whom could make the plan go awry).

It may be helpful to display the two gaps diagrammatically, as in Figure 2.

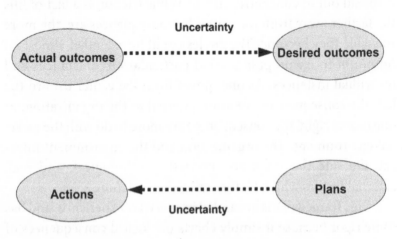

Figure 2 Clausewitz identifies two gaps

The problem of strategy implementation is often reduced to one issue: the gap between plans and actions. How do we get an organization actually to carry out what has been agreed? However, because of the nature of the environment, even if the organization executes the plan, there is no guarantee that the actual outcomes will match the desired ones; that is, the ones the plan was intended to achieve. The two gaps interact to exacerbate each other. In both cases there is uncertainty between inputs and outputs. The problem of achieving an organization's goals is not merely one of getting it to act, but of getting it to act in such a way that what is actually achieved is what was wanted in the first place. We have to link the internal and external aspects of friction and overcome them both at the same time. There is a third gap, the one between the two, which we must also overcome (Figure 3).

At first glance it looks as though there are four gaps here, but in fact there are only three. Only one of the two vertical gaps in this diagram is real: the gap on the left between actions and the actual outcomes that result from them. The other parallel gap between plans and desired outcomes is simply the recognition of the fact that the actions taken failed to realize the outcomes we desired. It is purely cognitive. So these two gaps collapse together,

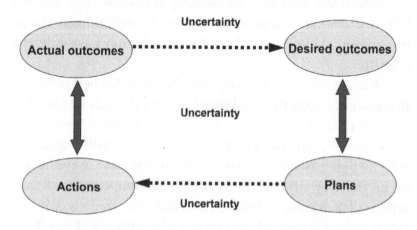

Figure 3 The two gaps have a gap between them

leaving three in all: the gaps between plans, actions, and the outcomes they achieve.

In the case of all three elements – plans, actions, and outcomes – there is a difference between the actual and the ideal. The ultimate evidence for this is that the actual outcomes differ from the desired ones. That means that the actions actually taken were different from those we should have taken. This in turn may have been because we planned the wrong actions (as in the case of the traveler) or because although we planned the right actions, people did not actually do what we intended (as in the case of the confused battalion). Or it may have been because of both. The *causes* of those shortfalls are different in each case.

Our plans are imperfect because we lack *knowledge*. We may not have gathered enough information about the situation or we may have interpreted it wrongly. We may have overestimated our own capabilities. We may have made false assumptions about the actions of others or about what will happen in a future which is fundamentally unknowable.

Our actions are not always those we plan because it is so difficult to *align* everybody who needs to act. The message about what we want them to do may not get through, or it may be misunderstood. They may act too early or too late. They may not believe that what we want them to do is the right thing to do, or they may not be willing to do it. They may simply have different priorities.

And even if we make good plans based on the best information available at the time and people do exactly what we plan, the *effects* of our actions may not be the ones we wanted because the environment is nonlinear and hence is fundamentally unpredictable. As time passes the situation will change, chance events will occur, other agents such as customers or competitors will take actions of their own, and we will find that what we do is only one factor among several which create a new situation. Even if the situation is stable, some of the effects of our actions will be

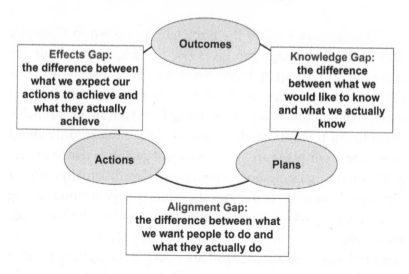

Figure 4 The problem: Three critical gaps

unintended. Reality will change like the movement of the pendulum. We are just one of the magnets.

So in making strategy happen, far from simply addressing the narrowly defined implementation gap between plans and action, we have to overcome three. Those responsible for giving direction face the specific problem of creating robust plans, and those responsible for taking action face the specific problem of achieving results in markets that can react unpredictably.

Having understood their underlying causes, we can now give the three gaps names which more accurately designate what gives rise to them. We could name the gap between outcomes and plans the *knowledge gap*, the gap between plans and actions the *alignment gap*, and the gap between actions and outcomes the *effects gap*. So the overall problem actually looks like Figure 4.

These three gaps constitute the system of *causes*. They explain why in the case of plans, actions, and outcomes, there is a gap between what we desire and what we achieve. All three are the result of friction.

We can now explain the uncertainties shown in Figures 2 and 3. The knowledge gap gives rise to uncertainty about the nature of the current and future reality (e.g., "Is the cause of our decline in market share poor service or the product offering, and do our competitors enjoy a large enough cost advantage to enable them to cut prices if we do?") and therefore uncertainty about how robust our plans are. The alignment gap gives rise to uncertainty on the one side about whether people will actually do what we want them to do (e.g., "Are the country organizations going to launch the customer service initiative?") and on the other side about what exactly the planners want us to do (e.g., "How can we launch the customer service initiative now before getting the new product suite and when we are also being asked to cut costs?"). The effects gap gives rise to uncertainty about what effects our actions are having (e.g., "Did the service initiative fail because the product is not as attractive as we thought or because we did not invest enough in the launch?") and about what other independent agents will do (e.g., "Or did our competitors pre-empt us by improving their service?").

These *real* uncertainties produce general *psychological* uncertainty. We do not like uncertainty. It makes us feel uncomfortable, so we try to eliminate it. Thus it is that each of the gaps provokes a common response, shown in Figure 5.

The examples described in Chapter 1 show a consistent drive toward more detail in information, instructions, and control, on the part of both individuals and the organization as a whole. This response is not only a natural reaction for us as individuals, it is what the processes and structures of most organizations are set up to facilitate.

A gap in knowledge prompts the collection of more data. In the case of the technology company, it was about the markets and more especially what was actually going on internally. Seeking to improve its information-gathering and processing capability, the company became more complex, adding committees and over-

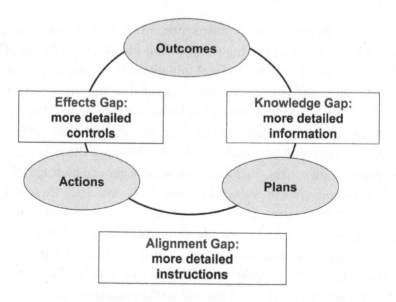

Figure 5 Usual reactions

lays, some permanent, some *ad hoc.* The pharmaceutical company was already immersed in information and had well-established processes for gathering and processing it, because developing drugs is fundamentally about gathering information and turning it into knowledge. So it pumped more data through its existing systems. No one took a decision to do so. It was just the natural result of how the organization as a system was programmed. In both cases, the data flow paralyzed decision making, because no matter how much there was, there was always more to obtain. Meetings were about analyzing problems rather than resolving them.

A gap in alignment is often indicated by top-level frustration and lower-level confusion. Both organizations exhibited this. Top-level managers felt increasing pressure to specify exactly what they wanted people to do. They began to stress actions rather than outcomes, in the one case by spelling things out "in painful detail" and in the other through SOPs and central processes. Some of the detail was translated into initiatives which began to proliferate, creating more confusion as well as more work. In their confusion, lower levels imitated the higher ones and identified problems of their own, which resulted in local initiatives. In a complex matrix organization when initiatives come from all directions they usually clash, creating dilemmas over what to do, like the one faced by the head of regulatory affairs in the drug company. Senior people began to intervene personally in details, throwing those actually responsible off course. Such behavior sends a general message that junior people are not trusted to make decisions. They therefore begin to delegate upward as a matter of course, ending in senior executives being asked to decide about such weighty matters as which color to paint a meeting room. Top-level frustration goes up a notch as people thereby demonstrate that they really cannot decide anything for themselves, and so the cycle goes on.

A gap in effects is typically responded to by an increase in control. The favorite control mechanism is metrics. As time goes on, the emphasis is switched from outputs to inputs, so that in the end everybody's actions are detailed, analyzed, and controlled by a few people who look to everyone else as if they are seeking to become omniscient about the world outside and omnipotent in the world inside. Controls have a cost. Overhead builds up around the controllers, and the reporting burden increases for the controlled.

In the technology company, the most telling effect was to focus attention on the internal world and numbers rather than the external world and what to do. In the pharmaceutical company, it was manifested in particular by layers of committees checking and reviewing the decisions of other committees. In both cases, leadership behavior was driven by risk avoidance, checking, and closer supervision. As senior people were constrained by the system to act as if they did not trust people ("I want you to report back to me every week"), so junior people began to mistrust the organization ("Why can't they get off my back – they seem to be just waiting for me to make a mistake").

The behavioral result on the part of followers was risk avoidance and the syndication of decisions, indicated by lengthening distribution lists in the email traffic.

These natural reactions do not simply fail to solve the problem, *they make it worse.* Because the cause-and-effect cycles are systemic and reciprocal, all three reactions interact with and exacerbate each other. Gathering and processing more information costs money and time. It is driven by a desire for certainty, a quest which can never be satisfied. Time passes and decision making slows down. Providing more detail is a natural response to a demand for clarity. But clarity and detail are not the same thing at all. The pursuit of detail actually increases noise and so makes it *less* clear what really matters. Details change quickly, so the more details we put in our plans the less robust they will be. Opportunities are missed, and by the time a decision has been made, the situation has changed, prompting further information gathering and analysis. The more detailed we make action plans, the more we constrain what people can do, which increases rigidity. Controls add to costs, slow things down further, and increase rigidity. People become demotivated and keep their attention firmly fixed on their KPIs, which become more important than what they were supposed to measure. Commitment is replaced by compliance, energy is sapped, and morale declines. The end result is a slow, expensive robot.

We need to find another way.

Any potential solution must address the three gaps. It must encompass planning effectively, finding a way of creating alignment and enabling people to take appropriate actions in the light of the situation they actually face at the time. We will have to work on how direction is formulated and given, how we communicate, and what behaviors and values govern the way we work together.

The literature about strategy execution contains much discussion of gaps, but it is not always clear what they are. The book about execution which has had the most impact in recent years speaks of "the gap between promises and results," which it claims is itself a result of "the gap between what a company's leaders want to achieve and the ability of their organization to achieve it"; that is, the alignment gap – getting the organization to do what its leaders want.[35] Reducing the problem to closing the alignment gap alone seriously truncates the issue, but it is by far the most common solution on offer. A recent academic article which tracked the fate of 150 strategic decisions from 30 organizations beginning in the early 1980s concludes that "managers can plan the implementation of a decision better when they know how to do so from previous similar experience." If they do not know how to do so, they should "hold back unless there is a general readiness for something of the kind to be done" and "under certain conditions" good planning helps.[36] Consulting firms also home in on how to close the "strategy-to-performance gap" by getting people to do what the management wants, and some even recommend more detail and more control.[37]

A survey conducted by the University of Michigan in 2005 identifies a range of barriers to execution, first among which is the "past/habits" of the organization.[38] In most cases the underlying problem was attributed to "leadership." The respondents' view was that the solution was to focus on alignment. The survey's author questions this, suggesting that although we put a lot of effort into developing and communicating strategy, "what we do not do is anticipate that things will change."[39] She then observes that "great companies excel at realignment." They listen to employees and customers "and they use that information to craft and recraft their strategies."[40] Here at last, someone has identified the effects gap. However, does closing it involve the "recrafting" of the strategy itself? She moves from the effects gap to the knowledge gap, from an unexpected outcome to a change in plan. Why not merely change the actions?

The reason for these oversimplified statements of the problem is a lack of theory, a deficit made good by developing an overall concept of friction. Without theory, all one can do is to observe what goes on in companies. What you see is a lot of people doing a lot of things which do not achieve very much. The reasons for these fruitless actions are varied, however, and so are the things we need to do about them. Some are fruitless because they are not what was intended in the plan, some are fruitless because the situation has changed and they no longer make sense, and some are fruitless because they were the wrong thing to do in the first place.

One of the most experienced teachers of courses on strategy implementation in the US recognizes that there are a range of problems requiring a range of different approaches. He traces them back to a fundamental failure to recognize that "strategic success demands a 'simultaneous' view of planning and doing."[41] Based on a survey of managers' views about the problems, he lists eight obstacles to be overcome: developing a model to guide execution decisions or actions; understanding how creating strategy affects its execution; managing change; understanding power; organizational structure; controls and feedback; creating an execution-supportive culture; and exercising execution-biased leadership. Handling these things well, he claims, "will guarantee execution success."[42]

That is a bold claim. The recognition that execution is not simply about getting people to do what you want is refreshing, and the list is unobjectionable. However, it remains a list, based on a review of symptoms rather than causes. It is not systemic. There is tacit recognition of the three gaps, and some sound advice about how to do a better job, but it is not grounded in any explanation as to why the problems arise in the first place. A business organization is a complex adaptive system. We need to understand it as a system in order to know where and how to intervene to change it.

Perhaps the most useful account of the problem and its causes is that by Jeffrey Pfeffer and Robert Sutton, who see it as aspects of yet another gap: the knowing–doing gap. They identify a range of symptoms: talk substituting for action; past habits constraining future action; fear resulting from interventionist and controlling leadership; the proliferation of metrics tied to reward systems; and the misplaced use of internal competition which suppresses cooperation.[43] The wide range of examples they offer is further evidence of how widespread and chronic the disease is. They all show organizations grinding to a halt in information, action plans, and controls. They offer a list of treatments based on examples of good practice. All and any of them could be efficacious, but a real cure to this systemic problem has to be systemic itself. We have first to understand the whole in order to understand the parts.

We have been examining a historical analysis of an ahistorical problem. The history does not end with Clausewitz. He was followed by others who elaborated and put into practice a solution which has been developed further to the present day. We are interested in finding a solution for today, but comfortingly, we do not have to invent one. History offers one already, along with some evidence that it works. We merely have to discover, understand, and apply it.

It is time to meet another crusty old Prussian.

QUICK RECAP

Before we do so, let us review the argument so far.

☐ Clausewitz observed that armies find executing strategy difficult and developed the concept of friction to explain why. Friction manifests itself when human beings with independent wills try to achieve a collective purpose in a fast-changing, complex environment where the future is fundamentally unpredictable.

❑ Friction is a universal phenomenon ultimately grounded in the basic fact of human finitude. Its universality means that it applies in some degree to all organizational life, including business. It also means that we can never completely escape it.

❑ Our finite nature means that we have limited knowledge, due to things we could know but happen not to (because we do not have perfect information) and things we could not know even in principle (such as unpredictable future events). It also means that we are independent agents. When we engage in a collective enterprise we therefore face the problem of communicating with each other and aligning our individual wills. While we cannot become God, we can deal with the more tractable implications of our finitude. The first step is to recognize it.

❑ Internal friction is exacerbated by the fact that in business as in war, we are operating in a nonlinear, semi-chaotic environment in which our endeavors will collide and possibly clash with the actions of other independent wills (customers, suppliers, competitors, regulators, lobbyists, and so on). The internal and external worlds are in constant contact and the effects of our actions are the result of their reciprocal interaction.

❑ Friction gives rise to three gaps: the knowledge gap, the alignment gap, and the effects gap. To execute effectively, we must address all three.

❑ Our instinctive reaction to the three gaps is to demand more detail. We gather more data in order to craft more detailed plans, issue more detailed instructions, and exercise more detailed control. This not only fails to solve the problem, it usually makes it worse. We need to think about the problem differently and adopt a systemic approach to solving it.

CHAPTER THREE

ELEMENTS OF A SOLUTION

Leading through intent

*Do not command more than is necessary, or plan
beyond the circumstances you can foresee*

CULTURE CHANGE

It is a melancholy fact that a disproportionate number of fundamental organizational innovations have their origins in disaster.
Only the prospect of perdition, it seems, releases real creativity
and radical change. Our story is no exception.[1]

It begins on a foggy day, 14 October 1806. In the course of
that day, two Prussian armies were shattered and scattered by a
French army at the twin battles of Jena and Auerstedt. Built up
by Frederick the Great in the eighteenth century, the Prussian
Army had been the most admired and successful in Europe. Its
defeat was militarily decisive and psychologically devastating.

Clausewitz was there, acting as adjutant to Prince August, who
had been given command of a battalion at Auerstedt. Clausewitz's
future mentor, General Gerhard von Scharnhorst, was Chief of Staff
of the Prussian Army. In the wake of the disaster, von Scharnhorst
led a group of men dedicated to understanding why and how it had
happened, and to transforming the organization which suffered it.[2]
"We fought bravely enough," von Scharnhorst pithily concluded,
"but not cleverly enough." The reforms he championed were a direct
consequence of his analysis of the catastrophe of the twin battles.[3]

The Army had been run as a machine which required iron
discipline to function because the motivation of its men was low.
Its training focused on processes which had been important in

the eighteenth century, but neglected others whose importance was growing. For example, it concentrated on perfecting marching drill rather than firing drill. Officers sought to counter the chaos of battle by handling troops according to mathematical principles. Nobody took any action without orders to do so. It was a highly centralized, process-dominated organization, assuming Douglas McGregor's Theory X of human motivation.[4] It achieved compliance through compulsion.

In 1806, of a total of 142 generals in the Prussian Army, 62 were over 60 years old and 13 were over 70.[5] Nor were they the brightest. A senior officer in Berlin was quoted as saying: "It is not a good idea to have too many educated officers; the commander, and then one other in charge of the advance guard is quite enough. The others are just there to get stuck in, otherwise there will be intrigues."[6]

The French Army of 1806, which Napoleon had inherited from the Revolution, was raised from citizen conscripts. It had no time to practice drill and perfect discipline, so it turned this vice into a virtue. It made extensive use of light infantry or *tirailleurs*, who engaged the lines of Prussians in an unordered swarm in which each man took advantage of the terrain and fired as he saw fit. The French were highly motivated. Their army was, in McGregor's terms, a "Theory Y" organization. It achieved commitment through conviction.

At the top level, Napoleon's dynamic young marshals, all of whom reached that position on merit, shared a few operating principles (such as "always march toward the sound of the guns") and were expected to act on their own initiative. They had the experience and ability to assess a situation and the authority to decide and act. Decisions were taken rapidly and action followed without hesitation. The result was an operational tempo which left the Prussians bewildered.

The Prussian Army needed to get cleverer and faster. Of the three fundamental variables in warfare – force, space, and time – lost forces could be replaced and lost space could be recaptured, but lost time could never be made good. It was essential to take actions which were about right quickly, rather than waiting to be told what to do. The only way of doing so was to develop a professional officer corps with the ability, authority, and willingness to take decisions in real time. With the introduction of general conscription in 1808, the officer ranks were officially opened to all, regardless of social position, and promotion was driven by performance rather than years of service.[7] So it was that the transformation of the Prussian Army began with people and culture, spearheaded by officer selection and training.

They were looking for a particular type: intelligent, independent minded, strong willed, impatient, and not overly concerned to bow to authority. In 1810, a "General War School" for officers was set up in Berlin to provide general education and professional training up to the highest level. Candidates were schooled in various disciplines, both academic and technical, so that they had a common outlook and language. A Prussian officer was expected to share a set of core values, defining his "honor," which took precedence over an order. If he acted in accordance with honor – or, as we might more commonly say today, with integrity – disobedience was legitimate. The right talent and the right behavioral biases were put in place as a first step.

However, in the long peace which followed 1815, the reforms lost urgency. Von Scharnhorst's great ally, August von Gneisenau, who was Chief of Staff of the Prussian Army at Waterloo, was too liberal for the Prussian court and was replaced in 1816. In 1831 he was carried off by the same cholera epidemic which killed Clausewitz.[8] The spirit of reform was kept alive by a few influential individuals. One was Prince Friedrich Karl of Prussia, the nephew of the future Kaiser Wilhelm I, and a practicing soldier. In a series of essays published in the 1850s and 1860s, he reinforced the growing idea that what made the Prussian officer corps distinctive, and gave it an edge, was a willingness to show independence of mind and challenge authority.[9] In an essay dating from 1860 entitled "The Origins and Development of the Spirit of the Prussian Officer," he tells the story of a staff officer dutifully carrying out an order without question, only to be pulled up short by a high-ranking general with the words: "The King made you a staff officer because you should know when *not* to obey." In contrast to other European officer corps, Prince Friedrich Karl comments, the Prussians do not allow themselves to be hemmed in with rules and regulations, but give rein to the imagination and exploit every opportunity opened up by unexpected success. Such behavior would not be possible if senior commanders were to demand full control over every unit.[10]

When Prince Friedrich Karl took over from the 80 year-old Field Marshal von Wrangel as commander of the Prussian Army halfway through its war against Denmark in 1864, he was accompanied by a shadowy adviser who had been Chief of the Prussian General Staff since 1857. The two of them led the war to a successful conclusion. Many operational commanders were not at all sure what the Chief of the General Staff was supposed to do, apart from handle administration and make sure the trains ran on time. When this Chief of the General Staff actually assumed command of the Prussian Army in the campaign against Austria in 1866, some of his subordinates were bemused. "This seems to be all in order," commented divisional commander General von Manstein on receiving an instruction from his Commander-in-Chief, "but who *is* General von Moltke?"[11]

HELMUTH VON MOLTKE AND
AUFTRAGSTAKTIK

Field Marshal Helmuth Carl Bernhard Graf von Moltke, a man born in the first year of his century, was the main builder of the German Army which emerged from it, and created the reputation of its General Staff as the pre-eminent body of professional soldiers in Europe. He was both a practitioner and a thinker in the fields of strategy, leadership, organization, and what we would today call management. His thoughts are contained in numerous essays and memoranda, but his influence at the time was more direct, for he was the leader and teacher of a generation of German generals.[12] In that role, he developed the Army's basic operating model, which has become known as *Auftragstaktik*. It is perhaps his most lasting legacy.

Von Moltke espoused the cause of independent action by subordinates as a matter of principle. In his appraisal of his own victory over the Austrians at the culminating Battle of Königgrätz in 1866, von Moltke commented that the independent actions of two Austrian generals in pressing forward, and so exposing their flanks, ultimately facilitated his victory. Remarkably, von Moltke exonerated them. It is easy enough to judge their actions now, he observed, but one should be extremely careful in condemning generals. Fear of retribution should not curb the willingness of subordinates to exercise their judgment. In the confusion and uncertainty of war, people who do so take risks. That must be accepted. The outcome of decisions involves luck and chance. Had they taken that aggressive action earlier in the day, or had they been supported by the rest of the Austrian Army, they could have reversed the result of the battle. "Obedience is a principle," he memorably asserted, "but the man stands above the principle."[13]

Von Moltke wanted to build on the Prussian officer corps' culture of independent thinking to create an effective system of command, one which also ensured cohesion. In his self-critical *Memoire* on the 1866 campaign, written for the king in 1868, two things he singled out for particular criticism are "the lack of direction from above and the independent actions of the lower levels of command."[14] This may seem surprising at first, until we see where he was heading. During the campaign, subordinates often acted independently without understanding his concept of how victory was to be achieved, which was to use one Army as an anvil and another as a hammer to take the Austrians in the flank.[15] He concluded that it was vital to ensure that every level understood enough of the *intentions* of the higher command to enable the organization to fulfil its goal. Von Moltke did not want to put a brake on initiative, but to steer it in the right direction. His solution was not to impose more control on junior officers but to impose new intellectual disciplines on senior ones.

In 1869, von Moltke issued a document called *Guidance for Large Unit Commanders*.[16] It was to become seminal, laying out principles of higher command which remained unchanged for 70 years, by which time the Prussian Army had become the German Army. Some passages are echoed in the doctrine publications of US and NATO forces to the present day.[17] It contains von Moltke's solution to the specific problem he identified in the *Memoire*, and directly addressed the general problem posed by the greatly increased scale of modern warfare: how to direct an organization too large for a single commander to control in person. As such, it is probably the first document of modern times to define the role of the senior executive in a large corporation.

The document covers a range of technical issues, such as the order of march and contemporary tactics. What is of interest here is the approach to command and control. The emphasis is on the former rather than the latter – if von Moltke's senior people could set direction effectively, control measures on his junior people could be less restrictive.

The guidance opens by emphasizing the importance of clear decisions in a context of high friction, which renders perfect planning impossible:

> *With darkness all around you, you have to develop a feeling for what is right, often based on little more than guesswork, and issue orders in the knowledge that their execution will be hindered by all manner of random accidents and unpredictable obstacles. In this fog of uncertainty, the one thing*

that must be certain is your own decision... the surest
way of achieving your goal is through the single-minded
pursuit of simple actions.

To accomplish that single-mindedness, orders must be passed down "to the last man." The army must be organized so that it is made up of units capable of carrying out unified action down to the lowest level. The chain of command and the communications process should ensure that instructions can be passed on. But the chain of command can get disrupted, and some tasks can only be carried out by mixed units put together for the purpose. So a clear chain of command is not enough, nor can processes dominate people. At all levels, people must remain in charge:

There are numerous situations in which an officer must
act on his own judgment. For an officer to wait for orders
at times when none can be given would be quite absurd.
But as a rule, it is when he acts in line with the will of his
superior that he can most effectively play his part in the
whole scheme of things.

An officer's readiness to act in this way depends on discipline. For junior officers, discipline means being ready to act on your own initiative in line with the will of your commander. For senior officers, discipline involves maintaining the chain of command, and:

not commanding more than is strictly necessary, nor
planning beyond the circumstances you can foresee. In
war, circumstances change very rapidly, and it is rare
indeed for directions which cover a long period of time in
a lot of detail to be fully carried out.

Specifying too much detail actually shakes confidence and creates uncertainty if things do not turn out as anticipated. Going into too much detail makes a senior commander a hostage to fortune, because in a rapidly changing environment, the greater the level of detail, the less likely it is to fit the actual situation. It also creates uncertainty about what really matters. Far from overcoming it, a mass of instructions actually creates more friction in the form of noise, and confuses subordinates because the situation may demand one thing and the instructions say another.

Furthermore, trying to get results by directly taking charge of things at lower levels in the organizational hierarchy is dysfunctional:

> *In any case, a leader who believes that he can make a positive difference through continual personal interventions is usually deluding himself. He thereby takes over things other people are supposed to be doing, effectively dispensing with their efforts, and multiplies his own tasks to such an extent that he can no longer carry them all out.*
>
> *The demands made on a senior commander are severe enough as it is. It is far more important that the person at the top retains a clear picture of the overall situation than whether some particular thing is done this way or that.*

Having issued some warnings about what not to do, von Moltke formulates his positive guidance on giving direction as follows:

> *The higher the level of command, the shorter and more general the orders should be. The next level down should add whatever further specification it feels to be necessary, and the details of execution are left to verbal instructions or perhaps a word of command. This ensures that everyone retains freedom of movement and decision within the bounds of their authority.*

The need for secrecy means that one has to be careful about spelling out motives, expectations, and future intentions in orders. However, it is vital that subordinates fully understand the purpose of the order, so that they can carry on trying to achieve it when circumstances demand that they act other than they were ordered to do.

Every command position needs to understand as much of the higher command's intentions as is necessary to achieve its purpose:

> *The rule to follow is that an order should contain all, but also only, what subordinates cannot determine for themselves to achieve a particular purpose.*[18]

The overall direction should be communicated in a cascade. Direction from the highest level should be kept high level. The levels below add appropriate detail. Each level is guided by the intention of the one above, which whenever possible was articulated in a face-to-face briefing as well as in writing. Understanding the context and the overall intention is what enables junior officers to take independent decisions if the specific orders issued to them become invalid because of a change in the situation.

Mindful of the realities of communication, von Moltke advises people to repeat verbal orders and, conversely, to examine orders received with great care in order to sort the information in them into what is certain, what is probable, and what is possible. Understanding an order means grasping what is essential and taking measures which put that before anything else.

So it is that by 1869, von Moltke had already outlined a way of closing the three gaps. His solution to each runs directly counter to our intuitive responses.

On the knowledge gap, he emphasizes the need to plan only what can be planned, the need for judgment and timely decision making based on what one can ascertain, and the acceptance of uncertainty. A decision maker will of course seek to gather whatever relevant information they can in the time available. However, some residual uncertainty will always remain. Rather than seeking to fill the gap completely by gathering more data, von Moltke suggests adjusting the scope of plans to the available knowledge and using it to identify the essentials.

On the alignment gap, he recommends a process whereby each level draws out the implications of the one above so that the lower levels are more specific and nested in the levels above. Plans should be appropriate to their level: the lower the level, the more specific and detailed they should be. Each level will know less about the overall context and more about the specific situation than the level above. So the higher level should tell the lower level what it needs to know about the situation of the organization as a whole, the overall purpose, the immediate intention of the higher level, the specific role the unit is to play and the roles of other units around it, the freedoms it has, and any constraints it has to observe. That is all it needs to know. With this knowledge of what to achieve and why, it should itself decide about how to achieve it. It will have more accurate and more up-to-date information about the situation it is facing and will therefore know best what specific actions to take. By exercising self-restraint in telling its subordinate unit only what it needs to know, the higher-level unit clears space within which the subordinate is free to take decisions and act.

On the effects gap, he encourages the use of individual initiative within boundaries and actually requires junior people to depart from the letter of their instructions if the situation demands it in order to fulfill the intent. Rather than tightening control, he suggests that as long as the intentions of the higher levels are made clear, individual initiative can be relied on to adjust actions according to the situation. The imposed discipline of controls and sanctions is replaced by the self-discipline of responsibility. There should be no fear of punishment if a calculated risk fails to pay off. Sins of omission should be regarded as far more serious than sins of commission.

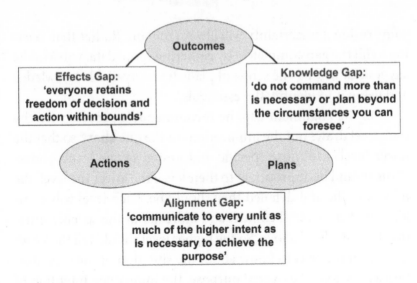

Figure 6 Von Moltke on the three gaps

His view could be summarized as in Figure 6. This is von Moltke's solution to the problem he identified in the 1868 *Memoire*. It is simple, but remarkable. Consider the more obvious alternative.

Faced with a situation in which junior officers had a high degree of *autonomy*, in the sense that they were prone to take independent action, but the organization's actions were not *aligned*, because direction was not getting through from the top, most of us would think about the problem as a trade-off like that in Figure 7.

We would interpret the observations in the *Memoire* as indicating that the organization had drifted too far to the right and was allowing too much autonomy. The answer would be to move it to the left and increase the degree of alignment – not all the

Figure 7 A choice?

way, perhaps, but enough to get a balance between two conflict-ing requirements. We would do some analysis of operational best practice to lay down the best solutions to specific tactical situa-tions, make our policy documents and orders more detailed, and institute tighter, more restrictive controls. It would be a compromise.

Von Moltke's insight is that there is no choice to make. Far from it, he demands *high* autonomy and *high* alignment *at one and the same time*. He breaks the compromise. He realizes quite simply that the more alignment you have, the more autonomy you can grant. The one enables the other. Instead of seeing of them as the end-points of a single line, he thinks about them as defining two dimensions, as in Figure 8.

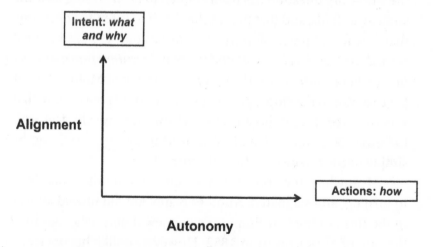

Figure 8 High alignment enables high autonomy

The insight is that alignment needs to be achieved around intent, and autonomy should be granted around actions. Intent is expressed in terms of *what to achieve and why*. Autonomy concerns the actions taken in order to realize the intent; in other words, about *what to do and how*. By requiring his commanders to distinguish between "what and why" on the one hand and "how" on the other, von Moltke creates an organization which is positioned at the top right of this chart.

The result is that the organization's performance does not depend on its being led by a military genius, because it becomes an intelligent organization. Rather than relying on exceptional – and by definition rare – individuals, this solution raises the performance of the average.[19] Being able to adapt to circumstances, the organization will tend to make corrective decisions while executing, even if the overall plan is flawed. That may not guarantee a great strategy, but it does make it unlikely that the organization would career headlong into disaster, as the Prussian Army had in 1806. By building this sort of capability, the risks of a flawed strategy have been mitigated because the intelligence of the whole organization has been applied to determining how the strategy unfolds, and that process has been so extended over time that it is for all practical purposes continuous. He has in effect *turned strategy development and strategy execution into a distinction without a difference.* The corollary is that von Moltke did not have to wait to develop a perfect plan. He could go with one that was 70 percent right, because the organization would deal with the other 30 percent. He did not need to know everything, he simply needed to be directionally correct.[20]

Meanwhile, the French Army waited for another Napoleon to turn up, and stagnated. Another Napoleon did indeed appear in the form of the first Emperor's nephew, Louis, who assumed the title of Napoleon III in 1852. However, unlike his uncle, he was not a genius. In 1870, rivalry between France and the increasingly self-assertive state of Prussia turned into war, and von Moltke, as commander-in-chief of the Prussian forces, faced the severest test of his career.

When the French Army met the Prussian Army on the field, the results of Jena–Auerstedt were reversed. A neutral observer of the campaign, the Russian General Woide, described the Prussian command doctrine as having the effect of a "newly perfected weapon."[21] It was like a secret weapon, for it was invisible. The miracle was that each man acted on his own accord, but in such a way that the actions of the army as a whole cohered. "Every German subordinate commander," wrote Woide, "felt himself to be part of a unified whole; in taking action, each one of them therefore had the interests of the whole at the forefront of his mind; none hesitated in deciding what to do, not a man waited to be told or even reminded."[22] The Prussian Army seemed to have mastered the fast-moving, ever-changing chaos which distinguished the modern battlefield to a remarkable degree. It appeared to have reconciled autonomy and alignment.

However, that was not how things felt from the inside. The Prussian Army had indeed won the war with France, but things had not gone smoothly. It was struggling to deal with new technology and the cultural clash between von Moltke's bright young things in the General Staff and the bulk of the line commanders.[23] It had got the essentials right and coped better with the mess and confusion of war than its opponent had, but many of its own people were critical of both performance and methods. Along with questions of tactics, the central issue under debate was how to retain control while encouraging independent action. Von Moltke had got the answer to precisely that question and so one might think that would have been the end of the matter. Not so. He had won the war but he had not yet won over everyone in his organization. Dogmatism was not in his nature and he encouraged debate. After 1871, the victorious army got into a furious argument with itself.

Technology was making the issue more acute. The increasing range and accuracy of modern rifles meant that formations had to be loose, rendering control yet more difficult. Battles were often won or lost by the actions of company commanders. Sometimes they made up for mistakes committed by their superiors. Sometimes, though, their headstrong decisions led to unnecessary losses. Cohesion was on a knife edge. Two ideas fomented the debate: the reinforcement of von Moltke's observation that a higher intent had to unify action; and the realization that every unit had to have a task or mission of its own to perform which made sense within that context.[24] To work out what worked, test cases from the war were refought and rethought on paper.

One particular incident became a *cause célèbre*. On 14 August 1870, the Prussian First Army under Lieutenant General von Steinmetz approached French forces holding high ground to the east of the fortress of Metz. In accordance with von Moltke's orders, it halted near the town of Colombey to observe the opponent's actions. Von Moltke's orders had also stated that his intention was for the First Army to hold the French while the Second Army enveloped them. In his general orders for the conduct of the war, he had stated that his overriding principle was to attack the enemy without delay wherever they were met, while keeping his own forces together.[25]

The commander of 26th Infantry Brigade, Major General von der Goltz, observed the French forces in front of him starting to withdraw. One of von Moltke's staff officers was with him and confirmed that the intention was to hold the French in position in order to allow an envelopment. Orders from the First Army were to remain on the defensive. There was no time for von der Goltz to ask his division, division to ask corps, corps to ask von Steinmetz, and maybe even von Steinmetz to ask von Moltke what to do, and then relay the order back again. So von der Goltz sent off a message to his division, his own corps, and his neighboring corps saying that he was going to attack, and at 3.30 p.m. he launched an assault.[26]

His men got into trouble, but his neighboring brigadier saw what was happening and joined in. So did the two divisions of his neighboring corps. The engagement ended that evening in a stalemate, but the French withdrawal had been delayed and the Prussians had maintained contact with them. Von Steinmetz was furious with the lot of them and ordered them to withdraw, so they sent back a few of their reserve troops to placate him. But in the morning the king arrived and forbade any withdrawal. Metz was sealed off and bypassed. Steinmetz accused von der Goltz of recklessness, and others agreed with him. The next day, one of von Moltke's staff officers assured von der Goltz that "his course of action had eminently furthered the objects aimed at; for the delay which the battle had caused the French was favorable to our projected operations and would facilitate their execution."[27]

The debate over this case continued for decades after the war in numerous publications. In a later history of the campaign, Steinmetz recorded his "disapprobation that so serious an action had been engaged in without orders from higher authority, and that it had been permitted to develop to such an extent, when the role of 1st Army was essentially defensive."[28] In his own account of the war, von Moltke expressed particular satisfaction with the spontaneous mutual support his senior officers gave each other, and observed that the outcome of Colombey prevented French withdrawal and allowed his Second and Third Armies to cross the Meuse.[29] The final judgment was passed in a tactical manual published in 1910: "His decision is one of the finest examples of spontaneous action taken within proper bounds."[30]

Passing final judgment on tactical methods also took years. The argument started as a three-way contest. The first group were the conservatives, who saw themselves as the upholders of the true Prussian tradition. They wanted to abandon the curse of loose-order tactics, which allowed the battlefield to descend into chaos, and re-establish disciplined, close-order formations. Their voices soon melted away.[31] The main debate was conducted by two schools, both demanding change. One was known as the *Normaltaktiker*, because they wanted to create standard specifications (*Normen*) for tactical procedures. They sought to establish coherence by training infantry leaders in the use of detailed methods of deployment and attack. The other school argued that no such recipes were possible. They were dubbed *Auftragstaktiker*, because they wanted to exercise control by specifying the mission (*Auftrag*) to be accomplished and leave decisions about how to do so to junior leaders on the spot.[32] Anything else would drive out the spirit of initiative. Junior leaders had to be properly trained and then trusted to make the right decisions. It was an argument between those who wanted to *manage chaos* by controlling *how* and those who wanted to *exploit chaos* by commanding *what and why*.[33]

The *Auftragstaktiker* of the Prussian Army, which after 1871 became the German Army, were developing a new concept of discipline. They argued that while in the eighteenth century it was possible to be successful on the battlefield by inculcating "passive discipline," which effectively meant breaking the will of the individual solider and turning him into an automaton, modern conditions required inculcating "active discipline." Active discipline did not mean following orders but acting spontaneously in accordance with intentions. A soldier did not have the choice *whether* to obey, but he was left free to choose *how* to obey. Military journals of the time contain much debate over the meaning of the words *selbsttätig* (spontaneous) and *selbstständig* (independent). The writers were looking for a definition of active obedience as independent thought leading to action which arose from a voluntary personal impulse. One of von Moltke's acolytes, General von Schlichting, coined the phrase *selbstständig denkender Gehorsam* – "independent thinking obedience." The moral and emotional basis of *Auftragstaktik* was not fear, but respect and trust.[34]

If every officer had the responsibility to exercise thinking obedience, they also had the responsibility to give clear direction. In the 1869 guidance von Moltke had made the distinction between an order – *Befehl* – and a directive – *Direktive* or *Weisung*.[35] This entered into general use. In 1877, General Meckel wrote that a directive had two parts. The first was a description of the general situation and the commander's overall intention;

the second was the specific task. Meckel stressed the need for clarity: "Experience suggests," he wrote, "that every order which can be misunderstood will be."[36] The intention should convey absolute clarity of purpose by focusing on the essentials and leaving out everything else. The task should not be specified in too much detail. Above all, the senior commander was not to tell his subordinate *how* he was to accomplish his task, as he would if were to issue an order. The first part of the directive was to give the subordinate freedom to act within the boundaries set by the overall intention. The intention was binding; the task was not. A German officer's prime duty was to reason why.

It was clear that if individuals within the organization were to tread the narrow path between the Scylla of rulebook passivity and the Charybdis of random adventurism, and so unify autonomy and alignment, they must also have a shared understanding of how to behave and what they could expect of their peers and their superiors. They needed a common operational doctrine and shared values. The organization had to have a high level of trust. The Army articulated the behavior it expected in the new Field Service Regulations issued in 1888, the year that von Moltke retired as Chief of Staff, and these were strongly influenced by von Schlichting. It recognized that battle quickly becomes chaotic. It emphasized independence of thought and action, stating that "a failure to act or a delay is a more serious fault than making a mistake in the choice of means." Every unit was to have its own clearly defined area of responsibility, and the freedom of unit commanders extended to a choice of form as well as means, which depended on specific circumstances. The responsibility of every officer was to exploit their given situation to the benefit of the whole.

The guiding principle of action was to be the intent of the higher commander. Officers were to ask themselves the question: "What would my superior order me to do if he were in my position and knew what I know?" An understanding of intent was the *sine qua non* of independent action.[37] It was official. By the time of von Moltke's death in 1891, the *Auftragstaktiker* seemed to have won through.

Nevertheless, the path of true change does not run smooth. Their opponents still did not give up; and now the master was gone. Perhaps the successes of 1866 and 1870 had all been down to his unique genius. Perhaps *Auftragstaktik* was merely a matter of personal style and would not work without him. The new regulations were subject to continual criticism in journals, and it is there in fact that the term *Auftragstaktik* is first found in the early 1890s, coined by its opponents.[38] The first attempt to define it in writing did not come until 1906, when Major Otto von Moser published a widely read but unofficial book about small unit tactics which devoted five pages to the concept. Von Moser emphasized its value as a means of reconciling independence and control.[39]

The arguments continued into the first decade of the twentieth century, which saw two events which finally drew the debate to a close. The first was the Boer War of 1899–1902, the second the Russo-Japanese War of 1904–5. Both were taken to illustrate the superiority of the new doctrine as mirrored in the tactics of the Boers in the one case and of the Japanese in the other. The Japanese Army had been advised by German staff officers who taught them the principles of the 1888 Regulations, which were confirmed by the new German Regulations of 1906.[40] The debate ended, but that did not mean that the new doctrine was a reality. The Germany Army was actually an amalgamation of the four armies of Prussia, Saxony, Württemberg, and Bavaria, each of which guarded its own traditions. The key figures in determining doctrine were the 25 corps commanders, and each of them had their own views. On the eve of the First World War, there was as much diversity as unity.[41]

In 1914, the methods which had overcome the French in 1870 served to overcome the Russians at Tannenberg, but narrowly failed in the west. They were made subservient to the vast and logistically impossible masterplan designed by Chief of Staff von Schlieffen and falteringly followed by his successor, von Moltke's less gifted nephew.[42] As the front became static, the principles of *Auftragstaktik* took a secondary role to principles of attrition, and so the First World War took its dreadful course until 1918. Even so, *Auftragstaktik* played its part in enabling the Germans to hold their lines against successive Allied offensives. In an environment in which communications between higher commanders and junior officers were uniquely fragile, the speed with which junior officers reacted to potential breakthroughs was critical to maintaining an effective defense. The willingness of German company commanders to change dispositions, commandeer reserves and launch local counter-attacks without further orders was one factor among many why so many Allied offensives stagnated.[43]

In March 1918, for the first time since late 1914, the German Army abandoned its reliance on artillery, machine guns, and trenches and flung a body of infantrymen called Stormtroopers, imbued with the principles of *Auftragstaktik*, at the British lines. In a few weeks they made larger gains in territory than the Allies had made in the previous three years. Nevertheless, slowed down by the resilience and firepower of their opponents, who were ordered by Field Marshal Haig to fight "with their backs to the wall," the Stormtroopers finally outran their artillery and their supply chain. On 18 July, the British gathered reinforcements and counter-attacked, and having themselves achieved a skill and a flexibility in the use of artillery unique at the time, joined their Allies to force the Germans back, until on 11 November 1918 the two sides signed an armistice. The 100,000 men the Allies allowed the Germans to keep as an army re-examined their 100-year-old traditions.

The new Chief of the General Staff, Hans von Seeckt, a veteran of the mobile war in the East, decided to turn his army of

100,000 men into an army of 100,000 officers. Training was centered on inculcating a spirit of initiative and von Schlichting's "independent thinking obedience." To further this and create greater levels of trust, all NCOs were trained as officers, and officers were expected to master the tasks of two ranks higher up the hierarchy and to take their place if needs be. Whereas von Moltke had restricted the use of directives to the higher levels of command, their use was now pushed right down the hierarchy.[44] In 1933, the German Army produced a new guide to its leadership philosophy called *Truppenführung* (literally "Troop Leadership"), which marks the next stage in the maturity of *Auftragstaktik*. It was issued to all officers. In it we read:

> *The basis of leadership are the mission (Auftrag) and the situation.*
>
> *The mission identifies the goal to be achieved and must always be the point of focus. A mission which tries to encompass multiple tasks can all too easily obscure what really matters.*
>
> *An uncertain situation is normal. It will rarely be possible to gain more accurate information about the state of the enemy. While you should obviously try to find out as much as possible, waiting for more information in a critical situation is seldom a sign of incisive leadership, and often a serious mistake.*
>
> *The mission and the situation lead to a decision. If the mission no longer provides a sufficient basis for action, or if it is made redundant by events, the decision has to take this into account. If anyone changes a mission or does not carry it out, he must report the fact and he alone bears responsibility for the consequences. He must always act within the framework of the whole.*
>
> *A decision should pursue a clear goal with all the means available. It is the resolution of the leader which*

carries it through. The will to succeed can in itself often bring about success.

Once a decision has been made, it should only be departed from in exceptional circumstances. In the vicissitudes of war, however, sticking rigidly to a decision can also be a mistake. Part of the art of leadership is to recognize the time and circumstances in which a new decision is called for.

A leader must grant his subordinates freedom of action as long as doing so does not compromise his intention. He must not, however, allow them to make a decision for which he is responsible.[45]

At 6 a.m. on 1 September 1939, Hitler unleashed the organization built around these principles on Poland, and on 5 October the last fragment of the Polish Army surrendered. On 10 May 1940, he unleashed it on France and on 22 June France surrendered, the British Army having in the meantime been evacuated from Dunkirk. On 22 June 1941 he unleashed it on the Soviet Union, and it proceeded to gain the largest and most spectacular victories in the history of land warfare.

In the end, of course, despite all the battles won by the German Army, Germany lost the war. It became a war of attrition like the previous one. Hitler's hideous ideology and murderous war aims gathered against him an alliance wielding massive superiority of resources, which was determined to extirpate the canker which had grown in the heart of Europe. The operational skills of the Wehrmacht were deployed in an attempt to realize a strategy which at the highest level was incoherent and irrational. Despite that, it took the combined forces of the two postwar superpowers, the British Empire, and the resistance of most of western Europe five years to defeat it. In its last battle, the Battle of Berlin in April–May 1945, what remained of the German Army inflicted 300,000 casualties on the three Soviet Army Groups which finally overcame it.[46]

A contributing factor to the German defeat was Hitler's contempt for the principles of *Auftragstaktik* and his attempts to reverse its practice, particularly on the Eastern Front from 1942 onward. Running through the whole conception was the principle of trust. Hitler had never trusted his generals. As long as they won battles for him he left them alone, but as the demands he placed on them grew and the scope of the war extended beyond Germany's ability to fight it, so success faltered. As half-victories turned into defeats, his mistrust grew, and with it his interference and the level of detail he tried to manage.[47] *Auftragstaktik* is not popular with tyrants.

FROM *AUFTRAGSTAKTIK* TO MISSION COMMAND

Among historians of the Second World War, attention has been increasingly devoted to the performance of the German Army and what can be learned from it. It was remarkable, as any of those who fought against it will attest. As one American veteran of Normandy and the Rhineland puts it: "Until you've fought the German army, you have never fought a real battle."[48] Scholars and researchers have tried to analyze why this was so. In 1977 US Army Colonel Trevor Dupuy reluctantly concluded:

> *On a man for man basis, the German ground soldier consistently inflicted casualties at about a 50% higher rate than they incurred from the opposing British and American troops under all circumstances. This was true when they were attacking and when they were defending, when they had a local numerical superiority and when, as was usually the case, they were outnumbered, when they had air superiority and when they did not, when they won and when they lost.[49]*

The reasons for this are many and various, but there can be little doubt that one of the major ones was *Auftragstaktik*.[50] After a while, some of those who defeated the German Army began to realize that the Germans were on to something and began to devote the subject some attention. As it crossed both the Channel and the Atlantic, so *Auftragstaktik* slipped into English as "mission command."[51]

It was some time before it did so, however. Once again, a crisis was required. Immediately after the war nobody bothered to examine the concept. After all, what did the winners have to learn from the losers? With the formation of NATO, the losers became allies, but very junior ones. It was in any case beginning to look as if technology would allow masterplanners to control everything, with perfect information becoming instantaneously available at the center. As the brightest and the best assembled in Washington to run the Vietnam War under former Ford executive Robert McNamara, they reveled in vast amounts of data and superb communications. They measured body counts and then told the generals in Vietnam what to do next. This created a "pathology of information."[52] The business paradigms and management theory of the 1960s invaded the Pentagon and it all went horribly wrong.

The impact of Vietnam on the US military bears some comparison with the impact of Jena on the Prussians. Digesting those lessons continued over a long period until, with the end of the Cold War in the late 1980s, the whole of NATO went through an identity crisis. NATO had been designed to fight the Red Army as it swarmed over the north German plain. There was a masterplan. Every NATO soldier knew exactly where he had to go and what he had to do when that happened. When it became clear that it was not going to happen, NATO had to prepare for something else, the nature of which no one could specify. Traditional methods of command and control clearly had to be replaced. The answer was mission command.

In the British Army, the ground had already been prepared

in the 1980s by Field Marshal Sir Nigel Bagnall. As commander of 1st Corps in Germany and then the Northern Army Group, he argued that NATO's "tripwire" approach was an inadequate counter to current Soviet doctrine. NATO troops occupied elaborately prepared forward defenses, and when that "tripwire" was activated, tactical nuclear weapons were to be used. Bagnall wanted to replace this with a flexible response based on maneuver and a counter-stroke. He realized that in order to achieve this he needed to transform the mentality of the British officer corps. In order to do that, he used the same instrument von Moltke had: training and education. He created a new Higher Command and Staff Course for senior officers to teach mission command, and stimulated a series of new publications dealing with doctrine. His influence spread beyond the British Army to other NATO forces. From 1985–8 he was Chief of the General Staff, and so was able to impose his will. As such, he was to mission command in Britain what von Moltke was to *Auftragstaktik*.[53]

Today, the operational manuals of organizations like the US Marine Corps or the British Army all contain passages which could have been lifted from *Truppenführung*. Mission command is part of official NATO doctrine. Something like it has long been practiced by élite forces. NATO has realized that it was not just a burdensome necessity, but something that actually improved the performance of regular army units. It was first applied on a large scale in the Gulf War of 1991.

Nevertheless, why should the results of these endeavors be of interest to us today?

First, they represent one of the earliest, well-documented attempts in the modern age to create a system of what we now call "empowerment," granting wide freedom of action to junior members of a large, complex organization. The desirability of doing so was not generally accepted in the business world until well into the latter half of the twentieth century. Indeed, during the first half of that century, business went the other way.

Frederick Winslow Taylor's slim volume, *The Principles of Scientific Management*, appeared in 1911. His approach to business exactly parallels von Bülow's approach to war, although Taylor was writing, to great acclaim, 100 years later. Taylor recommended the rigorous separation of planning and execution. "Thus all the planning which under the old system was done by the workman, as a result of his personal experience," he wrote, "must of necessity be done by the management in accordance with the laws of science... in most cases one type of man is needed to plan ahead and an entirely different type to execute the work."[54] Taylor was dedicated to analysis which went into unprecedented levels of detail, and so enabled a degree of control bordering on the obsessive. He describes his methods with pride:

> *The work of every workman is fully planned out by management at least one day in advance, and each man receives in most cases complete written instructions, describing in detail the task which he is to accomplish.*[55]

His most famous example was his analysis of the work of a Dutchman called Henry Noll, whom he called Schmidt, loading pig iron from a field into a railroad car at the Bethlehem Steelworks. Taylor had concluded that each of the loaders ought to be able to handle between 47 and 48 tons per day instead of the 12.5 tons they were in fact averaging. A man with a stopwatch stood next to Noll, telling him when to pick up a pig iron, when to walk, and when to rest, and gave Noll the incentive of being able to earn $1.85 a day instead of $1.15 if he did as he was told.[56] So he got compliance. Taylor got increased productivity. Businessmen across the world rejoiced, and businesses across the world mimicked the Prussian Army of the 1700s.

Scientific management worked for quite a while. It was not until the 1980s that some writers began to suggest that business organizations were more like organisms than machines and that they contained people with brains as well as hands and legs.[57] It is only since then that the environment described by Clausewitz has become recognizable as the world of business. It is what we have to deal with today and we are not having an easy time of it. The cumulative experience offered by the military is much greater.

Secondly, mission command is not something invented by a small, innovative organization which manages to be flexible because everybody knows everybody else or in which everything works well because of the personality of its leader. Mission command is *scaleable*. It does not work because a bunch of creative individuals team up and do funky stuff together. There have been and continue to be plenty of those. A few manage to grow and develop a culture which preserves creativity; many do not. Their experience is not transferable to large, established organizations which cannot afford to throw everything away and start all over again. Oil companies do not work like 20-person software houses and pharmaceutical companies do not work like biotechs. Exhorting them to learn from their smaller cousins is of limited practical help. In contrast, mission command has been made to work in organizations of hundreds of thousands of people with attendant levels of complexity.

Thirdly, neither *Auftragstaktik*, nor its descendant mission command, was developed as a theory, but as a *set of practices* which were continually modified in the light of experience. It was vigorously questioned and debated. Weaknesses were exposed and ironed out and the results were anchored in reality. Its effectiveness has been tested time and again in the most demanding environment any organization can face: battle. Not to examine it and try to learn from it would seem like looking a gift horse in the mouth.

We are helped here by the fact that as a set of practices which are themselves taught, techniques and processes have been developed which make it easier for other organizations to adopt them. There is a method for developing plans, breaking them down, and using them to brief subordinates. There is a procedure, which the military calls "mission analysis," to help subordinates to draw out the implications of what they have been asked to achieve. The subordinates then go through a process of "backbriefing" their superiors to check their understanding of the intent and its implications before passing it down the line to their own subordinates in a cascade. These techniques create internal predictability, which helps when the environment is chaotic, and allow scaleability. They can be adopted, in barely modified form, by any organization trying to have an impact on the world outside it. Using these techniques requires skill. The military invests an enormous amount of time and effort in training. Not for nothing did the Prussians set up the War Academy in 1810. This is a significant point. Adopting mission command as an operating model is not a matter of setting up some processes, but of mastering some skills, perhaps more precisely called "disciplines." Only when those skills have been mastered can the process be adopted. Taking over the processes without building the skills is simply pouring old wine into new bottles, adopting a dead form.

Finally, mission command is in principle *transferable*. Originating in observations made by Germans about the French, it has been adopted by other Europeans and by Americans. Behavioral norms constituting an organizational culture were channeled into a unified set of practices. Adopting those practices facilitated cultural change in organizations with very different traditions and cultural norms. They were not documented for a long time. The German Army had no wish to make its practices widely known, and for years passed them on through training and tradition alone.[58] It has been suggested that its roots in Prussian traditions make *Auftragstaktik* a uniquely and peculiarly German phenomenon.[59] Yet there was nothing inevitable about its development – it was highly controversial and its general adoption hotly contested, in part by people who argued that it was counter to Prussian traditions.[60] The case of the British Army in particular shows how mission command can be adopted by an organization

81

whose traditions run directly counter to it.[61] The Israeli Army has adopted a home-grown version of mission command, drawing on any and every source it could find about what led to military success as well as its own experience.[62]

Despite that, we have to recognize that the cultural soil out of which mission command grew is the hardest factor to reproduce and may act as a constraint in transferring it into some organizations. The Germans worked on their culture for decades. In those armed forces where it has been imposed from the top in a short period, the results vary according to the cultural roots and behavioral norms of different organizations within them. Anecdotally, it is generally accepted that mission command is most deeply rooted in special forces, airborne forces (who have always stressed the value of "airborne initiative"), and both the Royal Marines and the USMC. In regular units of the US Army and British Army, while the introduction of its techniques (such as the use of "mission-type orders") has had a positive effect, it has not penetrated as deeply. The author of a recent study of mission command in the British regular army concludes that since the Bagnall reforms, its principles "have still not been totally anchored in the organisational behaviour and working practices whilst in barracks," the core barriers being "linked to risk aversion and careerism."[63] It is more deeply rooted in the Royal Navy because the principles of mission command were normal practice in the eighteenth century and are hallowed in the Nelsonian tradition.[64] Within the Navy itself it is arguably best practiced in the submarine service, which has a tradition of being more maverick than the surface fleet.

So the cultural background of any organization attempting to adopt mission command should limit its expectations. That does not mean that it is not worth trying, as the example of the British Army shows. It is more a way of gauging the extent of the effort required. A dyed-in-the-wool bureaucracy which has systematically selected out the type of people who thrive in this environment will require a major transformation and experience a high turnover of people. Few businesses are as far gone as that. Most of them have drifted rather than rotted. A high level of discontent on the part of talented people is a sign that mission command could take root quite quickly, as it would liberate them. It is the silent, compliant ones who pose the greatest challenge.

FROM MISSION COMMAND TO LEADING THROUGH INTENT

The hazards of searching for universal principles behind what makes effective organizations are very great. Yet the rewards of identifying some things which at the very least are very important a lot of the time could also be great. Indeed, to positively deny that there could be any such things seems to fly in the face of evidence. Management is not a science but a practical art. Practicing it skillfully means applying general principles in a specific context. It helps to identify what the critical principles are.

The principles espoused by von Moltke 150 years ago are far more than 150 years old. One of the world's leading military historians has suggested that throughout history, "those armies have been most successful which did not turn their troops into automatons, did not attempt to control everything from the top, and allowed their subordinate commanders considerable latitude." He cites not only von Moltke's army commanders but the Roman centurions and military tribunes, Napoleon's marshals, and the Israeli divisional commanders in 1967. One might have added Nelson's captains.[65] "All these," he adds, "are examples, each within its own stage of technological development, of the way things were done in some of the most successful military forces ever."[66]

Clearly, this is not necessarily the way things are done in business organizations. However, we do find elements of this way of operating in some of the most consistently successful ones.[67]

Shortly after becoming Chairman and CEO of GE in 1981, Jack Welch read a letter in *Fortune* magazine written by Kevin Peppard, Business Development Director of Bendix Heavy Vehicle Systems. The letter is worth quoting in full:

Through your excellent series on the current practice of strategic planning runs a common thread: the endless quest by managers for a paint-by-numbers approach, which would automatically give them answers. Yet they continually fail in that pursuit.

I am struck by the parallel to military strategists. Before the French Revolution, generals had seen military strategy as a matter of geometry, with precise rules to observe... Precepts had abounded... then Napoleon disproved all the maxims.

Von Clausewitz summed up what it had all been about in his classic On War. *Men could not produce strategy to a formula. Detailed planning necessarily failed, due to the inevitable frictions encountered: chance events, imperfections in execution and the independent will of the opposition. Instead, the human elements were paramount: leadership, morale, and the almost instinctive savvy of the best generals.*

The Prussian general staff, under the elder von Moltke, perfected these concepts in practice. They did not expect a plan of operations to survive the first contact with the enemy. They set only the broadest of objectives and emphasized seizing unforeseen opportunities as they arose. In current American parlance, the art of the broken-field runner was the key to success. Strategy was not a lengthy action plan. It was the evolution of a central idea through continually changing circumstances.

Business and war may differ in objectives and codes of conduct. But both involve facing the independent will of other parties. Any cookbook approach is powerless to

*cope with the independent will, or with the unfolding
situations of the real world.*[68]

Welch took over the approach, calling it "planful opportunism."[69]
He quoted Peppard's words in a speech to the financial community in New York delivered on 8 December 1981, and it remained
a lasting principle of his celebrated term of office at GE.[70] Welch
describes that speech as "a disaster," because the analysts could not
understand why he put so much emphasis on "the human element." Undeterred, the whole of the next 20 years, he claims, "was
toward the vision I laid out that day."[71]

We need to find a name for mission command in commercial
organizations. "Command" is a military term not used in business.
It covers those aspects of leadership concerned with setting and
giving direction. "Mission" is simply a translation of *Auftrag* to
mean a task directed toward fulfilling a purpose. In business it
risks confusion with the meaning of "mission" found in high-level
mission statements, a far more abstract sense than the military use
of the word. Welch's choice of phrase captures von Moltke's
refusal to compromise and his insistence on achieving alignment
and autonomy. The result is an organization whose actions cohere
because it is following a clear direction, and seizes unexpected
opportunities because individuals and groups adapt as they go.

The name I have chosen for mission command in business
is "leading through intent." Its essence can be summarized as in
Figure 9 overleaf.

This solution constitutes a system and enacting it involves
going round a loop. It involves abandoning the linear model of
developing a strategic plan and then implementing it. Instead,
there is a cycle of thinking and doing. The horizon within which
actions are planned is limited, the effects of the actions are
observed, reflected on, and new action initiated. So the
thinking–doing loop becomes a learning–adapting loop. An
organization which behaves in this way will be observed to take

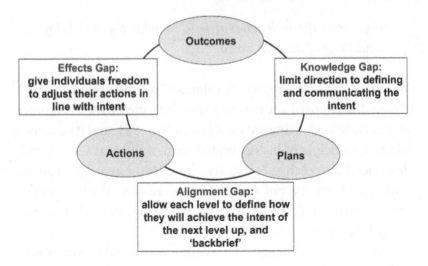

Figure 9 Leading through intent

action rapidly and keep adjusting what it does. So the "plan-and-implement model" of strategy becomes a "do-and-adapt" model. Strategy development and execution merge into one circular process, as in Figure 10.

The thinking–doing loop is kept as short as possible so as to reduce uncertainty and increase tempo. However, the intended outcomes may be far away in time. The key is not to plan the whole journey but to set direction and allow the organization to navigate. They will need a map before they set out, but they can add detail to the map as they go. They will be able to do so because as they go round the loop, they learn.[72]

With great consistency, mission command allows armies to make rapid decisions in an uncertain, fast-changing environment and to translate them, without delay, into decisive action. They can act faster than their opponents and *keep on doing so*, because speed is built into them structurally. By the same token, they can exploit unexpected opportunities and recover from setbacks. Mission command creates an organization which is not only more thrusting, but more resilient. If they have a clear understanding of

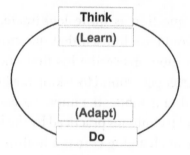

Figure 10 The do-and-adapt cycle

purpose, people understand what matters and can react quickly to whatever is unexpected, be it good or bad. Beyond this, mission command unleashes human energy and acts as a motivator. It demands, creates, and fosters large numbers of leaders and enables them to stretch themselves while working within limits. Leading through intent can achieve the same thing in business.[73]

Watching the Prussians in 1870, General Woide thought that they had perfected a secret weapon. He was right, in that the most important things happening were going on in people's heads. People whose self-understanding is a version of Noll's, who see themselves as functionaries, the servants of a process, or cogs in a machine, behave quite differently from those who understand themselves as independent agents bearing some responsibility for the achievement of a collective purpose and as part of a living organism. The ultimate test of how embedded the disciplines are is how individuals think. In his comparison of the US and German armies of the 1940s, van Creveld points to the difference succinctly:

A German officer, confronted by some task, would ask: worauf kommt es eigentlich an? *(what is the core of the problem?). An American one, trained in the "engineering approach" to war, would inquire: what are the problem's component parts?*[74]

The American's question is quite legitimate, of course. The German officer would ask himself that question as well, but he would ask it only after answering his first one. The American would typically never get around to asking the first one at all. The difference in mindset is subtle; the impact is enormous.

The command techniques practiced by the military continue to be refined. The unchanging core is a holistic approach which affects recruiting, training, planning and control processes, but also the culture and values of an organization. Mission command embraces a conception of leadership which unsentimentally places human beings at its center. It crucially depends on factors which do not appear on the balance sheet of an organization: the willingness of people to accept responsibility; the readiness of their superiors to back up their decisions; the tolerance of mistakes made in good faith. Designed for an external environment which is unpredictable and hostile, it builds on an internal environment which is predictable and supportive. At its heart is a network of trust binding people together up, down, and across a hierarchy. Achieving and maintaining that requires constant work.

It is now time to see how to turn the principles into practice. The first issue is how, with partial and imperfect knowledge, we decide what action we want the organization as a whole to take. We have in some way to plan what outcomes we want. We must close the knowledge gap.

QUICK RECAP

☐ The Prussian Army developed an operating model called *Auftragstaktik* which enabled it to consistently overcome the three gaps. This development began in 1806 and the first step was to change its culture by creating a meritocratic officer corps which valued independent thinking and initiative.

❑ The leader who turned the culture into a system was Helmuth von Moltke the elder, who fostered high levels of autonomy and worked out how to simultaneously achieve high alignment.

❑ His answer to the knowledge gap was to limit direction to defining and expressing the essential intent; he closed the alignment gap by allowing each level to define what it would achieve to realize the intent; and he dealt with the effects gap by giving individuals freedom to adjust their actions in line with intent. The result is to make strategy and execution a distinction without a difference, as the organization no longer plans and implements but goes through a "thinking–doing cycle" of learning and adapting.

❑ Such a model will only work if people are competent and share basic values. Von Moltke invested considerable resources, including his personal time, in developing people, an activity centered on the War Academy.

❑ The principles of *Auftragstaktik* have since been adopted by armed forces across the world, particularly those of NATO, under the name "mission command."

❑ The model is scaleable and transferable, and it is robust because it is not a new idea but a set of practices which evolved over a long period. The theory behind it stands in contrast to the scientific and engineering approaches which dominated management thinking until the 1980s.

❑ Some features of mission command are exhibited in some business organizations today. Grasping the principles as a whole offers a dividend over the value of the parts. I give mission command in business the name "leading through intent."

CHAPTER FOUR

THE KNOWLEDGE GAP
What and Why

*Strategy is a framework for decision making,
a guide to thoughtful, purposive action*

VON MOLTKE ON STRATEGY

Why does a business need a strategy in the first place? As a collective enterprise, a business organization needs to act cohesively. It may have a very clear vision or sense of purpose, and for some types of organization that can suffice to provide the cohesion needed. However, it is unlikely to suffice for a business. A business is a collective enterprise that has to prosper in a competitive environment. Before the 1970s, business success was widely regarded as a matter of participating in attractive markets. As everybody followed this precept, competition within these markets increased, making them less attractive, and returns became mediocre. To sustain good returns, each business had to work out not only which markets to participate in but how it was going to prevail against the others who were trying to do the same thing. Strategy had arrived.

The fundamental purpose of most businesses is to create value, often measured by – and sometimes identified with – the value created for shareholders. From the point of view of those responsible for directing the business, that does not specify *how* value is to be created. From the point of view of the members of the organization, it does not tell them *what* they are supposed to do. They need some direction, and what makes that direction *strategic* is that it answers the question: "How are we going to compete?" A good strategy is derived from insight into the basis of competition.

Answering the question "How are we going to compete?" prepares us for a collision with a series of independent wills outside the organization: those of customers, who may appear to be well disposed but who are ultimately unconcerned about our fate; and those of competitors, who, though they may share some common interests, are ultimately out to thwart us. We may have allies in the form of suppliers, but we must engage them too with our enterprise or face unreliability, or even a war on two fronts. Then there are others – such as regulators, legislators, the media, and money-lenders – who may help or hinder us, stick by us through thick and thin, or demand kilograms of flesh at inopportune moments, but all of whom shape an environment of shifting constraints.

Because it involves preparation, we tend to identify strategy with a plan. This is dangerous. Our quest for certainty can lead us to fall into the trap set by the knowledge gap and try to make perfect plans. This amounts to a failure to face reality.

In 1871, von Moltke wrote a three-page essay called "On Strategy" which confronts us with that reality. "The aspiration of strategy," he wrote, is "to achieve the highest end it can with the means available." In the case of military strategy, the ends are determined by politics. However, the military means available can make the desired ends unattainable. In that case the ends will need to be reconsidered. In the realm of organizational strategy, both ends and means are ambiguous and interdependent. The relationship between them is reciprocal.

The first task of the strategist is to make resources available and deploy them. Initial resource deployment has to be broadly correct, for it cannot be made good later on. Here, detailed planning is required well in advance of any action. Von Moltke and his staff made meticulous arrangements for deploying the army in different scenarios, down to the detail of railway timetables. They did so because detail mattered, the arrangements were complex, central coordination was vital, they had plenty of time to get things right, and no one was trying to stop them. Their mobilization plan meant that when war was declared in 1870, they beat the French to the frontier and were able to carry the war to their territory with superior forces. It gave them a competitive advantage. During the deployment von Moltke himself spent his time reading novels.

Things are different, however, in the next main task of strategy: the use of these resources on operations. For here, we encounter the independent will of an opponent, which we can constrain but not command. Von Moltke continues with what has become his most celebrated observation:

> *No plan of operations can extend with any degree of certainty beyond the first encounter with the enemy's main body.[1] Only a layman could imagine that in following the course of a campaign he is watching the logical unfolding of an initial idea conceived in advance, thought out in every detail and pursued through to its conclusion.*
>
> *Whatever the vicissitudes of events, a commander will need to keep his mind fixed unwaveringly on his main objectives, but he can never be certain beforehand which paths offer the best hopes of realizing them. Throughout the campaign he will find himself forced to make a whole series of decisions as situations arise which no one was able to predict.*

The first sentence of this passage is a necessary truth. From the point at which his forces meet the enemy, the strategist meets an independent will and is engaged in Clausewitz's wrestling match. The outcome of his actions depends on the reactions of his enemy – even if the enemy chooses to do nothing – and those reactions cannot be predicted with any degree of certainty. They may not even be rational. In the second sentence we hear the voice of experience. During the campaign of 1870, the French hardly ever did what von Moltke expected. His pragmatic rule of thumb was to work out what his opponent's best option was and to assume they would do that until proved otherwise. Once he was convinced that they were doing something else, he adapted his own moves accordingly. He remained calm and unruffled because he never expected his predictions to be correct. From the outside it looked like a genius following a masterplan, but it was in fact a prepared mind searching for the best path toward his goal. In the event, the blundering French commanders offered him some short-cuts which he followed with alacrity.

He had prepared his mind to make decisions during the process of executing the strategy. He refers to them as "acts of spontaneity" and they were as much part of the strategy as the initial planning had been. In a passage echoing his own advice to large unit commanders, he explains the intellectual discipline needed to make those decisions:

> *Every case is unique. It is all a matter of seeing through the fog of uncertainty in which every situation is shrouded, making an accurate assessment of what you do know, guessing what you do not know, reaching a conclusion rapidly and then vigorously and unwaveringly following it through.*

He expected to decide on a course of action with all the elements of friction working to create further difficulties: chance events, accidents and errors, misunderstandings and delusions, and, he writes, what some may choose to call "fate." This may sound like muddling through by making things up as you go along. It is not, however:

> *Even so, this does not mean that the conduct of war is completely blind and arbitrary. The balance of probabilities is that the sum of all those chance events is as much to the detriment or advantage of one side as the other, and*

that a commander who in each case issues directions which are at least sensible, even if not optimal, stands a good chance of success.

It hardly needs saying that to do this, theoretical knowledge is not enough. Mastering this free, practical art means developing qualities of mind and character which are shaped by military training and guided by experience drawn from military history or from life itself.

When all is said and done, the reputation of a commander rests on his success. How much of it is in fact down to his own efforts is very hard to say. In the face of the irresistible power of circumstances even the best man[2] can fail, and by the same token it can shield mediocrity. That said, in the long run, those who enjoy good luck usually deserve it.

In strategy there are no general rules or theorems of any practical value, von Moltke observes. It is not a science, and a good strategy is not enough to guarantee success:

Indeed, strategy provides tactics with the means of beating the enemy and can increase the chances of success through the way in which it directs armies and brings them together on the battlefield. On the other hand, strategy builds on every successful engagement to exploit it further. In the face of tactical victory the demands of strategy are silent – it must adapt to the newly created situation.

Strategy is a system of heuristics. It is more than science, it is the application of knowledge to practical life, the evolution of an original guiding idea under constantly changing circumstances, the art of taking action under the pressure of the most difficult conditions.[3]

Dating from the century before last, this is a radical view.

Von Moltke effectively rejects the notion, so well established that it is often taken as a given, that strategy is a long-range plan, standing in contrast to "operations" which are short-term actions. Yet, if we are not doing strategy now, when will we do it? Surely, if a strategy has any value, it must be something we are doing *now*. It must inform operations. What we do operationally must be grounded in strategy, it must provide its rationale. Operations must be the *manifestation* of strategy. Otherwise, the organization would be doing things without knowing where it was heading or what it was trying to achieve. It would be blind.

Von Moltke clearly rates the value of strategy very highly, as the articulation of an "aim" which the organization's leaders must always keep clearly in mind, and stick to whatever happens. It is not a path, but a direction. A direction could be set by giving a destination or simply a compass heading. It could be set by saying "Get to San Francisco" or "Go west, young man."[4] For the direction to be strategic, it would have to involve competition: someone else would have to be trying to stop us, or get there before us. Going west would require some planning so that we could muster and allocate resources and sequence events. A *race* to the west would require a strategy. A business in a socialist economy needs a plan, which requires the administrative resource-allocation skills of a manager. A business in a market economy needs a strategy, which requires the additional skills of a commander who can allocate resources so as to gain a competitive advantage.

A strategy seeks to realize the "highest end it can" given the means available. Means are limited, and so partly determine what the strategy should be. If we had unlimited resources, we would not have to worry too much about our strategy. If we were to try something and fail, we could write off our losses, gather more resources, and try again. No one is in that position, but the more constrained our resources are, the cleverer we have to be. Having limited resources, we must make choices about how to deploy them. We cannot do everything.

Ideally, we would set a direction by determining both the compass heading and the destination. However, we may not be able to set both. If long-term uncertainty is very high, we may not be able to say where we want to get to at a distant future point. For example, there may be big changes expected in technology or regulations which will affect our markets profoundly over the next few years but their exact nature and timing are unknown. We may not need to worry about that very much, though; arriving at Los Angeles might serve us as well as arriving at San Francisco. The important thing is to get going. With a broad sense of what changes are likely, we can get away with a compass heading like "Go west" and keep our future options open. On the other hand, if short-term uncertainty is very high because the markets are currently very turbulent, we may not be able to say whether to go west or north over the next few months. However, we may be clear about where we want to get to when things have calmed down. In that case the destination will give a capable organization enough direction to be able to duck and weave its way through the uncertain period and emerge in a better place than it started in.

The best that strategy can do is to offer the *probability* of success, to shift the odds in one's favor. Luck will play a part, but a good strategist can manipulate luck by loading the dice. While von Moltke does not shirk the original decision about resource allocation, he does not regard it as the end of the matter. Conducting a campaign will involve continuous decision making, seeking not to take perfect decisions, any more than we should seek to create a perfect plan, but ones that are sensible given the circumstances. We need to make decisions which are "about right – now,"[5] take action to change the situation, and then move on to the next decision. The laws of probability dictate that if our decisions are reasonably good, we will avoid disaster and are likely to do quite well. We will certainly outperform someone who tries to take one big decision about how to do everything or someone who makes no decisions at all. We manipulate luck by making a series of small choices which open up further options. To be good at this we need knowledge, but also judgment and skill acquired through native talent and training. Doing strategy is a craft which, like all practical skills, can only be mastered through practice, by learning from our own and others' experience.

So although the aim is constant, the path can change; indeed, it normally should. The existence of the original aim gives coherence to the decisions and provides criteria for subsequent decision making as circumstances change. However, the relationship between strategy and operations, between strategy development and strategy execution, is reciprocal: "strategy builds on every successful engagement to exploit it further." Strategy is about fighting the right battles, the important ones you are likely to win. Operations are about winning them. The intelligent way to manipulate luck is to observe the effects of actions and exploit successes. The organization thus goes round the thinking–doing loop.

So strategy and operations become a distinction without a difference. All we can observe is an organization taking actions. Whether the consequences were intended or not makes no *difference*, but we can still *distinguish* strategy from operations. Operations are about doing things right. They involve reacting to problems and eliminating weaknesses, because in conducting operations you are as strong as the weakest link. You can improve by imitating others, because achieving operational excellence means adopting best practice. Strategy, in contrast, is about doing the right things. It involves proactively shaping events and investing in strengths, because in creating a strategy you have to make choices, to decide to do some things and not to do others. You can shift the odds in your favor by differentiating yourself from others, because a good strategy seeks uniqueness.

Rather than a plan, a strategy is a *framework for decision making*. It is an original choice about *direction*, which enables subsequent choices about *action*. It *prepares* the organization to make those choices. Without a strategy, the actions taken by an organization degenerate into arbitrary sets of activity. A strategy enables people to reflect on the activity and gives them a rationale for deciding what to do next. A robust strategy is not dependent on competitors doing any single thing. It does not seek to control an independent will. Instead, it should be a "system of expedients" – or as we might say today "heuristics" – with the emphasis on *system*.

Von Moltke thought through worst-case scenarios and insured against the downside while being ready to exploit the upside. This kind of thinking created a surplus of space, time, and resources. When his opponents failed to do what he feared, he exploited his surplus.[6] He did not plan for one, but he was prepared for one. He created a system within which his expedients were available. His opponents always ran out of options before he did. So strategy becomes "the evolution of an original guiding idea under constantly changing circumstances." A strategy is thoughtful, purposive action.[7]

Though it is rarely articulated as succinctly as in this three-page essay from 1871, there is some reason to believe that von Moltke's conception of strategy is gaining support, if not consensus, in the business community.

STRATEGY, PLANNING, AND PREPARING

Since its high tide in the 1970s, the strategic planning school, led by writers like Igor Ansoff and Peter Lorange, has fallen out of favor. They were the heirs of von Bülow. Henry Mintzberg has played the role of a polemical Clausewitz, his efforts culminating in *The Rise and Fall of Strategic Planning*, a book of over 400 pages devoted to a detailed critique of the planners, the final chapter of which also tried to salvage something positive from their methods.[8] It is sobering to realize that this book appeared as late as 1994. It is sad that it expends so much effort on describing what you *should not* do, whereas Clausewitz and von Moltke concentrated on what you *should* do. Mintzberg points out that "formal planning does not create strategy so much as deal with the consequences of strategy created in other ways,"[9] ways he describes elsewhere as "crafting strategy."[10] The order is critical: first the strategy, then the plan.

If the notion of strategy as a plan is moribund, the notion of it as a framework for decision making is gaining ground. The change is being led by practitioners. In an article published in 2001 that rediscovers some of the principles of von Moltke's essay just 130 years later, Kathy Eisenhardt and Don Sull quote examples of companies including Yahoo! and eBay, Dell and Cisco, Miramax and Nortel as conceiving of strategy as "simple rules" which guide decision making.[11] The examples make the idea sound new and modern, whereas it is merely enlightened.

Among those adopting the more enlightened view are planners themselves. Daniel Simpson spent nine years as head of strategy and planning at a $3bn consumer goods company headquartered in the US. Disillusioned by the results of planning and the need to absorb much of the literature Mintzberg toiled through (some of which, he opines, is "not very helpful" and a portion of which he describes as "complete rubbish"), Simpson concludes that the keys to success are "an overall sense of direction and an ability to be flexible."[12] The example of successful practice he quotes is Welch's "planful opportunism," one case in which we know for certain that von Moltke was a direct influence. Welch himself had great influence in this area, not only because of the status of GE and his record, but also because at the beginning of his tenure GE was generally recognized as the leading exponent of strategic planning. Welch's view was that as a result strategic thinking had almost disappeared, and in 1984 he dismantled the planning system.[13]

Simpson adds an interesting comment after citing Welch. "I think more successful companies are developed through this sort of planful opportunism than through the vision of an exceptional CEO," he writes. "They aren't in the media spotlight as much as companies with the visionary CEO, but they are more common."[14] This is no surprise; exceptional CEOs are by definition uncommon. However, it also demonstrates that the original intention of the Prussian reformers, to create an intelligent organization whose performance did not depend on its being led by a genius, is as true in business. And if there is evidence that our thinking about strategy is catching up with von Moltke's, at this point we are still behind. We are extraordinarily reluctant to admit that luck plays a part in business success. The media create a cult of CEO heroes and their salaries are now such that restless shareholders have become rebellious. We would do well to remember that while a leader's reputation is ultimately based on success, "how much of it is in fact down to his own efforts is very hard to say."

This is a serious matter. A recent scholarly article argues that the greater a CEO's celebrity, the greater their perceived control over the actions and performance of their firm. This leads CEOs to continue to take actions associated with their own celebrity, and to create hubris.[15] This poses a double jeopardy: the delusion that one can control external events (i.e., a denial of friction); and the delusion that one is solely responsible for success, with a concomitant tendency to command a great deal more than is necessary (i.e., a reversal of a core principle of leading through intent). Hubris encourages a return to the deadly cycle of organizational stagnation we examined in Chapter 2. Because friction is rooted in human finitude, ignoring it is to play at being God. To attribute to CEO-heroes the ability to control events and be immune to good or bad luck is at heart a metaphysical worldview reminiscent of Greek polytheism or even, at the extreme, medieval theology.

Strategy, then, demands a certain type of thinking. It sets direction and therefore clearly encompasses what von Moltke

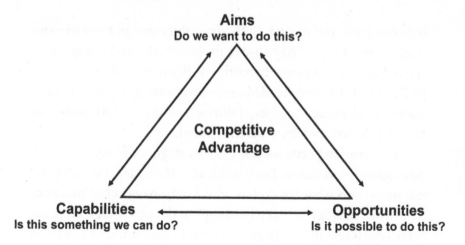

Figure 11 A good strategy is realistic and coherent

calls a "goal," "aim," or "purpose." Let us call this element the *aim*. An aim can be an end-point or destination, and aiming means pointing in that direction, so it encompasses both "going west" and "getting to San Francisco." The aim defines what the organization is trying to achieve with a view to gaining competitive advantage. How we set about achieving the aim depends on relating possible aims to the external *opportunities* offered by the market and our internal *capabilities*. The process of thinking strategically involves relating three points of a triangle, as in Figure 11.

A good strategy creates *coherence* between our capabilities, the opportunities we can detect, and our aims. Different people have a tendency to start with, and give greater weight to, one or other of these three factors. Where they start from does not matter. Where they end up does. The result must be cohesion. If any one of these factors floats off on its own, dominates thinking at the expense of the others, or is simply mismatched, then in time perdition will follow.

The strategy triangle confronts us with the first observation von Moltke makes about the nature of strategy: reciprocity between ends and means. Both are ambiguous and interdependent. In most of our day-to-day problems, the end is a given. It is fixed and we just have to work out the means of achieving it. In Figure 11, the two-headed arrows indicate that our consideration of the means (our capabilities and the opportunities we face) co-determines the ends (our aims).

Reciprocity pervades not only strategic thinking but decision making and action. Because the effects of our actions depend not merely on what we do but on the actions of other independent wills, strategy will need to adapt to the newly created situations which result. It is thus a "system of *heuristics*." The task of strategy is not completed by the initial act of setting direction. Strategy develops further as action takes place, old opportunities close off, new ones arise, and new capabilities are built. The relationship between strategy development and execution is also reciprocal. Doing strategy means thinking, doing, learning, and adapting. It means going round the loop. The reappraisal of ends and means is continuous.

In assessing ends and means, we have above all to be realistic. Developing strategy is an intellectual activity. It involves discerning facts and applying rationality. Leadership is a moral activity. It involves relating to people and generating emotional commitment. Developing a strategy around pre-existing emotional commitments is courting disaster. When people convince themselves that they have the capability to do something that in fact they do not, just because a lot of other people seem to be doing so, or convince themselves that the market will love the latest thing to pop out of R&D, just because their own engineers love it, strategies fail. When companies set themselves the aim of growing from an also-ran to a market leadership position in two years simply because doing so will boost the CEO's share options, shareholders' money is squandered on failed acquisitions and hopeless investments.

Many of the best-known strategy development tools – such as Porter's five forces and value chain models, the matrices for displaying competitive position used by BCG or McKinsey, cost analysis, supply curves, market segmentation, and so on – are in fact tools for analyzing the situation and trying to work out what drives success. Useful though they are, they do not produce strategies. They help to sort out information, simplify the complexities of reality, and focus attention on the essentials of the situation, internal or external. They are only effective if they generate insight into the basis of competition.

A notion central to Clausewitz's thinking about strategy was that war aims and the strategy adopted to realize them should be developed from an understanding of what I am calling the "basis of competition," and what he called the enemy's "center of gravity." "Making out this *centra gravitatis* in the enemy's war effort," he wrote, "to identify its spheres of influence, is a central point of strategic judgment."[16] The term, like friction, is borrowed from mechanics:

> *Just as the center of gravity is always to be found where the greatest mass is brought together, and just as every blow delivered against the load's center of gravity is the most effective... so it is in war. The forces of every protagonist, whether a single state or an alliance of partners, have a certain unity, and by virtue of this some coherence; it is where there is coherence that we find analogies to a center of gravity. There are therefore certain centers of gravity in these forces, the movement and direction of which govern other points, and these centers of gravity are to be found where the largest forces are gathered.*[17]

So it is in business too. Businesses engage in a vast range of activities. The art of strategic thinking is to identify which of them is the decisive differentiator, the determinant of competitive advantage. It involves mastering and sorting through a vast range of activities and simplifying them accurately down to the essentials which make the difference. The true strategist is a simplifier of complexity. Not many people can consistently do it well.

Clausewitz knew that. Indeed, so rare did he judge the qualities leading to strategic insight to be, that he gave the chapter in which he describes them the title "Military Genius."[18] We should treat this much-abused term with caution. Clausewitz was using it in the precise sense defined by Kant: genius is a gift of nature which intuitively develops the rules of human practices such as the arts.[19] Clausewitz's comments are worth quoting:

> *If he is to successfully prevail in this constant struggle with the unexpected, then two qualities are essential:* firstly a mind which even in this heightened darkness is not without some shafts of inner light which lead him to the truth, and then the courage to follow that dim light. *The first can be characterized with the French expression* coup d'oeil *and the second is* conviction.[20]

This sounds a bit dangerous. It could be an excuse for stubbornness, for not listening, for bees in the bonnet and private agendas. That is why it is rare. The key is determination based on insight. Clausewitz realized this:

> *There are people who possess a highly refined ability to penetrate the most demanding problems, who do not lack the courage to shoulder many burdens, but who nevertheless cannot reach a decision in difficult situations. Their courage and their insight stand apart from each other, never meet, and in consequence they cannot reach a decision. Conviction results from an act of mind which realizes that it is necessary to take a risk and by virtue of that realization creates the will to do so... the sign of a genius for war is the* average rate of success.[21]

The phenomenon of making good judgments in uncertainty has since been the object of careful examination. It is about the use of intuition.

Psychologist Gary Klein has made a study of intuitive decision making. By observing experts in a given field in situations in which they made decisions, Klein realized that they did not follow the conventional "rational model" of developing and evaluating options before choosing between them. They seemed to go straight to the answer, using what appeared to nonexperts, and indeed often to themselves, to be a "sixth sense." On analysis, the sixth sense turned out to be perfectly rational. It was based on pattern recognition. Through years of experience in their field, experts build up patterns of expectation, and notice immediately when something unusual occurs which breaks the pattern. These signals make the "right" decision obvious to them. It looks to others and feels to them to be intuitive, but the intuition is schooled, and rational. Clausewitz gives it the French name *coup d'oeil*, the glance of a practiced eye. Germans more usually refer to *Fingerspitzengefühl*, the "feeling in your fingertips." In the Anglo-Saxon world things take place more viscerally – it is "gut feeling." Whatever the language, schooled intuition is the basis of insight.[22] It was this discipline which von Moltke mastered in his domain of military strategy.

Insights into the center of gravity of a business and hence innovative strategies tend to come from people of long experience who have an unusual capacity to reflect on that experience in such a way that they become aware of the patterns it shows. This awareness enables them to understand how all the elements of their experience relate to each other so that they can grasp and articulate the essentials. Because of this, what to others is a mass of confusing facts is to them a set of clear patterns making the answer to many problems obvious. Hence they have the courage to act. Because they base their decisions on that understanding, and because that understanding is sound, they tend in the long run to get more things right than wrong and so demonstrate the above-average success rate that Clausewitz identifies as marking them out. We tend to speak of them as having "good judgment." In their field they do. But because it is grounded in pattern recognition, the quality of their judgment is dependent on context and they do not necessarily display it in every area of human activity.[23]

A short story may illustrate the point.

A few years ago, I visited a manufacturer of domestic boilers. At the time, the company was number three in the market and was not only making good returns but gaining share, closing the gap with the number two player. I asked all the top executives why the company was so successful. One said it was the quality of the product – but he admitted that the differences with competitors' products were small. One said it was the brand – but had to admit that the market leader's brand was also very strong. So it went on: R&D, technology, production efficiency, delivery times, customer service – all had their advocates, but none in itself felt compelling.

My last interview was with the managing director. I asked him once again why the business was so successful. "Let me tell you how our business works," he said. "Almost all of our domestic business is for replacement of existing boilers. People replace boilers when their existing ones break down. What do you do when your boiler breaks down? You call the installer," he continued, answering his own question. "When he tells you the boiler is too old to repair because he can't get the parts, what do you do?" He paused. "I'll tell you. You do what he suggests. And when you ask him which new boiler to install, he tells you that too. So 90 percent of all purchasing decisions are made by the installer." He paused to let this sink in. "Our business," he said deliberately, "is about *service to the installer*. But I am the only person around here who gets that. They all think I'm an old man with a bee in his bonnet." He looked me in the eye. "We are being successful because we offer our installers better service than any of our competitors. But we can do even better. I know that if we gear up the whole company toward optimizing service to the installer, right across the value chain, we can become market leader."

It all seemed very simple. It made perfect sense. The company was clearly doing more to enhance service to the installer than any other player in the market. Everyone knew that it was important – but so were lots of other things. The managing director was the only one there who regarded it as essential. He knew every detail of his business, built up over 30 years of experience. He did not only know every tree in his particular wood, he could describe the state of the bark on each one. However, he was the only one who could readily describe the shape of the wood. He had grasped the basis of competition, the center of gravity of the business, and hence the source of its competitive advantage.

This informed all his operational decisions. He wanted to increase the number of visits installers paid to the company's site – which was already more than any of their rivals – and build a new training center. He was obsessed with the quality of its installation literature. He was ready to invest whatever it took to increase spare parts availability at the distributors so that installers did not waste time waiting for a part. He wanted the new range of boilers the company was just developing to be energy efficient, quiet, and reliable, but above all he wanted them to be easy to install. And so on. And it was working.

He wanted to run some strategy workshops to focus all his top team on optimizing service to the installer. They were already making their implicit strategy happen, but as it became explicit and the top team grew more aligned, so decision making and execution became more focused. Within a few years the company overtook the number two player in the UK market and at the time of writing is the established market leader.

In this example, service to the installer is the *source of competitive advantage* my friends are seeking to exploit. Their *aim* is to achieve leadership of their chosen segments. They have identified becoming the supplier of choice to the installer as an *opportunity* across the market, and by excelling at that they are unhinging the position of their major competitors. They already have the *capabilities* to do so, but they are investing further in those capabilities and creating others. They are doing what all successful strategists do, which is to build further on their existing strengths. They therefore have a coherent strategy – they have linked up all three corners of the strategy triangle.

Their capabilities took time to build and have become complex and interlocking. They have allowed the company to build a position in the market which is sustainable because they also create barriers around it, making it difficult for competitors to do the same thing as well as they do. The proposition they offer installers is a powerful one. That results in further intangible advantages such as their reputation. Their proposition has become hard to copy, and by continuing to invest in its strengths, the company is maintaining its advantage. Their strategy informs all their decisions and their operational plans. It is being pursued as a central idea under continually evolving circumstances.

Their competitors are having to play a similar game, because service to the installer is the center of gravity of the business as a whole. Other businesses admit of more than one center of gravity. In the airline business, one can compete on the basis of service, focusing on the business traveler, but in the last decade some have realized that another option is to compete on price, and the low-cost airline – offering a very different value proposition – has changed the business as a whole, based on an insight into another set of market opportunities and a different set of corresponding capabilities. Centers of gravity are not static. For example, changes in technology have altered the basis of competition in the computer business from the period of the CPU, through the distributed server, to the PC, to the laptop. Failing to shift its position fast enough, the original dominant player, IBM, lost its position, went through a crisis, and has emerged as a survivor in a very different and more diverse competitive landscape.

Identifying the competitive center of gravity is a first step in setting direction and will inform further decisions. The most fundamental strategic decisions are those determining the compass heading and/or destination. From those follow further decisions about investment, resource allocation, and actions. The direction has to be turned into a path, the route of which is always informed by the center of gravity, but which also takes account of changing circumstances. That means that making the strategy happen will require a whole series of decisions on the part of a wide range of people.

Being made in the context of strategy, those decisions will have the reciprocal relationship between ends and means that is characteristic of it. As they involve overall direction, they will tend to be cross-functional and, as von Moltke observed, they will tend to be "one-offs" because every situation is unique. If we approach them with the natural, intuitive decision-making approach described by Gary Klein, we run a serious risk of getting things wrong. Unless we are strategy specialists (as some consultants are), it is unlikely that our experience base will be appropriate and we may tend to prejudge an issue as being of a certain type. That is the main reason most of the functional executives in the boiler company could not see that service to the installer was the center of gravity. They all knew that it was important. There is an enormous difference between knowing that something is important and realizing that it is the basis of competition.

Having an inappropriate experience base is dangerous when the nature of the issue itself is at stake. We are also liable to become emotionally anchored on a certain solution or type of solution. We therefore need to put together a diverse team and run a disciplined process of going round the loop, moving from the framing of the question itself, through option generation, to option evaluation, and back to reframing the question. It is a characteristic of high-performance teams that they go round the loop more quickly and reframe more often than average ones. It is usually reframing that generates creative solutions. It is because it involves systematic, "going-round-the-loop" thinking rather than linear thinking that von Moltke can refer to strategy as a "free practical art."

In order to provide guidance for decision making under continually evolving circumstances, strategy can be thought of as an *intent*.

INTENT AND MAIN EFFORT

What is important here is as much what strategy development does *not* do as what it does do. The need is in part to leave well alone. To understand what strategy could be in an environment characterized by friction, we are seeking a minimalist definition of its most essential elements.

Essentially, a strategy has to articulate an intent. An intent is the decision to do something now (a task) in order to achieve an outcome (a purpose). The decision will be a function of the situation and the aim. A good analysis of the situation will result not simply in a description of things that are going on, but insight into the basis of competition, the center of gravity of the business. Strategy is essentially an intent rather than a plan, because the knowledge gap means that we cannot plan an outcome but only express the will to achieve it, and the effects gap means that we cannot know for certain what the effects of our actions will be, and that we will probably have to modify our actions to achieve the outcome we want. We can only do that if we are clear about what outcome we desire.

If we are lucky, we may be able to penetrate the fog of uncertainty around us sufficiently to be able to set a compass heading and a destination. If we are unlucky, we may not be confident about either. Most of the time we will be able to do one or the other to some degree. Whatever the uncertainties, the organization has to have some idea where it is heading and what to do next. In all cases, but particularly in the worst case of high short- and long-term uncertainty, we can exploit the reciprocal nature of strategic thinking to help us. By going round the loop of ends and means, we can define the minimum that strategy needs. Even if we are unsure about the destination, we can specify an end-state; and even if we are unsure about our compass heading, we can specify a next step.

Suppose that we are unsure about the destination: We don't know if it is San Francisco we want to get to. However, we do know that it is a place on the coast, with a harbor and a fertile hinterland. Los Angeles might also fit the bill – we can't yet say, nor do we have to. Or we may not be able to say today which product market segments we will want to compete in in three years' time. But, based on our current position, we could say that they will be high-end segments where the basis of competition is customer service. If we think backward from that end-state, effectively "retrapolating" from a desired future rather than extrapolating from the present, we can work out what we will need to do between now and then in order to be able to compete effectively in that future. By thinking backward we can derive a next step.

Suppose that we are unsure about our compass heading: we don't know if we want to go west or south. However, we do know that we will have to move on from where we are now, and that we cannot do so without some means of transport. Getting a wagon and supplies becomes our current priority. Or we may not be able to predict how long current market turbulence will last, nor what the product priorities of our customers will be, but whatever happens we do know that we must reduce costs and improve customer service. Whatever the future holds, doing this now will open up more options than are currently available to us by removing constraints to which we are currently subject. By thinking through the essential demands of the present, we can also derive a next step.

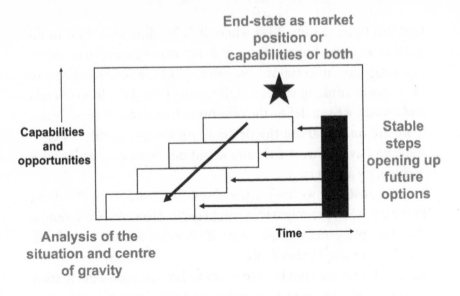

Figure 12 The strategic staircase

If we put end-state retrapolation and next-step analysis together, we can create what conceptually and diagrammatically might be called a strategic staircase, as in Figure 12.

Michael Hay and Peter Williamson, the developers of this model, have shown how the thinking behind it was used to guide the remarkable rise of the Japanese construction equipment company Komatsu from a subscale, local manufacturer of cheap and unreliable products to a world leader.[24] It took Komatsu some 20 years to attain an end-state which it memorably enshrined in the motto "Maru-C," meaning to encircle – and crush – Caterpillar, the world leader in 1971 when Komatsu embarked on its journey. While the ambition seemed fantastic at the time, it was not chosen at random. In the long run, unless it were to match and overtake Caterpillar, Komatsu could not survive. Its analysis of the situation concluded that even if it stayed in Japan, Komatsu could not avoid direct competition with the world leader and that it would be heavily disadvantaged unless it faced and overcame the challenge head on. Caterpillar's formidable capabilities specified

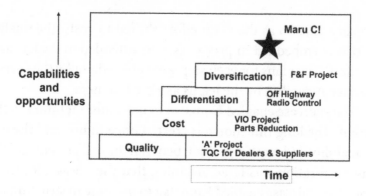

Figure 13 Komatsu's strategic staircase

the end-state Komatsu had to achieve. In creating it, Komatsu worked backward from there to create a series of decisive points, which Hay and Williamson characterize as the steps making up a staircase, each resting on the previous one, as in Figure 13.

The individual steps were identified and sequenced on the basis of economics and customer needs. No construction company would be interested in purchasing poor-quality products. If a piece of equipment were to break down on site, the costs of downtime and the expense of repairing and replacing it would quickly mount. Quality and reliability were worth paying for, so quality had to come first. If Komatsu offered the same quality as its competitors, the decision would then move to price. So cost was important, but only once quality had been achieved. After that, gaining share would have to come from developing specialized equipment, so product differentiation was next.

The steps formed the "President's theme" for the year. Each step began as a project. Quality was addressed by licensing technology and setting up total quality control systems inside the company. Once that had been achieved, cost was engineered out of the product with a parts-reduction project and by rationalizing the supply chain. However, the quality had to remain. In a staircase, each step rests on the one below it and the whole relies on every one. So as the main effort shifted to costs, the quality effort was embedded in processes, and extended to dealers and suppliers. The plans for each step were created not by the corporate executives, but by the teams assigned to them.

The staircase enabled Komatsu to link a distant future to the present. The long time horizon created uncertainty, and the gap in capability and market position between the real present and the future aspiration was large, meaning that there was a lot to be done. The staircase enabled Komatsu to use time to structure the large number of things which had to be done and so create focus. It would have been difficult if not impossible to make progress if the company had tried to do everything at once. It would have become mired in complexity of its own making. Instead, it worked its way through a huge change program by focusing on one theme at a time, each of which resulted in a stable position which improved on the preceding one, opened up future options, and was carried out with a view to what would follow. So, although the initial focus was quality, it could not be achieved at any cost, because everyone knew that cost would itself be the next area of focus – though they did not know at the time how they would address it. The long time horizon produced uncertainty, and the nature of the end-state was initially quite vague, only gradually acquiring shape. Defining direction in this way offered the company enough, but not too much, to make progress.

Complexity is the most insidious enemy of execution. If the environment is complex, the temptation is to mirror the complexity internally. If it is fast changing, the temptation is to match it with the pace of internal change. In fact, if an organization is to cope it needs to create as much internal predictability as it can and to make things simple.[25]

An organization can deal with complexity by doing many simple things, all of which are related to an overriding intent.

The steps of a staircase are not to-do lists but sets of tasks related to each other as elements of a whole. Not all tasks are equal. At each level, one task is defined as the "main effort." The steps of the staircase define the company's main effort every year (in Komatsu, the "President's theme") at the strategic level. There was a lot going on in the first year apart from quality. But the quality effort had first claim on resources, got the best people, and was the main yardstick of success. "Main effort" is the one thing that has to succeed, either because it in itself will have a greater effect than anything else or because other things depend on it. If resources become scarce, it is the last thing to be cut. If more become available, it is where they will go. If problems arise there, other things are left alone if necessary in order to fix them. As direction is passed down the organization, so every level has to work out what its own main effort is. As a result, execution gains in vigor and energy, and if a trade-off has to be made between different initiatives or priorities, everybody knows how to make it.

In management literature, the term "strategic intent" is most closely associated with Gary Hamel and C. K. Prahalad, who published a celebrated article with that title in *Harvard Business Review* in 1989.[26] It won the coveted McKinsey Award and remains one of the most requested of all HBR reprints, which suggests that it was answering a real need. It is instructive to compare what the authors thought they were doing with what they actually did.

As they were writing at a time when Japanese companies were successively rolling up western markets and sending their western competitors scuttling to their governments calling "foul," their article is positioned as a way of explaining Japanese success. The authors describe the ascent to world positions of small, disadvantaged Japanese companies like Honda, Canon, and Komatsu in terms of creating an "obsession with winning" sustained over decades. They argue that whereas western companies limit themselves by "trimming their ambitions to match resources," the Japanese develop capabilities which confer long-term advantage. They call this "strategic intent," which they characterize as envisioning "a desired leadership position" and also encompassing "an active management process."[27] As it is hidden from competitors, strategic intent works like a secret weapon. Hamel and Prahalad quote Sun-Tzu: "All men can see the tactics whereby I conquer, but what none can see is the strategy out of which great victory is evolved."[28]

Strategic intent is "stable over time," and involves capturing "the essence of winning" and setting a target that demands "personal effort and commitment."[29] It is what we have called an end-state. They explain how it is broken down into "milestones" (i.e., the steps of the staircase) and sequenced.[30] The elements of Komatsu's long war against Caterpillar are laid out, though not displayed as a staircase. They also mention that it gives scope for "individual and team contributions"[31] and is "flexible as to means – it leaves room for improvisation."[32] The authors then identify four generic approaches to competitive innovation deployed by Japanese companies.[33] They end with a critique of the reductive, formulaic approach to strategy found in the West, and note that in the 1990s "the challenge will be to enfranchise employees to invent the means to accomplish ambitious ends."[34] The route they are recommending "implies a new view of strategy."[35]

This prompts two initial observations.

First, there is nothing new about this view of strategy. Since the dawn of time, military commanders in a strongly disadvantaged position have recognized that they had to build capability over the course of a campaign in order to win it. It is common sense. What else are they to do?[36] Perhaps it would be more accurate to say that the view of strategy implied by strategic intent had been forgotten and neglected in the business world in the decades leading up to 1990.[37] In helping to remind us of it, Hamel and Prahalad did us all a service.

Secondly, there nothing particularly Japanese about using strategic intent as a method. Others can and do. Hamel and Prahalad were misled into thinking it was because between 1970 and 1990 a lot of Japanese companies were in the position of coming from far behind and having to build capability over a long period to match their western competitors. In the 1990s it was Chinese companies that faced a similar situation.

The *content* of western and Japanese strategies was different because of their fundamentally different *situations*.

Because they misinterpret the context in this way, Hamel and Prahalad also misunderstand the general value of the practices they describe and what is driving them.

The understanding of strategy behind what I am calling leading through intent is an implication of the fundamental nature of the environment and the demands it makes on any organization which hopes to be successful in it. They are derived *a priori*, and von Moltke and many others since have realized them in practice. Hamel and Prahalad reach their conclusions by extrapolating from a few examples which happen to be Japanese. Their method is inductive and *a posteriori*. In explaining the phenomena they observe, they are not always accurate in identifying the determining variables. That is hardly surprising – there was a lot going on. The situations were particular, the variables were many. Their problem is one that besets the inductive methods of writers on business, and the limited time horizons they set themselves in deciding which cases are "relevant." Hamel and Prahalad are indeed unusual in tracing Komatsu's history as far back as the 1960s. So much so that the long time horizon itself became a theme of the article. That was the next mistake.

The variable determining Komatsu's approach to strategy was not time, but *uncertainty*. It looked as if it was time, partly because uncertainty increases with time, but time was not the driver. What Komatsu did was to use a "do and adapt" approach over a "plan and implement" approach. Knowing it would have to compete with Caterpillar enabled it to determine an end-state in terms of a capability set, but it was uncertain about the full nature of that end-state and what exactly it needed to do to achieve it. At first it

117

was only able to identify the first three steps of the staircase: quality, cost, and variety. As it moved through them, it went through a cycle which it called the PDA process – plan, do, adapt. Stretching the staircase over such a long period is unusual, but the example is valuable because it shows how it can be done *even* over a 20-year horizon.

BP used a very similar approach to cracking the apparently insoluble problem of developing the Andrew oil field in the North Sea during the 1990s. That took six years to first oil, which was less than average. BP set an end-state without knowing how it was going to be achieved, and used a "do and adapt" method to get there because there was a lot of uncertainty.[38] Von Moltke used the same approach in campaigns lasting six weeks. In choosing to use the method of strategic intent, time is irrelevant. Because of their inductive method, Hamel and Prahalad only discussed examples in which the uncertainty was a function of the long time horizon and so conflated the two.

The two authors followed up with a book, *Competing for the Future*, which also drew on a second very successful article, "The Core Competence of the Corporation." This argues more extensively that all companies should adopt a long-term view of "unstructured arenas" in which there are massive opportunities to create customer value.[39] In order to do so, companies need to forget their past habits and instead of planning forward, use "strategic architecture" to develop "foresight," based on a view of broad trends and possibilities.[40] From this, they should develop strategic intent as an "animating dream"[41] to both stretch the organization and give general direction, build resources and capabilities accordingly, and exploit their "core competencies."[42]

With this, the authors have taken the elements of Japanese strategy which were situation specific and generalized them, while neglecting the general methodological insights they had about how to develop a consistent but adaptive strategy. Paradoxically, *Competing for the Future* includes many non-Japanese examples, and at one point the authors do in fact deny that there is anything Japanese about the approach they advocate, which is true.[43] However, the areas of main interest to them are capturing big future opportunities offered by technology (many of the examples are in consumer electronics), using long-term stretch goals, and deploying core competencies. None of these elements is essential to the model of strategy development they advocate, though all fit comfortably with it. A strategic intent need not articulate an "animating dream" to be effective. It simply has to provide a coherent framework for action within which the organization develops the strategy as it goes.

Competing for the Future became a bestseller. It said some of the things which needed to be said at the time. Some were ephemeral, but others have real substance. From my perspective, the work of Hamel and Prahalad sharpens up three points.

The first is the value of *intent* to provide cohesion in uncertainty. As they observe: "Brownian movement generates little forward progress."[44] It implies an exercise of collective will and the shaping of events, both inside and ultimately outside the organization. It implies persistence in the pursuit of a desired outcome. Circumstances change, opportunities come and go, but intent is constant.

The second is that *the end-state is not arbitrary*. Their emphasis on dream states located in the far blue yonder is misleading. The end-state is determined by insights gained from an analysis of the existing situation. Komatsu decided to set itself the goal of taking on Caterpillar because it had no choice, and the end-state clearly implied some immediate actions. The company could not survive, even in Japan, with poor product quality, and the business was scale intensive and going global even in 1970. Hamel and Prahalad equate intent with the end-state. However, the future end-state will remain a dream unless it shapes action in the present. Intent is a present task informed by a future purpose. Likewise, John Browne did not decide to develop the

Andrew field out of a whim. He knew that unless BP could do so, the North Sea business was condemned to decline within the decade. He also knew how much the company could afford to spend doing it. The original budget which seemed so impossible was simply the hurdle it had to surmount in order to make the field viable. In the case of BP, the key was not building resources but creating a new operating model. The direction-setting process was the same.

And thirdly, Komatsu's and BP's aspirations were not only rational but also *realistic*. Despite Hamel and Prahalad's rejection of calls for strategy to be realistic,[45] the examples they quote were quite in tune with reality. It was not clear how they could be achieved, but they were not illusory, because the aim was consistent with the opportunity in terms of time and resources, giving both companies the chance to build the capabilities they needed. It would have been unrealistic for Komatsu to set out to "encircle Caterpillar" in two years, and it would have failed to do so, though it would probably have improved quality. It was realistic to give the company 20 years, and, as Hay and Williamson point out in their more insightful account, the way it set the intervening steps strengthened its competitive position in sufficient time for it to survive to play the long game. Browne's ambition for the Andrew team was realistic because he too knew that the company had time, and he also knew the existing development process well enough to realize that it contained a lot of waste and opportunities for large savings. He just did not know how to realize the opportunities, so he gave the team the task of finding out, which they did.

Like any other goals, "stretch" goals work if they are realistic and fail if they are not. Executives who set them wisely know that there is some stretch left in the elastic band. If the elastic band is already fully stretched, giving it another tug will break it.

So, while thinkers like Hamel and Prahalad began to sketch out an alternative to detailed central planning, they were not always sure-footed. By the beginning of the twenty-first century, as frustration built up in boardrooms, the theme of strategy execution began to appear in articles and on bookshelves. The rise of the theme of "empowerment" suggests that most of us have some idea of what we would like in terms of an operating model, but not all the connections have been made, because strategy development has been seen as a separate theme from execution.[46]

If we deal with the knowledge gap by approaching strategy development in the way suggested in this chapter, we will have created the space to deploy an operating model that can close the other two gaps. In most organizations, the climate favors a strategy development process which allows a devolved operating model to flourish. In practice, it is not always easy for executives to know when they are and are not "commanding more than is necessary." It is now time to examine how that can be done.

QUICK RECAP

☐ A business strategy sets direction by considering both the ends to be achieved and the means of achieving them in a competitive environment. Means include execution. Strategy development and strategy execution stand in a reciprocal relationship and co-determine each other.

☐ A strategy is not in itself a plan, but prepares the organization for the future by providing it with a framework for decision making, based on some basic choices about how to compete. It is "the evolution of an original guiding idea under constantly changing circumstances."

☐ Depending on the nature of the uncertainties in the environment, a strategy can set direction by giving a compass heading or a destination, or both. A robust strategy does not guarantee success, but shifts the odds in one's favor.

☐ Thinking strategically involves "going round the loop" to establish coherence between aims, opportunities, and capabilities. It is a rational activity involving analysis, experience, and pattern recognition to generate insight into the basis of competition, the center of gravity of the business. Good strategies involve risk, but they are realistic, not heroic.

❑ A strategy is fundamentally an intent: a decision to achieve something now in order to realize an outcome; that is, a "what" and a "why." Even if our destination is unclear, we need some sense of the end-state to be achieved which gives our current actions a purpose. And even if the current situation is volatile, we need to decide what to do next in order to get into a better position than we are in at present. Strategic thinking can therefore be laid out as a staircase: a logical sequence of steps which lead to an end-state, which is either the destination or a position which opens up future options.

❑ The steps of the staircase define the organization's "main effort" at a strategic level. The main effort is that single thing which will either in itself have the greatest impact or on which all other things depend. It has resourcing priority. Defining main effort creates focus and energy, helps people to make trade-offs, and cuts through complexity.

CHAPTER FIVE

THE ALIGNMENT GAP
Briefing and Backbriefing

Tell me what you want – what you really, really want

VON MOLTKE WRITES A DIRECTIVE

After war broke out between France and Prussia on 19 July 1870, a series of unplanned engagements, all of which were initiated by Prussian Army, corps, or brigade commanders, resulted on 18 August in the main French Army being defeated in the Battle of Gravelotte–St. Privat, the first action deliberately brought about by von Moltke, and retiring into the city of Metz.

Von Moltke had never envisaged laying siege to Metz. His strategic intent was to seek out and destroy the French Army in order to be able to occupy Paris.[1] Now able to render a large part of the French Army harmless without another battle, he seized the opportunity. "Under the circumstances which had arisen," he wrote, "it was now necessary to formally invest Metz, which brought about the need for a complete change in the structure of the Army."[2] Orders for the reorganization were issued at 11 p.m. on 18 August, and it was completed within 48 hours. On 21 August von Moltke issued orders to the new formations to be ready to embark on a new phase of the campaign two days later.

The French had managed to build up another army in the town of Châlons, which lay to the west of Metz. That became von Moltke's new target. His reorganization had created two forces specifically to deal with it. Three corps were drawn from the forces around Metz to form the Army of the Meuse under Crown

Prince Albert of Saxony. They would join the four corps of the Third Army under the Prussian King's son, Crown Prince Friedrich Wilhelm, which was already heading for Châlons. Both commanders were experienced soldiers, and during the campaign so far had demonstrated both competence in handling their forces and a willingness to act in line with von Moltke's directives. One of his original Army commanders, the elderly von Steinmetz, had not always been willing do to so.[3]

On 23 August, the Army of the Meuse left Metz and marched west, leaving seven corps behind to lay siege to the city.[4] Von Moltke's first problem was to find the new French Army. As his two armies moved westward, they sent out cavalry patrols, interrogated locals, and collected newspapers, trying to pick up information from every conceivable source. The uncertainty created rising excitement in Prussian headquarters.[5]

The French moved north toward Rheims, from where it was expected to retire to Paris in order to defend the capital. It then appeared to change direction and head north east toward the Belgian frontier, probably in order to move south and relieve Metz. The information was partial and conflicting. A move to the east, exposing Paris, seemed to von Moltke to be "strange, even somewhat foolhardy," though it was being advocated by many commentators in the Parisian press, which the Prussians read carefully. In war, von Moltke wrote in his account of the campaign, one is usually only reckoning on probabilities and the balance of probability is usually that the enemy will do the right thing.[6] His enemy appeared to be doing the wrong thing.

During 25 August, von Moltke retired to his room. He worked out the French options and their consequences, and how to arrange his own movements to cover the eventualities. In the evening he received a telegram from London saying that an article in the generally reliable Parisian journal *Temps* had reported that the French Army was intending to relieve Metz. That was enough for him to make up his mind, despite the lack of reports from his own cavalry patrols.[7]

That evening, King Wilhelm I, Chancellor Bismarck, War Minister von Roon, and von Moltke met over dinner to discuss what was happening. It was von Moltke who took the decision to swing both his armies north. "Only Moltke's penetrating eyes," wrote Prince Leopold of Bavaria in his diary, "could settle the uncertain future into a concrete plan." Another officer in the headquarters called his ability not just to make sense of the disparate reports but then to risk the wheel north "veritable clairvoyance."[8] It was, of course, nothing of the kind.

On 28 August, von Moltke ordered the Third Army to stay on the left bank of the river Meuse, which ran north toward Belgium, and head for the village of Beaumont, while the Army of the Meuse marched up the right bank. The following day, they made contact with French forces. After a long fire fight, the French pulled back and camped around Beaumont. On the morning of 30 August, they were brutally surprised by part of the Third Army, and, after a day of confused fighting, retreated once more northward, crossing back to the right bank of the Meuse.

Von Moltke had moved to Buzancy, from where he heard and saw some of what went on. During the afternoon, Bismarck telegraphed the north German representative in Brussels to tell the Belgian Government that if French troops were to cross into their territory, Prussia would expect them to be immediately disarmed.[9]

In the evening, King Wilhelm arrived with his considerable entourage. He observed the events of the day from a hill and was able to confirm von Moltke's reading of the outcome.[10]

At 11 p.m., the Chief of the Prussian General Staff sat down and wrote the following directive to his two Army commanders.

Buzancy, 30th August 1870, 11 p.m.
Although up to the present we have received no news
about the positions of the individual corps after the day's

actions, it is clear that the enemy is pulling back or in retreat.

The advance is therefore to be resumed tomorrow at the earliest opportunity, and the enemy energetically engaged wherever he tries to make a stand on this side of the Meuse, and forced into the narrowest possible space between this river and the Belgian frontier.

The Army contingent of His Royal Highness the Crown Prince of Saxony has the specific task of preventing the left flank of the enemy from retiring to the east.

In this regard it would be advisable if at all possible for two corps to press forward on the right bank of the Meuse, and if any attempt should be made to take up a position opposite Mouzon, to attack it in the flank and rear.

Similarly, the Third Army should turn against the enemy's front and right flank. As much artillery as possible should be set up on this side of the river in such a way that it can disrupt marching or resting enemy columns in the valley on the right bank below Mouzon.

If the enemy should cross into Belgian territory without being immediately disarmed (by Belgian troops), he is to be pursued without delay.

His Majesty the King will be moving to Sommauthe at 8 a.m. Instructions issued by Army Headquarters are to be sent here by that time.

(signed) von Moltke

Each paragraph of the text, all but two of which consist of a single sentence, is devoted to a distinct point. The paragraphs cover in turn the essence of the situation, von Moltke's overall intention, the role of each commander, their main effort, what to do in an important contingency, and conditions for backbriefing.

It is a measure of von Moltke's authority and the trust placed in him that the subordinates to whom he is issuing instructions are heirs to the thrones of Prussia and Saxony respectively. This was an age when the right of a ruler to do as he pleased was still widely accepted. Von Moltke issued his directives on the authority of the Supreme Commander – the King – but he signed them himself.

He opens by saying what he does *not* know. He has no information about the precise whereabouts of the corps, two levels below him. Rather than complaining or demanding more information, he articulates the essential point which is clear enough from the reports he has received, his own observations, and his conversation with the King: that the French were withdrawing toward the north.

After a day of confused action, during which he would have heard a lot of gunfire and observed various bodies of men and horses moving about in the smoke, von Moltke might reasonably have wanted to find out what had been going on. He could have asked his subordinates to report immediately on the position and state of their forces, demanded casualty returns, enquired about ammunition stocks, and asked for information about the enemy. Had he done so, his armies would have stopped, turned their focus inward, and devoted their energies to information gathering. He could have effectively paralyzed his own forces by demanding more information. The only positive effect this would have had would have been to satisfy his own curiosity and relieve the psychological burden on him of acting under uncertainty. In fact, his burden was light. He already knew everything he needed to know: that the French were moving away to the north. They may have been in good order. If they were in confusion, so much the better; it did not matter. However much friction there was in the enemy camp, von Moltke meant to increase it.

The second paragraph articulates his overall intention. He wants to exploit the dynamic of the situation, and encourage the movement his opponent is already making while disrupting his ability to control it by taking aggressive action against any attempt to make a stand. The two Prussian armies are to act like sheep-dogs, herding the French into as narrow an area as possible between themselves on either flank, the natural boundary of the river Meuse, and the political boundary of the Belgian border. This will progressively constrain the French options, reducing both their space for maneuver and their freedom of choice. It will begin an envelopment. Von Moltke is not yet seeking decisive battle, nor does he care where the final engagement takes place. This is not a plan to get to a particular destination or a battle-ground he has chosen. The French could choose that for them-selves. What matters to von Moltke is that wherever it is, they will be hemmed in, if not surrounded. He has the initiative and he is shaping events, but he is not planning beyond the circum-stances he can foresee.

In these two paragraphs, he has conveyed to his command-ers a picture of the overall shape of things. They now share with him and each other a common view of the situation and what they are collectively trying to achieve. He then specifies the role of each army and the main effort of each commander.

The Army of the Meuse (on the right, eastern bank of the river) is to prevent any movement of the French left flank toward the east, and in particular to envelop any attempt to make a stand at the village of Mouzon. He recommends putting two corps out of three on the right bank, "if at all possible"; in other words, the Crown Prince of Saxony has the final call. This is to emphasize the need to keep the right strong and so prevent escape to the east.

The reference to Mouzon is to deal with a contingency which constitutes an anti-goal, something von Moltke does not want to happen. He wants the movement north to continue and not be held up. Mouzon was the obvious place to mount a delaying rearguard action. In suggesting envelopment of any such posi-tion, he conveys that he wants no set-piece battle to hold things up. He wants a decision, which means trapping the whole enemy force in a place from which they cannot escape. If they were to make a stand in Mouzon, the instruction to attack it in flank and rear would cover all eventualities. If it were held by a rearguard, this move would cut it off so that it could not hold up the main advance; if it were held by the whole French Army, his intended envelopment could begin and he could subsequently reinforce the Army of the Meuse with the Third Army. In the event, no such stand was attempted.

The Third Army is to prevent movement westward. The directive suggests using artillery to disrupt the French forces and prevent them from making a stand on the left (western) bank of the river. Using artillery means that von Moltke's own infantry and cavalry will not become embroiled in fighting, and so be able to continue marching to the north.

He then covers another contingency. Knowing of Bismarck's message to the Belgians, he simply states that if French forces do cross the border without being disarmed, they are to be pursued. He does not explain the diplomatic situation, he restricts himself to a clear statement of what action his commanders are to take. He calculated that a retreat into Belgium was the only option his opponents had to avoid calamity. In the event, this did not happen either, and the French commanders walked into his trap.

Finally, in line with the disciplines he preached, he makes sure his commanders know where his headquarters will be the following day, and when it will move, so that they can backbrief before then.

The Crown Prince of Prussia sent out his orders for the Third Army at 3 a.m. The orders for the Army of the Meuse were issued at 6 a.m. The speed with which thinking followed action and action followed thinking ensured that no momentum was lost.

In just 250 words, none of which is superfluous, von Moltke conveyed to his army commanders everything they needed to know to enable them to exploit a tactical success gained on the field outside Beaumont and create a decisive action. The following day, the tactical success was enlarged into an operational movement which pushed his opponent into a disadvantageous position.

On the evening of 31 August, 24 hours after the issuing of this directive, with his armies continuing their movements around each flank of the camp the French had made on the high ground north of Sedan, von Moltke observed to the king that he had them in a mousetrap. The overall intent expressed in his directive had been realized: the French were now hemmed in within a defensive triangle with a perimeter of no more than 15 miles.[11] Once again, von Moltke's tactical and operational moves were informed by his strategy. But because his strategy was an intent, not a plan, its realization was the result of tactical and operational developments which were entirely unforeseen.

The following day, 1 September 1870, von Moltke sprung the trap, turning the operational advantage of his encircling position into a strategic one.

Battle was joined at Sedan at 4 a.m. At 4.30 p.m, a white flag was raised over the town, and half an hour later Napoleon III, Emperor of France, asked for an armistice. At 11 a.m. the following morning, his field commander signed a capitulation. France no longer had an army, and on 4 September, the National Assembly in Paris was overthrown and the Third Republic proclaimed. The Prussians lay siege to Paris until January 1871 when an overall armistice was agreed. A peace treaty was finally signed on 10 May.

This directive is an example of how von Moltke trained all his officers to issue instructions. "Drafting orders was taken to a high art form in the Prussian Army," writes historian Arden Bucholz, "beginning right at the start of an officer's career at the War Academy." The instructors, who after 1872 were led by von Moltke himself, regarded it as a specific skill which needed constant practice, and, recognizing that clarity of thinking and clarity of expression go hand in hand, they taught their students how to write with a rigor only occasionally matched and never surpassed in the Humanities departments of today's best universities:

> *Orders were to be clear: logically arranged, short sentences, using universally understood expressions and railroad designations – 0700 for 7 a.m. and 1900 for 7 p.m. Orders were to be precise: subordinates were to be made acquainted with the intentions of their superior. Orders were to be complete – distinguishing the part that each unit was asked to perform. Orders were to be short. The rule was that they should never contain a single word by the omission of which their meaning would not be suddenly and completely affected.*[12]

These are high standards indeed. Perhaps they need to be high when you are issuing instructions to princes.

Peter Mandelson has revealed some of the problems that can arise at the top of a government when the standards are not high enough. Recalling a difficult period for the British Labour Government in 2004 under then Prime Minister Tony Blair, Mandelson reports Gordon Brown's view that "Tony's lack of 'intellectual rigour' was at the heart of our delivery woes." He then explains that "Tony's working style had become a lot more effective, but the change was not as transformative as we had hoped. 'The bewildering problem with Tony,' John Birt remarked at one point, 'is that while he knows what he wants, and he has the focus and direction of a good CEO, he doesn't give clear, direct orders.'"[13] Knowing what you want is not enough. You also have to be able to actually set direction.

Mandelson writes as if this were a matter of "working style." In fact, it is a skill. Nobody is born with it. Unless you deliberately practice giving direction, you are unlikely to be much good at it, no matter how talented you are. Small wonder Blair was not very good. He should have gone to the Berlin War Academy 150 years ago; then he would have been a more effective prime minister.

These skills clearly matter at the top. Do they matter to the thousands of humbler folk who simply need to get on with their jobs today?

TRACY'S DILEMMA

Tracy works on the check-in desk at a large airline. Punctual and hard working, she tries to put into practice all she has learned about how to deal with customers. She always smiles and treats them as individuals without being too chatty. She is efficient and professional. She wants to do the right thing. Usually, it is perfectly clear what the right thing is. Occasionally, it is not. That is when Tracy faces a dilemma.

One morning, 20 minutes before the flight to Frankfurt was due to depart, she was just closing down the desk and getting ready to leave, when a slightly overweight, besuited man approached the desk, weaving his way at high speed through the crowd of passengers in the departure hall. His face was flushed and his forehead glistened with sweat. He was somewhat out of breath and his shoulders moved from side to side under the weight of two heavy bags. Loosening his tie, he fixed his eyes on her.

"Don't close the desk," he gasped. "The 7.25 to Frankfurt. I've got to get on it. Bloody traffic…" He slapped a passport, a ticket, and a frequent flyer Gold Card down in front of her.

"I'm sorry, sir," Tracy said, "the flight is closed."

He stared at her. The color in his face turned a deeper tone of pink. "I've got to get on it," he said. "There's a client meeting. It's important. I've got to be there. *You must get me on that flight.*"

She glanced at his bags. He would certainly have to check one of them. Even then, the other one was too big for hand luggage.

Tracy looked around her. "Is there a customer service agent around?" she called over to the desk next to hers. "I think they're all tied up at the moment," said her distracted colleague. "There should be one available in about five minutes or so." That would be too late. She picked up the phone and called her supervisor. The phone rang several times. There was no reply. Tracy was alone.

In front of her was a business passenger with a Gold Card. He represented a potential future revenue stream for the airline running into hundreds of thousands. He had friends and colleagues who also flew a lot. She knew that what she did in the next few minutes would become a story he would tell.

It was all his fault, of course. He knew the rules about luggage and he knew the traffic conditions, so he should have left more time. He also knew it was his fault, and that made him all the more upset. Check-in was closed. The flight had to leave on time. It could not be held up because of one passenger. If word got round that the airline was lax about departure times, all sorts of people would take all sorts of liberties. And these days, there was no bending the rules with security.

What was Tracy to do?

At this point, everything depends on her. She is in a trench in the front line and has unexpectedly come under fire. She must make an immediate decision and act on it. But what she does depends almost entirely on what the organization she works for has done for her already, and how she can expect it to react to what she decides to do. She needs two things: information in order to make a decision; and support in order to act. There is no one to issue direct instructions. It is too late now to wait till someone can tell her what to do. She has to work that out for herself. The organization can make that easy or well-nigh impossible. Either she is prepared or she is not.

She first needs to be able to orient herself. What is the situation? How important is this? Does this guy matter? Does what *she* does matter?

To work this out she needs to have some understanding of her company's strategy and her role in it. If the basis of competition is clear, that will be a good start. Someone needs to have understood and articulated the center of gravity, and made clear to her what that means for her. The acid test of whether she understands that or not is whether she is able to make trade-offs.

Had Tracy been working for BA in 1995, she would have had some guidance, because the then Chairman, Colin Marshall, had a clear intent. The company had a mission statement: "To ensure that British Airways is the customer's first choice through the delivery of an unbeatable travel experience." The center of gravity was customer service. Marshall had not decided this on a whim. In an interview he gave that year he commented: "We know that 35 percent of our customers account for more than 60 percent of our sales."[14] The critical customer was the full-fare-paying frequent flyer. So Tracy would have known that this out-of-breath man was important.

She would also have known that at that moment, *she* was important. Making the company's strategy happen was in her hands. Marshall was clear about that: "People on the front line are the ones who ultimately create value since they are the ones who determine the kinds of experience that the company generates for its customers." He also knew that he could not keep that belief to himself: "Our employees must understand their role in delivering superior service and must have the power and ability to deal with customer problems."[15]

In order for her to decide what to do and to act on it, Tracy then needs to understand the space she has and its boundaries – she won't act until she knows how far she can go, how much power she has. If people do not know the boundaries, a few of them will go off like loose cannons, making undeliverable commitments and spending money like water. Most, however, knowing full well that there are boundaries somewhere, will stay rooted to the spot and do nothing. Specifying boundaries is like marking out minefields – it enables the troops to use the space between them. If they are known or even rumored to be there, but are unmarked, advances usually come to a halt. If Tracy is to help her customer, how far can she go? Can she ignore security? Certainly not. Can she hold up the flight? Probably not. But she needs to know.

Marshall was quite clear about how he got employees to understand what was needed and act on it:

> *By giving them freedom to act within specified boundaries. I try to impress upon our people that in a service business the customer doesn't expect everything will go right all the time; the big test is what you do when things go wrong. If you react quickly and in the most positive way, you can get very high marks for the customer. Recovery matters as much as good service."*[16]

So, if she were working for BA in 1995, Tracy would have known the following:

- ❑ The company's overriding aim is to deliver "an unbeatable travel experience," so she must try to help.
- ❑ Gold Card holders are the most valuable passengers, so she should pull the stops out and do whatever she can for this man.
- ❑ It is how you recover when things go wrong that earns high marks from customers, so the situation represents an opportunity.
- ❑ Speed matters, so she must act on the spot.
- ❑ She was free to do anything that would not delay the flight, and could expect the organization to back her up.

She knew all this because all these things had been made clear in training programs. At the time, BA put every employee through a program every 2½ years. It first used one called Putting People First, and more recently had used one called Winning for Customers. Marshall himself turned up to take questions at all the sessions he could on the original program. If he could not make it, he made sure another senior manager went in his stead and reported back to him.[17]

So what did Tracy do when she was working for BA in 1995?

She called the flight departure desk to book a seat for her sweaty charge and tell them she was coming through with another passenger. She asked them to see if he could carry bulky hand luggage, and if not to let the baggage handlers know that she would be bringing a bag direct to the aircraft hold. She took his ticket and passport, bypassed the queues, and rushed him through security. The flight was still on time and had a slot, so she only had 20 minutes. She walked the man briskly through, chatting to him to make him feel more at ease. They arrived with a few minutes to spare, which was enough for her to take one of his bags straight down to the handlers loading the hold and make sure that got on as well.

The specific result was never measured, but Marshall would have been willing to bet that her actions secured a considerable revenue stream for the airline for years to come. In the aggregate, of course, the impact of service was measurable, but this was an act of faith.

Had Tracy been working for a low-cost airline in 2005, she might have acted differently. In that case, the basis of competition would be price, not service, and no single customer group would be as valuable as the Gold Card-holding business passenger. Rapid aircraft turnaround, low cost, and efficiency would be crucial, so she would not be able to risk causing long queues at check-in by attending to the needs of a single passenger. With a common check-in for all flights, there is always work to do at the desk and she would not have been able to leave it. Customers know that the modest cost of their ticket means many restrictions.

Expectations would have been clear. Tracy would have been polite, but she would have had to remain at her post.

Tracy's decision and actions were based on her company's strategy. Different strategy, different actions. For us, what matters is not the content of the strategy but how the strategy, whatever it is, is made to happen. In the case of BA, what to achieve and why was made clear in universal training programs, directly supported from the top. However, following the example of von Moltke's "directives," it is possible to formulate a statement of intent which contains "all, but also only, what subordinates cannot determine for themselves to achieve a particular purpose." The quality of the direction coming from the very top can make an enormous difference to performance.

If Peter Drucker first urged managers to *manage* by objectives, von Moltke could be said to have *led* with directives. We can take over his principles in formulating strategic intent at the highest level. Such a statement needs to contain the following:

❑ *An account of the situation*, bringing out the essential features which bear on the course of action to be taken. It is useful to cover the state of knowledge, distinguishing what is known, what is probable but uncertain, and what is not known but could be relevant. The description of the situation should make it clear what the implications are for what the organization has to do. It may be appropriate to include an end-state if this is quite distant – for example: "Become the market leader in domestic boilers, generating returns of X percent."

❑ *A short statement of the overall intent.* This is classically stated as a task plus a purpose. In other words, what we need to achieve now and why – for example: "Strengthen service to the installer in order to gain market share." This will represent a step toward the overall end-state. Given all the possible goals, objectives, initiatives, and priorities one could and does have, this is the real focus, the thing that lends coherence to all the others. Achieving it defines success. It answers the question everyone in the organization can and should ask of their leaders, the one which is hardest to answer. The question was once succinctly formulated by The Spice Girls: "Tell me what you want – what you really, really want."

❏ *An extrapolation of the more specific tasks implied by the intent.* These will have to be turned into responsibilities for the next level in the organization, and will thus define their role in making the strategy happen. At the strategic level (typically therefore that of the board or the executive committee of a business unit), these will probably be themes or priorities which involve different contributions from several organizational units. It will be the job of the directors or senior executives to work them through and turn them into projects for their direct reports. At this level, as at each subsequent one, one should try to define the main effort.

❏ Finally, *it should give any further guidance about boundaries,* in particular the constraints to be observed, and indicate future decisions which may have to be taken. This helps people to think ahead and warns them of things on the horizon of which they may not be aware. Constraints do not only define boundaries, but help to clarify what is wanted by making explicit what is not wanted. They may take the form of what have been called "anti-goals"; that is, "Whatever you do, do not allow this to happen."[18]

These are not binding prescriptions. The statements should reflect variations in the complexity of the task, the stability of the situation, and the expertise of the subordinates. However, experience suggests that if one of these items is left out, clarity will be lost. Experience also suggests that the more that is added – and the greater the level of detail – the more clarity will also be lost.

Companies communicate their strategies in many ways. There are plans, presentations both internal and external, lists of objectives and goals, conference speeches, webcasts and videos. There are also the meetings, workshops, and forums in which strategic themes are discussed, and without which the words may not be understood. Strategy is not developed in a vacuum, and most of the audiences will be partly initiated. Different audiences will be familiar with different parts, and the laws of friction will rule here to ensure misunderstandings, varying interpretations, and the operation of local interests. A statement of intent is needed to clarify the essential points. In many cases, it might well replace some of the noisier alternative forms.[19]

Tom Glocer, who became CEO of Reuters in 2001, used this form of communication to clear away some of the confusion besetting a company which needed to work its way out of a crisis.

When Glocer took over, the crisis was beginning to break. A series of acquisitions and rapid growth throughout the 1990s had led to spiraling costs with a lot of duplication. Reuters' main customers in the banking industry faced shrinking markets, which led to reduced demand for Reuters' key products, the information systems used in dealing rooms. Focused competitors were gaining share, and scoring higher customer service ratings. In 2003, Reuters' revenue fell by about 11 percent, which included a loss of share, and the company announced the first loss in its history. Its share price fell from £16 in February 2000 to 95p in June 2003. The very existence of one of the most famous names in corporate history was in question.

To get moving, Reuters needed a compass heading. It was not clear what was going to happen to its markets, and it was quite possible that the company would itself radically restructure. However, it was clear that under any scenario, certain capabilities would be needed. They had to be built in a logical sequence.

In 2002 Glocer and his team plugged the holes in the dyke by cutting costs. In 2003, they announced a three-year recovery program called Fast Forward. It involved radical cost reduction, simplification, and culture change. Everything had to be

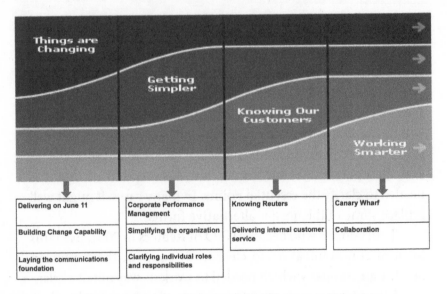

Figure 14 Main effort map: Working up a staircase

addressed: costs, complexity, the product range, information systems, service, the organizational structure, and the culture. They needed focus. So they used what was in effect a staircase in order to define the strategic main effort for the organization. Fast Forward consisted of six workstreams, and Figure 14 is a "main effort map" for the culture change component called "Living FAST."[20]

Each step was broken down into more specific elements, down to the level of projects. Within this overall framework, different product groups had main effort maps of their own. The main effort map gave shape to the overall intention and linked it to the actions of individual groups.

The strategy development process was simplified and Glocer gave direction through statements of intent which specified the essentials of what and why on a single page. Here are some edited extracts from one example dating from the transition between the first and second steps in Figure 14, with some comments:

Over the next three years Reuters needs to switch from our "self help" phase, where profitability has been driven by cutting costs, to profitable growth driven by revenue gains. (The implications of the situation – which itself was well known – are a switch in main effort over the next three years.)

I have distilled the strategic guidelines… generated at the beginning of the year into two key themes for next year (the next step in the staircase):

1. *We must ruthlessly simplify and streamline our infrastructure, systems, products and processes. Not only does this complexity drive cost, but it also hampers our efforts to deliver superlative service.* (The current intent, expressed as a "what" and a "why": we have to simplify in order to reduce costs and improve service.) *In this effort, we must ensure that we focus on those capabilities, assets and products which are differentiating… those capabilities, assets and products which are not key to our future success we should either stop, outsource or sell as appropriate.* (Guidance on decision making implied by the intent. Decisions about marginal business areas should be on the side of ruthlessness.)

2. *We must treat our growth businesses and our maturing businesses differently. We must make our maturing businesses more efficient year-on-year and ratchet down our costs. In addition, we need to fund selective adjacent growth opportunities. To date, the most promising areas meriting investment are A, B and C. We also need to start investing in longer-term growth opportunities, including D.* (Specific guidance for the leaders of different businesses – some are to optimize margin and cost and others to optimize growth. This helps each group of

141

executives to make trade-offs, and indicates how funds will be allocated.)

In terms of overall ambition, in financial terms, we are aiming for organic revenue growth of X%, operating margin of Y% and annualized cost savings of £Z million. (The end-state three years out defined in financial terms, which is all that was needed at the time.)

The biggest single project to further simplification is our investment in a new technology platform to renew the product suite. Our ultimate aim is revenue growth. At present, if there is a conflict, the new technology platform should be given priority. (Definition of main effort.)

Defining main effort had a real impact on people in the field. When someone managing part of the renewal of the technology platform got a call from a country manager asking for some engineers for a few months to sort out a problem with a client, he refused. He simply pointed out to the country manager that the new platform had priority. There the discussion ended. The country manager went back to the client, offered a temporary solution, and told him he would get a new and better set of products in six months. The products arrived on time because the people producing them refused to dissipate their resources. The decision was made on the phone in five minutes, required no approval, and in the end everyone was happy.

In February 2006, Reuters announced its results for 2005. Group profits were up 28 percent on 2004. Revenue in 2005 grew by 3 percent, the first year of growth since 2001. Customer satisfaction had risen by 2.5 points.

STRUCTURING THE ORGANIZATION

In their different ways, Marshall and Glocer got their message across to everyone. There are some things that everyone needs to know. However, the overall intent implies some different things to different people. As the strategic message is passed on, it may need to be modified and made more specific. The first thing that needs to be in place, then, is a channel of communication. This is provided by the reporting lines of the organizational structure. Sometimes the reporting lines facilitate the passing on of the message; sometimes they make it difficult; sometimes they make it so difficult that they block the message. When that happens the problem has to be addressed.

This is not the place to expound a methodology for organizational design. That has been done by others many times already.[21] We need not worry about how to make the structure perfect. However, unless the structure of the organization broadly reflects the structure of the tasks implied by executing the strategy, the strategy will not be executed. Every organizational structure makes doing some things easy and doing other things difficult. If the structure makes doing some things so difficult that there is a *conflict* between structure and strategy, the structure will win. So if you are serious about the strategy, in the case of conflict you have to change the structure.

For example, if your strategy depends on consolidating manufacturing on a regional basis, and your structure is based on countries with a manufacturing plant in each country under the control of country heads, there is a conflict. It is a fair bet that unless you change the structure and create, for example, a head of manufacturing in each region, reporting to a head of global manufacturing, the strategy will not happen. Instead, the launching of the strategy will be accompanied by much nodding of heads, a lot of discussion, and deadlock.

The issue comes down to people. They are both the problem and the answer. Nothing happens unless the key people involved in it want it to, and if the top team does not stand four-squarely behind the strategy, it is doomed. They may not say that they disagree, but if there is a conflict between the strategy and their real convictions, you may as well not start. Curiously, people's convictions tend to correlate with their interests. Their interests are largely determined by the structure and the compensation system. Both, therefore, must be examined in order to identify and remove any conflicts.

To claim that organizational structure should reflect task structure is simply to say that it be "fit for purpose" given the nature of the task and the environment. As we have seen, when the situation and the tasks it required changed, von Moltke was able to reorganize his forces in the middle of a campaign, cannily sidelining a recalcitrant subordinate in the process. He did it in two days. The German Army retained this ability to change structure rapidly at all levels, forming "battle groups," often named after their commander, to carry out specific tasks. It also gave them the ability to throw together disparate forces at short notice to act as fire brigades in an emergency. It was an ability their opponents in the Second World War never mastered.

The general environment is characterized by friction. Friction means that there will always be less information available than we would like, that identifying the essential information is difficult, and that understanding each other will require special effort. That leaves us with some choices. Historian Martin van Creveld has delineated them with startling clarity:

> *Confronted with a task, and having less information available than is needed to perform that task, an organisation may react in either of two ways. One is to increase its information-processing capacity, the other to design the organisation, and indeed the task itself, in such a way as to enable it to operate on the basis of less information. These approaches are exhaustive; no others are conceivable. A failure to adopt one or the other will automatically result in a drop in the level of performance.*

Van Creveld considers the alternatives from a historical point of view:

> *The former approach will lead to the multiplication of communication channels (vertical, horizontal, or both) and to an increase in the size and complexity of the central directing organ; the latter, either to a drastic simplification of the organisation so as to enable it to operate with less information (the Greek phalanx, and Frederick the Great's robots) or else to the division of the task into various parts and to the establishment of forces capable of dealing with each of these parts separately on a semi-independent basis.*

Whereupon, toward the end of his survey of some 2,500 years of attempts to create strategies and make them happen, van Creveld concludes:

> *It is a central theme of this book that, through every change that has taken place and given any level of technological development, the first two of these approaches are inadequate and in danger of becoming self-defeating and that, the likelihood of further change notwithstanding, the third one will probably remain superior to them in virtually every case.*[22]

There are many reasons for adopting any particular organizational structure, and no single structure is good for all circumstances. Reasons may include the strategy, but are as likely to encompass the availability of people, the need to provide platforms for them, the need to emphasize some things at the expense of others, the need to separate some business units from others in order to protect their culture, and so on. For our purposes, we need to check that there are no blocks, and, if there are, we must stop and remove them. Following van Creveld's principle, we have to structure the tasks implied by the strategy and the units responsible for carrying out those tasks in such a way that the units can perform the tasks with the available level of information. The bottom line is that organizational structure should make doing the most important things easy. That will inevitably make doing other things difficult. There are ways of compensating for that, but the basic trade-off must be made. No structure is perfect.

In the light of that requirement, here are three questions to ask:

1   Can we identify organizational entities which can be made wholly or largely accountable for executing the key elements of the strategy to the extent that controls are in place to measure how well they are doing so?

If a major plank of what is implied by the strategic intent is split across more than one unit, think again. Those activities which most need to be coordinated should fall within unit boundaries. If, as in the above case of manufacturing plants, a major plank is dependent on the cooperation of all the main units and is also in conflict with their interests, stop. Coordination because of interdependency is fine: for example, launching a new product range will require R&D, manufacturing, marketing, and sales to work together, but accountabilities can be defined. However, a strategy based on being first to market with global products will founder if power is with country heads – rapid global rollouts imply strong central functions. Sometimes difficult links will remain. If so, they should not be ignored but addressed explicitly, through an overlay mechanism like a task force or project. Do not allow structure to get in the way, but do not expect it to do everything.

2   Are the leaders of these units skilled and experienced enough to direct their units on a semi-autonomous basis and are they committed to the strategy?

It is obvious that the people in leadership positions matter, but not quite obvious how much they matter. With the right leadership, even a unit which has been used to carrying out orders blindly can learn to play a part in executing a strategy more flexibly. The difference between compliance and commitment grows with the seniority of the people concerned. The reason for this is that senior people have more room than junior ones to affect others and to actively undermine something they do not believe in. Total commitment of an entire senior team is rare. A reasonable aim is adequate consensus. A consensus is adequate when everyone agrees to give the strategy their best shot and not get in the way. There will always be doubts and always room for other preferences. Anyone not willing to put them on one side should be put on one side themselves or they could do great damage.

3   Is there enough, but not too much, hierarchy, and does each level of the hierarchy have the decision rights it needs to play its part?

Hierarchy is valuable. It allows one to take decisions on behalf of many, enabling an organization to carry out different collective actions simultaneously and cohesively. We are familiar with cases of having too much hierarchy – roles overlap and become unclear, effort is duplicated, decision making slows down, costs rise, and power becomes more important than knowledge. However, it is also possible to have too little. If there is not enough hierarchy, effort fragments, local interests are optimized, scale and focus are lost, and cohesion dissipates. A hierarchy only works if it encompasses appropriate decision rights and responsibilities. Decision rights are appropriate if the person or group with the best knowledge and expertise in any given area is able to act in a timely manner without asking for permission. So, for example, prices may be set by central marketing, regions allocate marketing budget, countries decide about the weight given to different distribution channels, and local sales organizations decide which customers to target. If there is not enough hierarchy and local sales organizations report directly to the center, then either the center will dictate everything, resulting in massive information flows and rigidity, or there will be chaos as prices vary from place to place in a single market.

If the answers to these three questions are positive, there is a communications channel available that does not have crossed wires or lines that lead nowhere, and we can start to align the organization behind the intent.[23] The structure has to be used to pass on the message. The message to be passed on is: "This is what we want you to achieve and why."

What does anyone need to know in order to take action?

They need to know something about the overall intent. Armed with this knowledge, they themselves need to say what they are going to do as a result. In other words, they need to break down their task into further tasks implied by their main one, assign them, and pass the message on. In order to close the communications loop, they need to repeat the message back up, adding the specific tasks they intend to undertake. This simple but critical step – which is as obvious in theory as it is rare in practice – is called a "backbrief." Once the backbrief has been carried out, they are ready to go. Briefing and backbriefing are repeated at each level, with the tasks becoming ever more specific, until they result in actions which are no longer open to more analysis into further, more specific tasks. In a military organization using mission command, this discipline is called "mission analysis." In the language I have developed for business, I call it "strategy briefing."

In the real world, managers will often have to brief themselves, based on information gleaned from multiple sources.

Arriving at sufficient clarity to allow action is an iterative process.

To understand what this involves, let us enlist the help of a young American called Joe.

THE STORY OF JOE

Joe had a new job. He deserved it. He was one of the rising stars. Having read engineering, he had gained an MBA and joined a large, well-established information services company. A year after moving into new product development, he was offered a major challenge – to set up a new development center in Asia.

His employer was facing some big challenges itself. A new competitor was gaining share with a set of simple, low-cost products. As a result the company was losing revenue, and margins were under pressure. Joe's job was to get the new development center running in order to reduce the cost of new products.

The following months were hectic but exciting. While finding a new location and recruiting staff, he also had to get clear about the technical aspects of the job, which were very complex. He had a good team, and they hit the ground running.

Meanwhile, the pressure around him was building up and everybody felt it. The markets were bad and getting worse. Revenue would have fallen anyway, but the loss of market share was more serious still. As margins also fell, the inevitable came and corporate began a series of cost-cutting rounds. The customer service units were having to do more with less and were groaning under the burden of a complex product line in the installed base. Joe was spending lots of money, but the new products were not arriving. Life was not a lot of fun.

The team were working all hours and there was a sense of having a mountain to climb. About six months into the new job, Joe called an off-site meeting in which everyone put their cards on the table and they all took stock. Though they had covered a lot of ground, there was little sense of achievement. Then it all came out.

"I don't want to sound negative," commented a weary technician, "but what exactly are we trying to achieve here?"

Joe was a bit taken aback. "Look, that's one thing that is perfectly clear. We are creating a new center to develop low-cost products. We've got two years. You know the situation and you know the company's strategy. It's been talked about long enough. It's all in the communications pack – and on the website, for that matter."

"Yeah, sure," came the reply. "I've seen all that. And frankly, I'm confused. There's lots of stuff about shareholder value, about reinventing ourselves, thinking globally, and embracing change. There's stuff about being the most innovative player in the industry, and about delivering superior customer satisfaction, and there are targets about increasing revenue, lowering costs, and raising margins. Well, I don't get it. From where I am the sky's falling in. We're in deep recession, the competition is eating our lunch, revenues are falling, margins are shot to bits, customers are starting to hate us, and all anyone seems to care about is getting rid of people to save money. Some of *us* are probably next. Where are *we* in all of this? What are we supposed to do?"

Joe sensed that this was a time for some of the stuff he had learned about leadership. Time to get control, get people on board, get them to buy in – stuff like that. Start with the basics. He had thought they were clear enough, but they did not seem to be so clear after all.

"OK," he said, "I hear you. And you're right. Let's sit down right here and now and work it out for all of us so we're all singing from the same song-sheet. Let's not just talk, let's write it down, and we'll all know exactly what we're about."

That did not rouse much enthusiasm, but there was no opposition either. The silence gave Joe the chance to think back to something he had heard once on a course: The first questions to ask are "What?" and "Why?" He went over to the whiteboard and wrote down "task + purpose." Under task he wrote "What" and under purpose he wrote "Why."

As he turned back to his audience, he saw to his surprise that they had perked up a bit. "So we'll answer those questions, right? Here and now. OK?" There were nods.

"Yeah," said his challenger. "For God's sake, unless we can answer that, what the hell are we up to? And frankly, I can't answer it."

Good, thought Joe. This will be a quick win.

The discussion started with the team's purpose. It began, as such a discussion usually does, with an aspiration, an ambition which was meant to be inspiring. It was not long before the words "world class" were uttered, and the team's purpose was to "Build a world-class development facility." Some of the team liked that, but Joe noticed that others were rolling their eyes.

"Look," somebody piped up, "that's an aspiration anyone could have. It makes no difference, it's vague and vacuous and has nothing to do with our situation. What are we actually doing *now*?"

The first version was crossed out. The purpose became: "To build a new development facility." "But that's just a description of what we're doing," came the objection. "Isn't that the 'What'? The question is what we are trying to achieve."

"We need to reduce costs," came the answer. So perhaps that was the "Why."

The discussion then opened up. "We aren't only trying to reduce costs," someone observed. "We are trying to improve service and raise quality. They have to be in there somewhere."

"But we can't improve service," someone else objected. "All we can do is to provide products that allow others to do so."

"Any more than we can grow revenue," added another.

"So what does the organization want from us?" interjected another.

151

"It wants new products," answered Joe. "It's really quite simple. We haven't actually launched a significant new product for two years. Nothing is happening. We have to get something out of the door."

"Just a minute before we rush off here," came another voice. "Are we talking just about new product development, or about enhancements and support? That's where half our people are working."

Joe called a halt to the increasingly raucous discussion. "Let's step back a second," he suggested. "What is the situation?" He tried to sum it up, both for himself and the others: "The company's revenues are declining by about 10 percent a year, in part because we're in the worst market in history but in part because we are losing share. Our cost base is 30 percent too high, our products are old, and customer satisfaction is falling. We claim to be an innovative organization but we have stopped innovating. New product development is blocked. Our job, surely, is to unblock it. If we do that, it will reduce operating costs and improve customer satisfaction and that will help the sales force sell more and increase revenue."

Joe felt there was something strangely liberating about what he had just said. He, like everyone else, had a list in his mind of what needed to be done. There were always costs, revenues, margins, and service. But he had articulated the relationship between them for the first time. New product development was a link in the whole chain, and he had made it clear to himself that success for him meant getting product out now. They had to speed things up.

The discussion continued. Half an hour later, they had their first answer on the whiteboard:

What: to significantly reduce time to market for development, enhancements, and support of high-quality products to our customers in a cost-effective manner
Why: in order to help aggressively grow our revenues and increase our margins

Over lunch, Joe wandered off outside to have a think. He had been so busy over the past six months he had hardly done any thinking at all. He did not like what they had written. It was unrealistic and confusing. How were they going to grow aggressively in the current market? How were they going to start? What were they going to do now? He wanted something more incisive. He also ruefully realized that he should have thought about these things long ago. He had been told to do something, but how did that fit into the overall plan? He needed to set the scene for his people. It was complicated. He realized that the things they needed to know were things that had consequences for what they were going to do. The rest did not matter.

Joe went back in and started on a new sheet on the flipchart. At the top of the page he wrote "Context." Then he filled in the rest of the sheet:

> *The company's market share is being eroded by competitors under some of the most difficult trading conditions in our history*
> *The loss of share must be halted or we will have no basis for future growth*
> *Customer service is the key to halting this decline, but the existing product line makes it impossible to deliver outstanding service at acceptable margins*
> *With the current loss of accounts, every day that passes makes recovery more difficult*

The group were coming back in as he finished writing. "Does that help?" he asked. There were a few nods as people read it through.

"Actually, we've got a crucial role in all of this, haven't we?" observed one of the head programmers. "I hadn't realized that. I thought we were just back-room boys."

"And," somebody added, "if it's true, it means that what matters is time. We've got to speed things up."

"Is that right?" someone else asked. "What is the company trying to do? I'm sure there's a strategy document somewhere."

Joe remembered reading something on the internal website and hearing a lot of stuff as well. "I think I know what you mean," he said. "Let's see if we can find it."

A few minutes later someone with a laptop shouted "Eureka!" They plugged it into the beamer and the words of the corporation filled the screen. It was part of the strategic plan, endorsed by the board. It was official. This is what it said:

> *We are committed to delivering great service to our customers. This will require us to build a strong service-based culture. This will be achieved by a combination of improved customer and market segmentation capability, improved customer service processes and tools, and, significantly, specific customer-focused behaviors being constantly demonstrated both internally and with external customers. The goal is to reshape the business to deliver superior shareholder value over a sustained period.*

They stared blankly at the screen. "Sounds like marketing are behind that," someone commented.

"More like HR," said another. "Though finance finally got their oar in at the end."

"What the hell's a 'segmentation capability'?" someone asked plaintively.

"Don't worry about that," said another. "It only means they ran it past the consultants before going live. It's just stuff they do in marketing."

"What's a 'customer-focused behavior'?" asked another. Nobody knew.

"Probably cutting prices," offered one.

"Junkets in Thailand," suggested another. Sniggers ran through the room.

Joe decided it was time for a bit of that leadership stuff again. "Let's think about what's behind it," he said. "It says there is going to be a change. This is not business as usual. The clock's ticking. We have to give customers better service than our competitors if we are to get them back, and we've got to make money as well."

"So how do we fit in?" someone asked.

"If the company is going to compete on service they need us to give them the products to enable them to do so," Joe replied. "It used to be all about technology and features, but it isn't any more. Our competitors have matched us. It's a service game. I was talking to the boss about it the other day."

"Which boss?" someone asked, helpfully.

"David," Joe replied, "the Head of Technology. He wants a coherent suite of products, not the mess we've got now, with different things for every region and every client. I've talked to my other boss about it too, the Head of Asia. We can't continue to do special things just for the region, let alone for individual clients. The costs are killing us. That's one reason they are so high. We have to bite some bullets and make choices. Sales don't like it, but there it is. It's our call. We've only got so many people. Why don't we try to write it down, simply, and work out what it is they want us to do, both in technology and in the company as a whole. What was their intention when they wrote all this?"

So they had a go. Forty minutes and several sheets of flip-chart later, they had a formulation. They decided to call it "Higher intent." It read:

One level up – Technology Group:
To develop and support a coherent product line that is easy to service in order to allow sales and marketing to grow revenues
Two levels up – Corporate:
To transform the company within the next three years in order to deliver superior service and financial performance

"Our job," said Joe, "is to do that in Asia. It tells us a few things that should drive every decision. The new products have to be simpler to service or they are no good. They have to fit in with what is being done globally, and the local sales people will have to live with that. No more bespoke modifications for so-and-so. We've got to design them with the sales and marketing people to make sure they can sell them, or they are useless. And they have to be low cost or we can't make money selling them. We have to think radically – we are building the future while the sales force fight the fires today. But we've got to move fast. Now let's look at the 'what' and 'why' again."

Looking again at what they had written down before, they realized that it was a bit of a muddle. So Joe asked the group to think again and answer the question: "What do we have to do *now*?" The immediate purpose was actually defensive. There was no way anyone could grow revenues and margins in the current climate. But they had to stop the erosion of market share. That was feasible. Growth would come later. It was also becoming clear that the critical factor was time. Cost and quality were *constraints*. If those hurdles were not met, the products would be useless, but they would not in themselves solve the problem. They had to get something new out of the door that year and create a process that could continue to do so. There were over 250 products. They could not possibly do that with all of them. In the pipeline some were new, some were enhancements, all at different stages, requiring different levels of effort. None would be any good without field support. They had to focus their effort and decide which ones made the most difference.

Finally, they came up with a new statement:

What: to accelerate delivery to market of critical products
Why: in order to enable sales channels to halt market share erosion by year end

"Funny," someone observed, "we've never had anything before that said we were supporting sales. I guess this means we've got to work with them pretty closely."

"Is this ambitious enough?" someone asked. "It doesn't sound particularly inspiring."

"This is stretching enough for me," said Joe. "It's ambitious but it's doable. If we give ourselves a target we can't achieve we're just setting ourselves up for failure, as we usually do. That doesn't inspire, it demoralizes. Though that reminds me, we've not got any targets here. We need some measures so we know if we're succeeding or not."

They got back to work. They talked about deadlines. They discovered that the deadlines depended on the products chosen. Some could be got out in weeks, others in months. Setting an appropriate target was the job of the people working on them. However, from where they were, they had an overview of costs and a fairly good idea of what was needed. They could set that. They decided that in order to keep on track they had to measure three things: time, market share, and costs. They expressed each measure in terms of a goal:

1 Delivery of agreed product set on time and on budget.
2 Total market share in Asia at the end of the year = share at the beginning of the year.
3 Reduce operating costs of development in the region by 20%.

There was a pause. They were all studying the flipchart. Someone narrowed his eyes and frowned. "We ourselves cannot stop market share from declining," he said. "Do we want to measure ourselves on that?"

"Strictly speaking, no," replied Joe, "but it is the purpose behind everything we are doing now. If the rate at which we are losing share goes down, we will know that what we are doing is working, even if we don't hit the target of making it stop. If we don't look at it, we might be barking up the wrong tree. It's part of the situation we want to be in at the end of the year, the end-state we are working toward. We may not be measured on that ourselves, but we have to monitor it to know if we are being successful."

"What about what we *are* measured on?" someone piped up. "We've all got targets. Dozens of them." Indeed they had.

Joe had targets of his own. Part of his bonus was tied to the number of new products they delivered. Optimizing that was not difficult – he could merely go for the easy ones nearest completion. Whether they had any impact or not was somebody else's problem. Or so he supposed. "Look," he said, "I'll make a commitment to you. I will renegotiate the targets for this group. I will explain what we are doing and that the measures are just there to tell us whether we are successful or not. What we are trying to optimize is the outcome. The measures are the dashboard. We've got a speedometer, a milometer, and a fuel gauge. We need to watch them, but we should not confuse the readings on them with what we really want to do, which is to arrive on time at our destination. When we've worked out who is doing what I will measure your performance on how well you accomplish that. One thing I will want to know from you is how you're going to measure your own success. Which brings us to the next question: How are we going to do it?"

They started by taking a look at what they were actually doing. It turned out there were three main things: growing an offshore facility, working on costs and efficiency, and working on various corporate and local initiatives. They decided only to do what they needed to do, which was quite a lot, and that put paid to many of the initiatives. There was no time for them. Too bad.

"Look guys," said Joe to some of the more nervous, "if we do what we are aiming for here, we'll be heroes. Let's not get sidetracked."

The next thing they realized was that they had left something out. No one was working out which products were critical. That was the first task. They needed to keep some work going on the cost side, but the central thrust was to accelerate the process and deliver something good to the sales force. They decided that to get sufficient drive and focus they should divide that up between development on the one hand and enhancement and support on the other. Each could work independently. So there were four main tasks implied by the intent:

- ❑ Identifying the critical product set
- ❑ Accelerating development
- ❑ Accelerating support and enhancement
- ❑ Reducing costs.

If they achieved all of those they would achieve their intent – and be heroes.

But suppose they could not do it all? Suppose they had to play their part in the headcount reductions? Suppose resources became more constrained and they had to short-change something? Joe looked at the list. "Among all of these things," he asked, "what is really vital? If we had to cut, where would we cut last?"

They had a debate. They needed to define the critical products, but they only needed to get that broadly right. They had to reduce costs, but even if they failed they could accept low margins for a time. The big difference was with new product development – if they did not speed up that process this year, all else would be in vain.

Joe went back to the board and drew a red circle around "Accelerating development." Next to it, he wrote "Main effort."

It was time for a break. Joe went for a brief stroll outside and reflected about what they had been doing. They had started with a list of things to do which only had a loose relationship to each other and were of very different levels of importance. Putting that on one side, they had thought through what needed to be done so that the tasks had a structure. They had identified and closed a gap in the "to do" list – identifying the critical products. And they now had something that had no overlaps, so the tasks could be assigned without people getting in each other's way. No gaps, no overlaps. Each task would become the most important thing somebody had to do – so Joe could be sure it would get done. He was thinking about the team he would need. Given his organizational structure, he had someone responsible for development and another for enhancement and support. So that was clear. He would need to create a temporary cross-functional team to identify the critical products, and form another one to address costs.

Then he began thinking about what they would need. He wanted to be able to assign them the tasks and let them come back to him with a plan about how they were going to achieve them. What else did they need to know? He did not want to tell them how they should set about doing things. They all knew their jobs better than he did and achieving what they had agreed would require some creative thinking. He wanted to give them space. But how much and how could he define it? What he needed to do was to simply say what they were free to do and what they were not free to do. He had to define their boundaries.

Joe went back in and as the team reassembled he wrote a new heading on each of two flipcharts: "Freedoms" and "Constraints." "Right," he said. "Next step. Let's write down a list of the resources we have and other things which can help us and the things we must make sure we do not do or allow to happen."

That seemed like a sensible thing to do. The brainstorming began. A quarter of an hour later, they had a list under Freedoms including "senior management support," "motivated employees," and "the importance of new products." There was a longer list under Constraints. This included "concerns about our ability to deliver," "customer reluctance to adopt new products," "competitor activity," and "organizational complexity."

Joe stepped back. Everyone looked a bit blank. Those lists weren't very helpful. They looked like lists of good things and bad things. There were more complaints than constraints, plus a few worries. That did not tell them what they were free to do or constrained not to do.

"Let's try again," he said. "Let's now really try to think through the things we can do and the things we can't do. Let's try to define the limits of our authority and the conditions we have to meet, and the freedoms we have within the limits which we can use to help us. We can begin with the constraints. Some constraints are a direct result of what we are trying to achieve."

It soon became clear as they thought back to their earlier discussion that there were two big constraints: cost and quality. They were trying to optimize time, but cost and quality imposed boundary conditions. How could they decide what those were? Someone started a discussion about quality and within a few minutes there was an earnest debate going on which started to get passionate and technical at the same time as old opinions clashed. Joe stopped it. "We've just identified another aspect of the tasks," he said. "We're going to have to work this out as we go. Let's not assume we know the answer already." He wrote down two constraints:

> *Product quality to be defined with reference to customer needs/service organization*
> *Product cost requirements set by budget and competitive benchmarks*

Those things were not under their control, but they had to find out what they were. They realized that by defining their boundaries, they were also identifying who they had to talk to in the organization and the outside world. The discussion became more concrete and more focused. They identified two more constraints and a question:

> *Development center rationalization decision must be agreed with head of Asia*

161

*Obsolescence program must be agreed with global prod-
uct management
Unclear who has final decision on new product development projects*

As he looked at those, Joe realized that he had defined his own
role. His job as leader was to manage the boundaries of the team.
He had to work on the constraints. The first two meant he had to
prepare the decision makers and ensure that the team's proposals
were good enough to be accepted. The third was something he
had to clarify, or they could waste a lot of time. He needed to
manage the matrix and made a note to himself to raise the issue
with both his regional boss and his functional boss when he saw
them next. He wanted some decision rules to avoid the bun fight
which he knew would otherwise be inevitable.

They then turned to "Freedoms" again. Things weren't so
bad. They had the authority to prioritize requests within the
region, which meant that they could control their own resources.
They also had the authority to build cross-functional teams with
Operations to improve reliability. So they decided to do that.
And they could make their own capital expenditure decisions
within the existing centers. In fact, they could do quite a lot to
control their own destiny.

The shadows were lengthening and people were tired. Time
to call it a day. Joe had one more question: "Looking at all that
lot, can we do it?" he asked. They ran through it all again to check
it was consistent, whether they really had the resources to carry
out the tasks, and whether doing all the tasks would achieve what
they wanted. No one could be sure, but it looked plausible. It was
certainly worthwhile. If they did it, it would make a huge difference to the company.

"Well," said Joe, "I want each of you leading the four main
tasks to come back to me with a plan by the end of the week. In the
meantime, let us all commit to each other here to do whatever we

have to in order to make it happen. Let's have a drink before we head for the airport."

Around the bar, they agreed that now things had been made clear, they did not seem as daunting as they had done. They had been weighed down by concerns which really did not matter much and they had all been doing things which were peripheral and could now be stopped. In fact, they could stop doing quite a lot of things. That would be good news when they got back. Now everyone could start playing a real role in things that mattered and they might start to achieve something.

Which, as it happens, they did.

STRATEGY BRIEFING AND BACKBRIEFING

What Joe did was common sense. In its essence, his thought process was no different from Tracy's. For Tracy the context was obvious: she was confronted with a valuable passenger who was going to miss his flight unless she did something about it. She knew the higher intent: to gain full-fare passengers by offering superior service. She knew her freedoms and constraints: she could leave her post and override the normal boarding process, but she must not delay the flight. From that she could quickly decide what she had to do and why: she had to get the passenger on the plane in order to secure his long-term loyalty to the airline.

Tracy had no time, but the task was simple and she did not have to involve anyone else, so she went through all of this very quickly in her head. Joe had a lot more time, but he needed it because his situation was more complex and it involved a lot of other people. Tracy could think in her head and act immediately. Joe had to write things down in order to engage with others and needed some structure to help him think through the issues. He needed some moments of quiet reflection and the problem required some iteration before he got to an acceptable solution.

But the thinking Joe and Tracy did to align their actions with their company's strategy was the same.

The core principle of their thinking was to understand "what" and "why," and the consequences. If you are a soldier you will call a "what" and a "why" your "mission." If you are an executive you can call them a "goal" or an "objective," if that is more in tune with your company's terminology. The word I have used is "intent." Up to a point, the words do not matter, as long as everybody knows what they mean. In some companies toward the end of the year everyone does "objective setting," while in another they do "goal setting." The best choice of words depends on the local usage.

The term I have chosen for the overall process is "strategy briefing" and its basic structure is given in the template on page 249. It is a way of structuring thought so as to concentrate the mind on what matters *now*, and leave out what does not matter. It looks deceptively simple.

Briefing is difficult to do well and has a major impact, for it essentially determines how people are going to spend their time and what outcomes they are going to try to achieve. Few things could be more important for any business. In view of its importance and its difficulty, it is remarkable that it is little taught.

The story of Joe's off-site meeting is a composite of several real examples, and is designed to reveal some of the thinking which typically goes on and why it is difficult. To an outsider, the result often looks banal. A good part of the value lies in the quality of the thinking which has gone on, and how deeply the protagonists engage with the strategy and their own dilemmas. The end result should give all involved an image of what is going on and their part in that.[24]

A briefing is not a project plan. Plans come afterward. Moreover, it assumes that some planning, at the strategic level, has already been done. Ideally, there would be a statement of strategic intent. The purpose of briefing is to enable people to act independently.

It is a skill which improves with practice. At each stage Joe's people moved from confusion and complexity to clarity and simplicity. Their thinking characteristically meant going round the loop between ends and means. Their final attempt may not have been perfect, but it was good enough to enable them to organize themselves. It involved paring things down to their essentials by leaving out more and more. It stated everything anyone in the unit needed to know and no more, and did not attempt to pre-judge decisions which could better be made at lower levels. Deciding what those decisions are is part of the discipline.

Briefing is radical in the way in which it unifies effort. The effort is directed toward a *desired outcome* – everybody has an ultimate goal which is defined in terms of a state of affairs to be attained in the real world. The effort is expressed as *action to be taken*, a task – something to be done – which will be something which makes a difference. Before the off-site, Joe's team had been generating a lot of activity. They turned some of the activity into purposive action and stopped the rest. That produced a degree of calm in his overworked department. Their time on task increased and they made themselves more productive. As their effort became purposive, so – diverse though it was – it became *unitary*, which immediately created focus. By defining what really matters, when other things start to get in the way, as they will, people still have the torchlight of intent to guide them.

Of course, we all have many things to do. We tend to put them on a list, which helps to get through the day. Lists do not help to get through a strategy. The discipline of briefing turns lists into a structure. A structure reveals how things are related to each other. If there really are things on the list which are totally unrelated, you have a problem which should be raised with your boss. In most cases, though, you can discover, or create, unity of effort.

A typical list of things a manager has to achieve in a year might look like this:

1   Increase revenue by 8%
2   Raise average net margin to 15%
3   Open a new office
4   Reduce costs by 5%
5   Hire five new sales people
6   Increase employee satisfaction
7   Complete negotiations on a long-term contract
8   Introduce the new credit control system

Using the concepts of the strategy briefing, a first run through the list could reveal the following:

1   Increase revenue by 8% – our potential intent
2   Raise average net margin to 15% – our potential intent
3   Open a new office – implied task supporting 1; delegate
4   Reduce costs by 5% – implied task supporting 2
5   Hire five new sales people – implied task supporting 1; delegate
6   Increase employee satisfaction – an outcome; possible metric
7   Complete negotiations on a long-term contract – implied task supporting 1
8   Introduce the new credit control system – separate task; delegate

We now need to identify the main task which forms part of our intent. To do so, we need to understand the higher intent. What comes first, revenue or margin? Either is possible. If our intent is to gain market share in order to strengthen our long-term position, the main effort is revenue and holding margin at 15 percent is a constraint. If our intent is margin improvement, but we want to grow with the market in order not to lose position, revenue is a constraint.

We need to know which it is because we may need to make a trade-off. If come next December, someone is sitting in front of a customer ready to take a large-volume order which will lift revenue growth to 10 percent but with a low margin which will

166

reduce our average net margin for the year to 12 percent, what should we do? Will we be congratulated for landing a significant order and beating our target, or told off for loading up our books with poor-quality business and missing the all-important profit figure? We need to talk and get some clear direction. It might be "Aim for revenue of 8 percent but on no account allow margins to fall below 15 percent," in which case the margin figure is a hard constraint; or we may learn that a 15 percent margin would be nice but what really matters is that it should not fall below 12 percent. Whatever the answer, we need guidance. Good guidance allows us to make trade-offs. With that guidance, we can put together a proper briefing and pass the message on.

We will need to think through the implications of opening a new office and hiring new sales people while reducing costs. And if we are running the unit, we may want to think about our own role. Item 7 could be something which we would want to lead personally. Item 8 does not directly support this year's effort, but it should improve cash flow and have an indirect effect on margin improvement. If we delegate it to someone and tell them its purpose is to support margin improvement, that will focus their mind on the operational effectiveness of the system and help to guard against getting mired in purely technical issues. If we brief everybody well, they will have a strong sense of purpose. If we do everything we intend, we will have something to celebrate, and should remember to do so. As a result, employee morale should go up. So there is unity in the apparent diversity.

An important corollary of unity of effort is the emphasis on *clarity and simplicity*. What matters about creating alignment around a strategy is not the volume of communication, but its quality and precision. In order for something to be clear, it must first be made simple. Joe needs the intellectual skills to grasp the essentials of his situation just as much as his CEO does. What is not simple cannot be made clear.

The observation made by Meckel in 1877 that "every order

which can be misunderstood will be misunderstood" still stands unrefuted. Hence the discipline of backbriefing.

Joe now needs to talk his boss through the results of his briefing session and check that he really has understood his intent and is doing what is wanted. Likewise, his direct reports need to work through the implications of the session for themselves in the same manner and backbrief him.

In the backbrief three things happen. The first obvious thing is that the unit being briefed checks its understanding of the direction it has received or worked out. Secondly, and less obviously, the superior gains clarity for the first time about what the implications of their own directions actually are, and may revise them as a result. Thirdly, it provides an opportunity to ensure alignment *across* the organization as well as up and down it. If everyone backbriefs together, the results can be checked for gaps, overlaps, and coherence. Adjustment follows. It is very difficult – and indeed is a waste of time – for someone to try to think through for themselves all the implications of what they are asking people to do two levels below them. It is in this way that the senior people themselves get to grips with what the organization is going to do as a result of what they have specified. It is normal for them to get it slightly wrong the first time around. It is also quite normal for a strategy brief to require revision.

Useful as it is for a team, a single strategy brief is only the starting point in closing the alignment gap for the organization. The briefing cannot stay within the team. Its implications need to be thought through by those responsible for each of its elements, as in Figure 15.

At each level, the starting point is the intent of the level above. Given that context, each unit has to work out its part in the plan, its own "what" and "why." Joe's team are typical in first putting down everything they had to do and then thinking it through, giving their activities structure, and working out priorities. They then broke this down further into the tasks it implied: identifying the

Translating the intent into action: each level is more specific

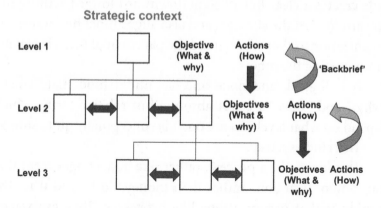

Strategic context

Figure 15 Unpacking intent: Each level is more specific

critical product set; accelerating development; accelerating support and enhancement; and reducing costs. These four *implied tasks* laid out how they were going to achieve their overall task, and each was made the responsibility of one member of the team.

Back in the office, the process continued by having each of those team members further specify how they were going to achieve their task. Joe's "what" – "to accelerate delivery to market of critical products" – would thus become their "why." Whereas for Joe each of their tasks was an element in *how* he would achieve his objective, for them it was *what* they would do. So for the first of his direct reports, the main objective was "to identify the critical product set in order to accelerate delivery to market of critical products"; for the second "to accelerate development in order to accelerate to market the delivery of critical products," and so on. Each of their direct reports would then themselves work out their implied tasks, and pass those on. The process would continue until no further analysis of tasks was necessary. At each point there would be a backbrief.

In this way, the strategy is broken down into relatively discrete elements and then fitted back together again, so that each level nests in the level above, like a set of Russian dolls. The cascade creates a clear line of sight downward toward actions and upward toward the strategy, and also aligns functions across the organization as they understand the part each of them is playing in supporting the others.

It is logical, and once one has understood that "what," "why," and "how" are not absolute but relative terms which depend on what level you are on, it is conceptually quite simple.

Therein lies a trap.

This looks like a process, rather like budgeting, except that the content is actions rather than money. So indeed it is. The trouble is that organizations like processes. They are warm, familiar things and can be rolled out fairly easily. It is therefore tempting to understand strategy execution as a process, distribute the forms, get everyone to fill them in, and relax. The result will be resentment, rigidity, and stagnation.

Although closing the alignment gap involves a process, the process is merely a way of linking together briefing and back-briefing between levels. The essence of briefing is not a process, but a skill. Although the strategy briefing template looks like a form, it is really a set of concepts to help to structure thinking. Tracy, after all, took her decision without using the form at all. Unless and until the thinking skills are in place, a briefing cascade will be stillborn. It not only will not work, it could be damaging. It will be another time-wasting hoop to jump through. The skills must be developed first, before the cascade process. Strategic briefing works because it helps people to do their jobs effectively and stops them from wasting time. But they have to learn how to do it through practice. The organization cannot jump the gun.

The steps required to achieve alignment in the context of friction have been famously and memorable enumerated by the Austrian psychologist Konrad Lorenz. Drawing on his observations about what is needed to make people change, we might modify them for an organization as the following:

1   What is said is not yet heard.
2   What is heard is not yet understood.
3   What is understood is not yet believed.
4   What is believed is not yet advocated.
5   What is advocated is not yet acted on.
6   What is acted on is not yet completed.[25]

There is an understandable tendency for leaders of organizations to concentrate on the first step – demanding enough in itself – and assume that once that has been achieved, their work is done. In fact, it has just begun.

If the organization does not jump the gun, it will have a powerful weapon to combat friction. How does a briefing cascade address Lorenz's steps?

STEP 1

First, a briefing is written down. This ensures that it has been *heard*.[26]

There is a great deal of noise in an organization. There are strategic plans, initiatives, projects, operational plans, budgets, and targets. In all of this, everybody has to have a clear answer to the question: "What do you want me to do?" Writing a strategy briefing ensures that this at least has been heard.

STEP 2

Secondly, it ensures that what has been said and heard is also *understood*.

The acid test of understanding is being able to say what the message implies about what an individual should do. What ultimately defines understanding is being able to *extrapolate implied tasks now* and being able to *make trade-offs in the future*.

To the discipline of structuring implied tasks so that they have no gaps and no overlaps is added the further refinement of identifying a *main effort*. We have seen that creating a shifting main effort directed at a center of gravity can be an effective way of executing a company's strategy over time. The same principle applies at business unit, department, and team level.

Joe's main effort was "accelerating development." The *company's* main effort was halting the decline in market share. By identifying this as *his* main effort, Joe was deciding that this was the single biggest contribution he could make to that overall intention. It meant that if he lost people mid-year because of headcount reductions, he would transfer engineers from working on enhancement and support onto development so that it should not be delayed. If achieving his own cost-cutting goal were to come into conflict with accelerating development, he would likewise decide against making the cuts, or would make them in other ways. Thinking through main effort helped Joe to work out how he would make such possible future trade-offs.

Rigor is added here by demanding the explicit articulation of the intention both one and two levels above. In other words, I have to understand both what my boss and their boss in turn are trying to achieve. Everybody understands the intentions of everybody else two levels up in the hierarchy.

This practice has been arrived at by trial and error. Experience suggests that understanding the immediate intention one level up is not enough to give full alignment if things change, and that understanding the intention three levels up is of little additional help. Two levels up is like Goldilocks' porridge: it is just right. It puts people in the position of being able to answer the question: "What would my boss want me to do if they were here now and knew what I know?"

In a matrix structure of the kind prevalent today, thinking two levels up also has the benefit of helping to resolve the dilemmas the matrix naturally creates. The "next level up" may well be ambiguous. Two bosses might point in different directions. Understanding the level above them generally resolves the issue and allows action. Reality is never black and white but actions always are. A matrix is like a set of traffic lights. If a driver at a crossroads is to move, then at any point in time, one set of lights must be red and another green. The level above sets the lights. A few months later, they may change. But at any given point in time, the direction must be clear.

STEP 3

Understanding gets compliance. Only *belief* gets commitment.

There are many reasons why people might only go through the motions. Two of the most common are that they do not believe a course of action is feasible or that they do not believe it makes sense. Strategy briefing flushes this out. It requires the stipulation of resources and constraints. It is perfectly valid to come back and say: "I can do this, but not that, unless I have more resources or more time." The process checks the realism of the direction. It also checks its relevance. A nice idea which is impractical or not making a contribution to the real objective will not survive a strategy briefing.

STEP 4

In an organization, what needs to be done must be promulgated. It requires *advocacy*.

After the backbrief, the owner of each task has to brief their own people and cascade the process down. The tasks they identify as constituent of their part in the plan have to be owned by the next level. If they have done a rigorous strategy briefing exercise themselves, it will make the job of doing so easier for the level below them. Indeed, it gets simpler as it goes on.

STEP 5

The identification of tasks enables the mission to be *acted on*.

As the process cascades down, the tasks become increasingly concrete and specific until no more analysis is necessary or possible. However, by that point, actions taken will all be relevant and cohere. It is simply a matter of structuring what needs to be done. Simple, perhaps, but something which requires effort.

Hence at the end the question of the mission's validity is explicitly posed. I have to assess whether or not the situation has changed from when I was first briefed and what that implies about what I ought to do now. I have several stepped options. If there has been a change and I can still fulfill my original part in the plan by modifying what I was planning to do, I carry on. However, if the change is so substantial that I can no longer carry out my original task, or carrying it out no longer makes sense, I should refer back. If that is impossible, I do whatever I judge to be most in keeping with the guidance I have been given about the intent.

STEP 6

Action can begin, but how do we know that it is the right action and when enough is enough? Only if we can measure the effects. It is through measures that we know how to adjust and when a task is *completed*.

Some businesses are run "on the numbers" because their strategy is designed to optimize them. In a military context, this is rarely the case. Nevertheless, even in a military context, some effort is made to measure the outcome in order to improve clarity. For example, if the mission is "to make town *x* safe in order to establish stability," what does "safe" mean? In the end it will be a judgment call, but some measures help. So a peacekeeping force will monitor the number of shooting incidents, the number of teenagers on street corners, the number of refugees returning, the level of economic activity, and so on.[27] This provides some data for whoever has to form the judgment that the town is "safe" and that the peacekeepers can be withdrawn. However, making that judgment cannot be bucked. No set of measures will give an automatic answer. That this is equally true in business is something we are wont to forget.

In the final analysis it is behavior that counts. If we close the knowledge and the alignment gaps in the ways suggested so far, we will be able to gain traction, focus effort, and deliver a strategy – until something unexpected happens, which sooner or later it will. To move away from the plan–implement model and become a do–adapt organization which is flexible enough to learn as it goes and determined enough to fight its way round any obstacle, we need to close the effects gap. To do that we need people who are ready, willing, and able to use their freedom.

QUICK RECAP

❑ People at all levels can find themselves in situations where they have to exercise independent thinking obedience.[28] They can only do so if the organization has already prepared them by providing them with the information they need to take decisions.

❑ That information can be formulated as a statement of intent, which distills the strategy for everyone. That statement can then be broken down into its component parts and used to start a process of briefing each level.

❑ A briefing should cover the higher intent, up to two levels up, the tasks that this implies for the unit concerned, where their main effort should lie, and their freedoms and constraints.

❑ Working this through in a structured way pays dividends in aligning the organization both up and down levels and across functions.

❑ The whole organization can be aligned if briefing is done at each level, with each one adding more specificity to the tasks implied by the higher intent, and then presenting the results to the level above in a process called backbriefing. This checks mutual understanding, allows for adjustment of the original brief, and, when done collectively, helps alignment across functions.

❑ Unpacking the implications of the intent on each level will only work properly if the organizational structure broadly reflects the task structure implied by the strategy. If it is in conflict with the strategy, it should be changed before anything else. It requires an appropriate level of hierarchy of entities that can be made wholly or largely accountable for critical tasks, led by people who are skilled and experienced enough to make autonomous decisions.

CHAPTER SIX

THE EFFECTS GAP

Independent Thinking Obedience

Sins of omission are worse than sins of commission

BUILDING THE ORGANIZATION

Von Moltke was clear that his job was not merely to develop campaign strategies and set direction on campaign, but to build an organization capable of taking decisions and acting in line with the direction he set. In fact, he spent most of his time doing this. He saw the outcome in terms of success or failure as being as much down to the organization as a whole as to his own decisions. He had humility, a quality that has only recently been noted in the business literature as a characteristic of many leaders of outstanding companies.[1]

To create that organization, von Moltke needed to recruit and develop the right people. While doing so did not depend on finding individuals of genius, it did depend on identifying and developing a body of people with the right talent and putting them in the right place in the organization. Here, there was a problem.

By the time von Moltke became Chief of the General Staff, the aristocracy had lost its historical grip on the officer corps as a whole, but it still dominated senior positions. In 1860, only 35 percent of Prussian generals had middle-class origins, an indication that there was a glass ceiling. Von Moltke meant to break it.[2] The vehicle he used was the General Staff and the instrument he used to create the vehicle was the General War School, which in 1859 was renamed the War Academy (*Kriegsakademie*). In 1872, the General Staff itself took over the running of the Academy.

The purpose of the Academy was twofold. The first was to act as a rigorous selection mechanism. The second was not only to train professional skills, but to develop a group of people who would make similar judgments and behave in similar ways because they shared a common doctrine. The best junior officers with at least three years' service could apply for a "high potentials" course which would lead to entry into the General Staff.

Selection was by competitive examination, so although most made the pass mark, only the best 10–15 percent were accepted. Results were adjusted according to each candidate's educational background, especially evidence that he had used a "crammer." Of the eight papers, five were on military subjects requiring a modest amount of technical knowledge. The questions were mainly problems requiring a solution, and marks were awarded for the quality of the decision, the reasoning behind it, and the originality of approach. The objective was to identify potential based on clarity of reasoning and decision-making ability.[3]

Once accepted, the student was taught in ways which were later taken over by the world's business schools. Most of the courses were designed to develop professional rather than academic skills and delivered in open lectures in which active debate between teachers and pupils was regarded as essential. There were only six full-time instructors. Of the remainder, 20 were active General Staff officers and 16 were university professors. The General Staff course culminated in a three-week staff ride in which historical and potential battlefields were visited and candidates were required to assess the ground, the situation, and the options and describe how they would have acted themselves. The "Order of Teaching" issued to the Academy in 1888 stated that this final exercise was to test "the capacity, knowledge, and endurance of each officer – to find out what he can do." Its author was von Moltke.

That was not the end of it. Successful candidates were put on probation and given a further two years of training, which had to be carried out alongside their day jobs. They had to do a tactical map exercise every week. Von Moltke himself was the senior tutor. He led two staff rides a year and supervised the conduct of wargames, which sometimes lasted for months.[4] The staff rides and wargames were designed to develop powers of decision making in circumstances dominated by friction. Von Moltke had been an early enthusiast for the wargame system designed by Georg von Reisswitz in 1811 to simulate brigade-level engagements on a board using dice to reflect chance.[5] He replaced the original dice with an umpire to increase realism and add to the level of friction.[6]

Von Moltke regarded the War Academy as one of his most important instruments for building the organization he wanted. The General Staff course passed out only the best of the best.[7] The syllabus of the War Academy was designed not simply to build skills, but to impart a shared approach and ethos. The single aspect of performance emphasized more than any other was individual initiative and responsibility.[8]

Adopting a unified set of common practices has advantages in itself by raising the level of internal predictability. Rather than being left entirely to "individual style," the way leadership is exercised is constrained within acceptable boundaries. There were set ways of giving direction. If a commander's intent was not clear, subordinates had the right, indeed the duty, to demand clarity. They had the right to exercise freedom of judgment. Everybody knew that. Everybody also knew that when, as expected, things started to go wrong, they could expect the organization to help them and they were expected to help others. People knew how they could expect others to behave. That built confidence.

Von Moltke supervised his high potentials program himself, and spent two weeks of every year from 1858 to 1881 leading 20–40 officers on a staff ride, and so directly influenced the thought processes of the people at the top of his organization. They were taught to identify the essentials of a situation and act rapidly and incisively. They were taught to recognize patterns and use their intuition, to take decisions which were "about right – now" rather than wait for more information, and then take another decision as they saw the effects of the first. They were taught to think independently and use their own judgment; one exercise put officers in a position in which they had to disobey orders in order to be successful.[9] The result was, von Moltke said, that in a given situation, 99 out of 100 officers would react as he would himself.[10]

He created a unified operating model by working on the minds of his generals, allowing them to absorb a common doctrine based on principles rather than rules. His methods did not only develop what Argyris and Schon have called "single-loop learning," in which an organization learns to correct its actions so as to carry on its current policies and fulfill its current objectives, but "double-loop learning," in which the organization's policies, objectives, and behavioral norms are modified.[11]

Von Moltke reinforced the behavioral norms in the way he reacted to mistakes. He knew that punishing one case of misjudgment would kill off every attempt to foster initiative in the officer corps for years to come. "It is easy to pass judgment after the event," he wrote. "For that reason, one should be extremely careful before condemning generals."[12] That notion was made official, and applied not merely to generals but to all officers. The Field Service Regulations of 1888 contain the sentence: "All commanders must always be aware that *an omission or failure to act is a graver charge than making a mistake in the choice of means*."[13] Superior officers were instructed to refrain from harsh or wounding criticism of mistakes lest it undermine the self-confidence of subordinates, to praise the fact that they did show initiative, and to correct them in such a way that they learn. Otherwise, as one general wrote, "you will extinguish a hundred positive initiatives in order to prevent one error, and thereby lose a tremendous amount of energy."[14]

Von Moltke went further still, only admitting to the General Staff those among his high potentials who had proven that they were willing to *disobey* orders, at least in an exercise. Not many of us are prepared to be that radical today.

However, Colin Marshall for one would have endorsed the 1888 Regulations:

> *We realise that employees – all of us – won't always be right, but it is better that they make mistakes than not try to solve customers' problems. We discourage our managers from coming down on an employee like a ton of bricks if the decision the employee made was wrong. Instead, we want managers to explain why the decision was wrong and what the right decision should have been, so that the next time the employee is confronted with a similar situation he or she will get it right.*[15]

Creating a common culture is a long and difficult process, but some things can have a big impact. BA changed its culture quite radically in a period of less than five years. It did so by focusing on the things von Moltke worked on. In Marshall's words, it "begins and ends with the way employees are trained, nurtured and led."[16] If Tracy's employer wants her to use the space it gives her to be adaptive, it will be careful about how it selects her, the training she gets, the environment it places her in, and what it expects of those who lead her.

DEVELOPING PEOPLE

Let's go back to Tracy at the point at which we left her standing behind the desk, making up her mind what to do. She has all the information she needs to take her decision. She has understood the company's strategy and what it means for her. She has made the trade-off decision. She is ready to use all the space she has been given to get her sweaty customer on his plane.

Yet sometimes, Tracy hesitates.

She is ready because she has understood what to do. But being ready is not enough. In order to act, she must also be willing and able to do so. To be willing and able she needs support, both physical and moral. The organization must provide her with the means to deliver what is needed, and she requires confidence – in herself, in her boss's reaction, and in the rest of the organization. Willingness and ability often go together. If she is not sure whether she or someone else is able to do what is needed, Tracy may not be willing to act.

We would be well advised to bear in mind the difference between being ready, willing, and able. If things are not happening as we want, we tend to assume that people have not understood. Sometimes, however, repeating the message does not have any effect. Sometimes, people understand it quite well, but do not see what is in it for them, do not believe the organization is capable of doing it, or doubt that it means what it says. People only show independent thinking obedience if they have the means to do so, and are operating within a network of trust. The first thing is to get the right people into the network in the first place.

McKinsey has popularized the theme of human factors in terms of a '"war for talent." Because of adverse demographics and more intense global competition, many companies are finding it increasingly difficult to find enough "A players." The core piece of advice is that companies have to make themselves more attractive to the scarce number of high potentials looking for jobs, and invest heavily in those they do attract.[17] Given that their instinctive reaction to the three gaps leads many companies to wage a war *on* talent, particularly their own, a measure of enlightenment is in itself likely to improve their position.

In the end, the war for talent will be won by the few banks and professional service firms who depend on recruiting A players and therefore pay whatever it takes to get them. Most organizations will by definition mainly employ average people most of the time. The real challenge is how to create an organization which enables average people to turn out above-average performance. The A players are important because, like von Moltke's General Staff, they can act as a multiplier on the performance of the average. What really matters is not the performance of the individual stars but the performance of the collective. Most organizations could improve that performance significantly if they could unlock the potential of their existing people, whether or not they are unusually talented.[18]

It is important who you let through the door in the first place, and what positions you put them in. Just as some can act as multipliers, so others are dividers. Some people are not suited to the principles of leading through intent. They fall into two main groups.

Those in one group like being told exactly what to do and following procedures. They are uncomfortable with responsibility and lack the self-confidence to exercise independent judgment. So their default behavior pattern is to delegate upward by continually asking for direction. The other group consists of natural authoritarians who only feel safe if they have total personal control. They are uncomfortable with uncertainty and lack the trust in others to delegate. So their default behavior pattern is to micromanage and punish deviation from set procedures. Our message is a threat to both groups, and although they may say they agree with it, in practice they will not follow it. Both groups are a problem, though the severity of the problem varies widely.

Upward delegators will tend to reveal themselves as such and are unlikely to progress beyond a certain level. There is a process of natural selection. They will tend to join organizations where they can feel comfortable and have a role to fulfill. They can be identified because their behavior is chronic. Trying to change these chronic cases will only make them suffer.[19] However, some people delegate upward because they think they are doing the right thing, because of the demands of the organizational system they are in, or through lack of confidence. Past behavior patterns are not always a reliable guide to potential. They can change.

Micromanagers are more of a problem because of their impact on those working for them. Micromanagement can also be an adopted behavior pattern which can be unlearned; behavior and personality are not the same. Sometimes, if their subordinates are relatively inexperienced or of low competence, micromanagement may be appropriate. The type of direction and the amount of space given to any subordinate must be appropriate for their particular skills and experience.[20]

The most serious problem is the chronic micromanager who is also an authoritarian. Such individuals micromanage under all circumstances because their psychology leads them to fear uncertainty and seek control. The psychological makeup of the authoritarian character was studied after the war by an international group led by German philosopher Theodor Adorno, which published a seminal study in 1950.[21] Authoritarians are conventional, are uncritical of and submissive toward those of higher status, are inclined to think in rigid categories, and tend to follow rules and procedures. The more extreme of them are also cynical about human motivation, aggressive toward those who challenge the hierarchy or deviate from established procedures, and like to appear "tough." As individuals they are unpleasant to deal with. If they gain positions of power, they become a social problem. Within organizations they are dysfunctional, and if they reach the top they can be destructive.

Norman Dixon has examined their impact in military organizations in a celebrated work first published in 1976.[22] He attributes most of the military disasters described in his book to the influence of authoritarians and their mindset. Such people are attracted to peacetime armies because they offer a very stable environment characterized by detailed rules governing all aspects of behavior ("bull"), and personal relations dominated by hierarchy. They have the opportunity to be "tough" by punishing even trivial deviations from rules or challenges to authority as insubordination. Their impact in peacetime is nefarious because they are unwilling to sacrifice cherished traditions in favor of technological innovation and they suppress original thinkers. In wartime, however, their impact is often disastrous. In the face of the uncertainties of friction, they panic: they make bad decisions or no decisions at all, avoid big issues and fuss about detail, and react to the anxiety they feel in the fast-moving external environment of war by trying to exercise tight control over the internal environment, bullying subordinates, and blaming others when things go wrong – as they usually do.[23] The opening phase of a major war usually involves the identification and removal of these people and their replacement with another type who is psychologically adapted to the environment.[24] Such a type, who bears some superficial resemblance to the authoritarian, is characterized by Dixon as an "autocrat."[25]

In contrast with the authoritarian, the autocrat is not interested in details, but is conceptual enough to be able to grasp the essentials of a situation and self-confident enough to be comfortable with uncertainty. Autocrats seek responsibility and are able to trust others if they have grounds to do so. They are thoughtful and humane. Wellington was an autocrat.[26] Authoritarians micromanage under all circumstances because it is the only approach they are comfortable with. An autocrat only does so if the circumstances render such behavior appropriate.

Armies do not have a monopoly on authoritarians. They turn up in business as well, though probably in smaller numbers than in peacetime armies because the modern business environment does not attract them as much.[27] They can be identified through the consistency of their behavior patterns under all circumstances. They should not be allowed to reach positions of power. If they do, the only way to deal with them is to sideline or remove them.

Most managers are more flexible and will adapt their behavior to circumstances. The organization can influence that by offering them the appropriate form of development.

Jack Welch used GE's training center at Crotonville in the way von Moltke used the War Academy and, just as von Moltke ran staff rides, Welch regularly appeared personally in "the pit." Such a level of investment by the CEO remains the exception rather than the rule, but it had very high returns. It enabled the man at the top to get to know people he was probably going to work with and to exercise direct influence on their thinking and behavior. There could be no better way of guiding their future decisions and shaping the organization as a whole, for they spread the message. If you want to change the way people think and act, even if you do not want to found a religion, you need to create disciples to send among the people as well as preaching to the people yourself.

It can be argued that the military have the luxury of times of peace when they can train for "the real thing." In business, "the real thing" is always going on, and finding time for training is difficult. One could equally well reverse the argument, however.[28] History suggests that it is in times of peace that an army can lose its way and most readily be infiltrated by authoritarians. Businesses do not have that problem. They do not have to spend vast resources trying to simulate "the real thing" in exercises, but can work at improving all the time, building skills as they go and taking time out occasionally to reflect on the learning.

Nevertheless, few business organizations are large enough to be able to afford a Crotonville. The answer is to focus the training and development effort on the critical groups of people, to do some training on the job, and to propagate the methods required outside of the classroom.

It is not necessary to train everybody in the organization in order to inculcate leading through intent. The key group is upper–middle management, people running a department or unit who are senior enough to have to make strategic decisions. Typically, this is two levels below the executive board. They need to master the disciplines of strategic thinking and briefing. If the development effort is focused on them, they will then pass down the skills and develop them in those working for them. Because they have day-to-day operational roles, they will have a greater influence on culture and behavior than more senior executives.

They are usually the best place to start. It may seem more logical to start at the top. In practice, it is more difficult. It is very hard to craft a good statement of intent without first understanding the implications for the lower operational levels. The top management has usually set some broad direction. They need to agree with the approach and give their blessing to it. When it comes to making it happen, they are best brought in by being backbriefed. They can have a huge influence if they model the desired behavior, but the skills they need are not merely working out "what does it mean for us," but crafting strategic direction and identifying the center of gravity. Doing that will be far easier if those reporting to them have first worked on their own briefing. The strategy will improve and sharpen through iteration.

Training of this kind cannot be theoretical. It only works if it takes the actual situation as its starting point. The best way to do that is by running workshops designed to support the development and promulgation of the current strategy. First time around the results will not be perfect, but they will be better than otherwise. The second time, things will go more smoothly and the results will generally be clearer and more incisive. After that, occasional reinforcement will maintain quality. Doing it for real every time speeds up learning.

Training can be backed up by an articulation of the approach and the implied behavioral norms in internal publications analogous to Field Service Regulations, which can be made available to all. However, such publications need to affirm what is already an established, or at least emerging, reality. If they are at odds with the actual culture, they will backfire.

High-performing organizations tend to have a strong culture. By having a strong sense of "the way we do things round here," they offer potential employees a choice about what sort of working environment they want. The sense of culture can become "cult like." Sometimes, as at P&G, the culture is not explicitly articulated; in others, like Nordstrom, it is documented. At Nordstrom it is embodied in an employee handbook, which is simply a single five-by-eight-inch card stating: "Our number one goal is to provide *outstanding customer service.*" It then lays out what it calls the Nordstrom Rules: "Rule #1: *Use your good judgment in all situations.* There will be no additional rules."[29]

The reason that this document is powerful is that it simply sums up the reality a new employee will encounter at Nordstrom. The company creates "customer service heroes," and stories are told about what they did to earn the title. It takes letters from customers very seriously and it is regarded as "a real sin" to get a bad one. They measure sales per hour and post up individual rankings on the bulletin board. They give special rewards to "Pacesetters" who set and exceed high sales targets. If someone is seen to get irritated with a customer, they are sent home and put under close observation for a few weeks. They employ secret shoppers to check on service standards and the demeanor of individual sales staff. Such an environment is not for everyone, but it ensures that the intent is clear and that behavior is aligned with it.[30]

Statements and documents should be used to reinforce and consolidate rather than lead change. The best ones are short, simple explanations of the principles guiding behavior which help people to make choices, and are best illustrated with stories. If the principles are so universal and bland that no trade-offs can be made, they will have little impact. A principle such as "Be honest and open" only makes sense if people understand what it stands in contrast with, and the reality mirrors that. If it just means "We don't like people who lie and are deceitful," it means nothing. If it means "We want you to tell it as it is, stand up for your opinion even if it is in conflict with others, and challenge authority," it does mean something, but it will fall flat if bringers of bad news

are punished for being negative and those who challenge authority are told to shut up, sidelined, and get poor evaluations for not
being team players.

Fear is not a word commonly used in management literature
and it may sound overly dramatic. In reality, there is a lot of it
about and it is often a reason why people decide to play safe, and
do as little as possible.[31] They may not be congratulated, but at
least they will avoid punishment. Most people working in organizations have a lot at stake. The stakes probably include their
prosperity, their security, their reputation, and their self-esteem.
People tend to be risk averse and compliant. That can pose a
problem both for those who delegate responsibility and for those
who are asked to accept it.

One of the greatest fears of senior people is of letting go and
thereby losing direct control. In delegating authority for decision
making one gives away power without giving away accountability. A lot of people who do not suffer from the pathology of
authoritarians find that a scary thing to do. It implies trusting
your people. If you have been brought up to believe that leadership is about knowing how to do something better than your
followers, it is difficult to see the task of leaders as enabling followers to perform their jobs better than they otherwise would,
and admitting that they may know how to do those jobs better
than you do. Letting go is hard to do but can bring great rewards.

The answer to this type of fear is to create controlled situations in which you can test how much trust to place in people.
Such a situation arose for one manager who was in charge of the
property department in a company which runs chains of pubs
and restaurants in the UK. There was a fire in a pub in Wales and
he received a call from his regional manager late one night to
report on the incident. The regional manager had never had to
deal with a serious fire before. The property manager had dealt
with several, and knew what to do. Instinct told him to get into
the car, head off to the scene of the fire, and take control. However,

he decided instead to talk through the issues with his subordinate and ask him to backbrief by faxing over a plan the next morning. He went through the plan for an hour on the phone and then said, "Off you go – get back to me every evening and if you need any help in between times, call me."

So they went on, until after a few days they spoke every other day, then every week. The fallout from the fire was contained and everything sorted out. The result was not merely to solve the problem, but to develop an individual so that in future if there is another fire, the regional manager will be able to handle it himself. He is now more valuable to his organization and the property manager will have more time to get on with his job instead of the next one down. The most important thing he did, he said, was to stay where he was. It was also the hardest thing to do. He felt anxious. The anxiety dissipated over the next few days as he grew more confident in his subordinate.

The other side of this is the fear felt by the more junior people who have to accept responsibility. This is natural in many who are not chronic upward delegators. It means feeling exposed and having to take decisions. It means the possibility of making mistakes, and hence the risk of punishment.

We may not have to be as radical as von Moltke in fostering disobedience. People will be willing if they are confident that the organization as a whole will not punish them. If they are confident of that, they need to feel confident in their own ability. That often depends on being offered support of the kind the property manager gave his subordinate.

There are two dimensions to trust. One is moral – I will trust you if I am confident in your *motives*. In the end, people who optimize their own interests over those of the collective should depart. We can usually identify them, and a good briefing process will help to flush them into the open. The other is practical – I will trust you if I believe you are *competent*. Competence is a function of context. I may be quite willing to trust you to drive me to the airport, but not trust you to fly me across the Atlantic. So it is up to me to create a context in which I can trust you.

The framework of strategy briefing allows me to do this. I can determine how much space to give you by setting the boundaries and the control loop. The default is to give you as much as possible, but if I have doubts (for example because you are inexperienced or we have never worked together before), I can make the boundaries narrower, and I can make the control loop tight or loose. The boundaries should be set so that failure is not catastrophic. In the above example, the main mechanism was the control loop: daily at first, then every few days, then weekly. But it remained the regional manager's responsibility to say *how* he was going to deal with the fire. That responsibility was never usurped.

Leading through intent is a tough approach, but it is enlightened. It is not about being nice to people, but respecting them. The bedrock of morale is feeling confident that you are making a contribution to a collective purpose. Morale drops if an organization wastes people's time. They get resentful because time is all any of us has got. Using an effective briefing technique renders the motivational task of leadership far easier by making the connection between the individual and the collective, and forming the basis of mutual respect.

Experience suggests that managers who have the courage to let go are often surprised by just how much their subordinates are capable of achieving when given good direction. It exploits and develops human potential. Making a start is simply a matter of having faith that the potential is there. It is remarkable how seldom that faith is disappointed.

DRIVERS OF BEHAVIOR

Nevertheless, people sometimes get in the way. Our default reaction when people are not doing what we want is to use the carrot of incentivizing them to do so (for example by offering them more money if they do) and the stick of punishment if they do not (for example by not promoting them or giving them a poor evaluation). This is to seriously limit our own options as managers.

Some rather obscure academic work has been done on this issue by organizational sociologists. Based on the teachings of Frenchman Michel Crozier, The Boston Consulting Group has been able to distill the essentials of the matter to produce a usable tool. Organizational sociology starts with the empirically verifiable assumption that most organizational behavior is rational given the position of each individual within a particular organizational subgroup.

In its essentials, the model claims that the behavior exhibited by groups of actors in organizations is a function of their goals, their resources, and the constraints under which they operate, as illustrated in Figure 16.

Map of Organizational Dynamics

Actors	Goals	Resources	Constraints	Resulting behavior

Figure 16 Behavior as a result of a human system

In order to explain behavior in an organization we need to understand:

❑ Who the groups of similar actors are and how they interact with other groups who have different levels and sources of power.
❑ The real goals these groups have, be they explicit or implicit.
❑ Their resources, which are not only physical (such as money,

equipment) but mental or moral (such as authority or the expectation of mutual support).

❑ Their constraints (time limits, other demands, limits to power and authority, including the ability to influence others, and problems they face in achieving their goals).

In order to influence the resulting behavior, managers can change the system either directly (by changing the actors, setting new goals, giving more resources, or removing some constraints) or indirectly (by, for example, changing reporting lines, processes, information, training, and so on), as in Figure 17.[32]

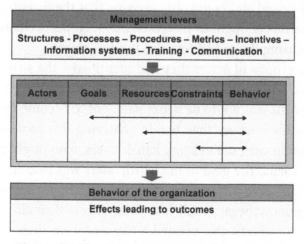

Figure 17 The human system can be managed

We are usually alerted to dysfunctional behavior because we notice effects which will fail to add up to the outcomes we want. The systems appear to be malfunctioning, although on their own terms they are functioning perfectly well. To get them to deliver what we want, we need to modify some or all of the variables in the system, watch what happens, and carry on modifying them until we get the behavior which achieves the effects we are after. In doing so, we have to be careful to analyze the system correctly. As we will see, dysfunctional behavior may be producing undesirable effects elsewhere in the system. A group of actors who are failing (in our terms) may simply be responding to pressures originating elsewhere. We must also know what effects will add up to the outcome we want. Sometimes this is clear, sometimes less so.

The value of this model in understanding human systems can be shown by a simple illustration. A cosmetics company was seeking a new distribution channel for some innovative shampoos. It decided to train shampooists in salons to sell the new products, and gave them generous financial incentives to do so, allowing them to boost their meager income substantially. Few sales resulted. The marketing experts at the cosmetics company were surprised and could only imagine that the incentives were not generous enough, so increased them. Nothing changed. An analysis using the model revealed the real reason.

The groups of *actors* they had identified – the shampooists – worked with another group – the hairdressers. The *goal* of the shampooists was not to be better paid, but to become hairdressers. The key *resource* they had in achieving this goal was their relationship with the existing hairdressers, who might possibly mentor them. The goal of the hairdressers was to cultivate and defend exclusive personal relationships with their clients. Hence if a shampooist began to talk knowledgeably to their clients about haircare products, this created a *constraint* on their ability to retain exclusivity; in fact, it sabotaged it. Selling shampoo would wreck the shampooists' relationships with hairdressers. It was about the worst thing a shampooist in a salon could do.

The answer was to go to another group of actors altogether, the salon managers, who were celebrity hairdressers. They did not look promising at first. One of them remarked, "I'm not a shopkeeper, and I don't sell soap." But by changing the packaging of the shampoo to emphasize its technical specifications it became a resource for the salon managers, who were then happy to recommend the products to their clients as part of their service. Sales grew rapidly.[33] The company managed to align its own goal with the goal of the salon managers, which was to be experts in the art of coiffure.

This behavioral model, derived from academic research and successfully applied in its simplified form by BCG, mirrors the categories used in what I have called "strategy briefing," a technique developed completely independently by the military in a long process of trial and error. It is in fact strategy briefing in reverse.

In briefing, we begin with the actors and their context, and define their goals, resources, and constraints. Examples such as the above show what can result when that does not happen and things are left to nature. The organisms adapt to the fitness landscape in which they find themselves – the systems of their organization – and seek to survive and prosper. While in their specific form their goals can be many and various, they will all further survival and prosperity. The cosmetics story shows how the imposition of a strategic goal (selling shampoo) onto an alien system will fail.

This suggests the alluring thought that behaving in the way required by the philosophy of leading through intent is natural, *if we internalize the outcome we are seeking to achieve.* In trying to achieve what we all really want, obeying orders is in fact an unnatural learned behavior. Nature programmed us to think for ourselves, take risks, and seize unexpected opportunities. This in turn suggests that if an organization wants to *encourage* such behavior, the most important thing it can do is to *identify and stop doing whatever is currently inhibiting it.* To put it bluntly, it should get off people's backs.

Another case described by BCG shows how acute people can be in working out the true situation and setting rational goals for themselves, and how creative they can be in adapting their behavior to achieve those goals. People are very good at finding and using resources even if they are less than obvious. And not only are they good at working around constraints, they can manage to actually turn them into resources. When we don't like the result we call this "playing the system." From a neutral point of view it is a compliment to human creativity. The challenge is to harness this energy productively. Doing so usually means changing the system, not the players.

A software development function was turning out bug-ridden products and taking 25 percent longer to do so than others in the industry. The function contained three sets of units: a design unit, development units which wrote the software, and a testing unit which finally released the products. The company tightened controls on quality and time for all three sets of units. Things got worse.

The heart of the problem was in fact one of the software development units, though according to the metrics it was performing best of all. This unit worked on those subsystems of the products which had to conform to industry norms. For the company, having to comply with industry norms was a constraint. For the unit, it was a resource. So were the delays. Knowing that the designers would be late and were also dependent on them for knowledge of the industry norms, the developers began writing the software before the design was complete. This enabled them to hit their time targets. The designers had to comply with the developers or face delays themselves. In order to avoid being held responsible for further delays, the testers did only minimal quality checks. The clever developers turned the company's constraints into resources for themselves and did very well, making a bad situation worse. For them, the target of on-time delivery which the organization had given them became the goal of maximizing their own autonomy within the system. That goal was a perfectly rational one given the nature of the system.

The answer was to increase the power of the overall project managers, measure all units on the final outcome in terms of customer satisfaction, hire some designers with marketing experience, and redesign the process to give more weight to customers' needs.[34] The goals, resources, and constraints of all the units were thereby changed. Internal uncertainty was reduced and the efforts of all were directed at managing the remaining external uncertainty: customer satisfaction.

Constraints are often a valuable resource, and not only for canny software engineers. They have triggered major innovations in all fields of endeavor, not least in business. They were at the root of the development of the Toyota production system. The man credited with starting it in the 1950s and 1960s, Taiichi Ohno, has written that the system "developed out of need." At the time, Toyota was financially vulnerable and faced the problem of producing the "small quantities of many varieties" required by the Japanese market simply in order to "survive in competition with mass production and mass sales systems of an industry already established in Europe and the United States."[35] Ford and GM had vastly greater resources. In looking for another way, Ohno was inspired by a visit to a supermarket, observing that every customer took whatever quantities of whatever product they wanted straight away. He decided to create a production system that functioned in a similar way and began by eliminating waste. Ohno is credited with the saying that "having no problems is the biggest problem of all." The result is the most productive automotive manufacturing system in the world today, which is sustaining its lead despite every attempt by its rivals to copy it. It has its origins in the need to overcome a constraint.

These stories also show that one of the challenges of strategy execution is to meet not only the company's objectives, but the objectives of the people who work in it as well.[36] If company objectives are in conflict with personal ones, only one of them will win. Either the employees leave the company (as regularly happens in the most obvious form of conflict – forced redundancy) or the strategy will be sabotaged, consciously or unconsciously. If company objectives and personal objectives are not in conflict but are indifferent to one another, employees will generally be compliant, and some things will get done, at least until the going gets tough. Only if the two are aligned and mutually supportive will employees feel commitment.

While it will not guarantee such alignment, good formalized or semi-formalized briefing and backbriefing will tend to flush out incongruities. It is not designed to make personal goals and aspirations explicit, but it does force people to reflect about whether they are really willing to undertake the task assigned to them, and gives them the opportunity to challenge it. If they are of good will, it can counteract unintended consequences of the kind described. If they are not of good will, it makes it harder for them to hide. If they are not of good will and clever enough to keep their real motives hidden, one has a different kind of problem.

Even with good will, undesired effects such as those described above will still occur, and one should be ready to address them as they appear.

ALIGNING PROCESSES

The right sort of people, given good direction and led in the right way, can start to make a difference. They may be willing to do the right thing, but still unable to do so if the processes of the organization get in their way. They need processes which support them by being *aligned* with the strategy and with each other and by being *flexible* enough to enable adaptation to changing circumstances. The two most important organizational processes are budgeting and performance appraisal. They form part of corporate body language, more powerful than anything anyone says, which shapes organizational culture.

Strangely, it is not common to link strategy and budgeting.[37] In many companies, there is a strategic and operational planning process run by the strategy function, and budgeting is run by finance. Sometimes they even try to separate them in time so as not to overburden people. There is often also an objective-setting and performance appraisal system run by HR. Performance appraisal has an effect on one's career and is often tied to pay. This separation is courting disaster.

While the separation may be organizationally convenient, creating a single process is not all that difficult. The "what and why" cascade offers a neat parallel to the budgeting process. It cascades actions, budgets cascade money. A budget is a resource and a constraint, and so needs to be considered as part of briefing. Logically, briefing should come first. Practically, they co-determine each other and the process can be iterative.

After briefing, backbriefing, and budgeting, each unit is in a position to write an operational plan with more detailed actions, responsibilities, and timelines. These plans are not needed for control purposes, and can be left to the individuals directly concerned. Briefings should contain all the important metrics and these can be put into a scorecard, balanced or otherwise. That in itself creates a performance management system which should form the basis of appraisals. Creating further objectives is not only superfluous, leading to unnecessary work, but creates confusion. The more objectives someone has, the harder it is for them to focus on what really matters and the more their freedom of action is constrained.

People want to survive and prosper. They try to act in ways that will enable them to do so. They watch who is promoted and draw their conclusions. Dispensing medals or money is part of corporate body language. It reveals what is really valued, whatever people say. Appraisals are dependent on the judgments of various superiors, whom it is therefore wise to please.

If you are exhorted to be innovative, but the person who writes your evaluations prefers tried-and-tested methods, you will tend to follow a policy of "steady as she goes" rather than risk their ire or possible comments to the effect that you are a loose cannon or lacking in judgment. If you are exhorted to take risks but know that nobody who made a mistake was ever promoted, you will tend to keep your head down, for taking risks implies a certain rate of failure. If you are exhorted to be critical and challenging but know that your evaluation criteria include being a "team player," you will be careful about what and whom you challenge.

In assessing the performance of the organization and of individuals, do not try to replace judgment with measures. Measures offer some objectivity, so they are a valuable support mechanism. In the final analysis, assessment requires human judgment. As the word itself suggests, organizations are organic. They are human systems and only work if the people in them can trust each other's judgment. We should do our best to ensure that the judgment is informed, but the ultimate judgment is about the fulfillment of the intent. Performance appraisal should therefore be driven by the briefing process and is a result of it.

If an organization systematically builds the strategic thinking and briefing skills of its executives, it can create something very powerful. It can turn a set of principles into an *operating system* for the whole company. Building the skills will take sustained effort, but creating a unified process is just a matter of bringing together disparate elements which for the most part already exist. Because the process is unified, there is a greater chance of coherence, and less danger of one element getting in the way of another. Figure 18 is a real example.

For many organizations, institutionalizing such a process in the annual planning cycle would generally improve alignment between plans, actions, resources, and incentives. However, if it is only an annual process, it will not in itself encourage adaptive behavior or make the organization more agile. It will allow for some change at lower levels, but objectives and resources are set for a year. In many business environments that is no longer enough. We need to create room for more frequent reviews to ascertain what effects are being achieved and changing our actions. We may also need to reallocate resources. Writing in 2001, Kaplan and Norton quote a study which claims that "78%

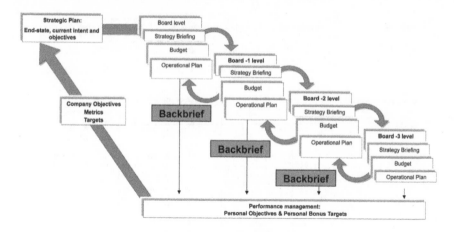

Figure 18 A unified process

of companies do not change their budgets within the financial cycle."[38] The reasons for this are not clear, but two factors probably loom large.

One is that the budget is seen as a financial matter, so there is no need to depart from the annual financial cycle of planning and calculating results. Budgeting is hard enough work as it is – doing it once a year makes many companies almost grind to a halt, so why invite more pain? The answer is that the budget is a business matter, and all that is generally needed are adjustments. The bulk of most cost bases will remain unchanged, but if we are to be agile, we do need to be able to invest more here and tighten things up there in the course of a year.

The other is that financial markets like predictability. They like strategies to be plans, and everything to go according to them. Deviation is seen as a "failure to deliver." Although this is intuitively plausible and comfortingly macho, it is about 150 years out of date and unrealistic. The answer to the analysts is that agility is valuable and an agile organization will not only suffer less when hit by unpredictable external shocks, but will also be able to exploit unforeseen opportunities. It is therefore more likely to exceed expectations, which is the only way to

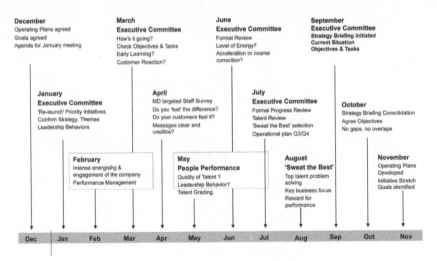

December
Operating Plans agreed
Goals agreed
Agenda for January meeting

March
Executive Committee
How's it going?
Check Objectives & Tasks
Early Learning?
Customer Reaction?

June
Executive Committee
Formal Review
Level of Energy?
Acceleration or course
correction?

September
Executive Committee
Strategy Briefing Initiated
Current Situation
Objectives & Tasks

January
Executive Committee
'Re-launch' Priority Initiatives
Confirm Strategy, Themes
Leadership Behaviors

April
MD targeted Staff Survey
Do you 'feel' the difference?
Do your customers feel it?
Messages clear and
credible?

July
Executive Committee
Formal Progress Review
Talent Review
'Sweat the Best' selection
Operational plan Q3/Q4

October
Strategy Briefing Consolidation
Agree Objectives
No gaps, no overlaps

February
Intense energising &
engagement of the company
Performance Management

May
People Performance
Quality of Talent ?
Leadership Behavior?
Talent Grading

August
'Sweat the Best'
Top talent problem
solving
Key business focus
Reward for
performance

November
Operating Plans
Developed
Initiative Stretch
Goals identified

Dec	Jan	Feb	Mar	Apr	May	Jun	Jul	Aug	Sep	Oct	Nov

Figure 19 Operating rhythm

increase the value of its shares, or at least beat the trend.[39] It is unwise to make promises to the financial community which make the company a hostage to fortune.

So the process cannot be allowed to create stagnation. It must form an *operating rhythm*, which allows flex in the course of a year. A quarterly cycle is quite manageable. The annual budget becomes a rolling forecast. Figure 19 is an example.

During the year, the strategy and the budget are reviewed in March, June/July, and September. The following year is prepared in November. The reviews take place within each business unit, but the calendar is the same for all units in order to keep people together, save time and money on travel, and allow corporate committees to give and take resources. In practice, it is not that difficult. In the example above, the person responsible for the process claimed that if the CEO were to change his intentions midyear, shifting budgets and adapting to the changes would be easy.[40]

The main theme of the reviews is the question: "Has the situation changed?" This is where the measures come in, but they alone are not enough. Participants must also be able to address the questions "Why" and "What does that imply about what we should do now?" In order to answer those questions, direct observation is required and causality needs to be debated. The final decision may be based on one of three conclusions:

1   What we are doing is right, so we need to continue – the desired effects have not come through yet.
2a Our overall objective is still valid, but we will not achieve the desired effects in this way, so we must change what we are doing in order to achieve it.
2b Our overall objective is still valid, but we observe some unpredicted effects which represent an opportunity, so we must change what we are doing in order to exploit them.
3   We need to change our objective.

Most commonly, the conclusion will be 1 or a variant of 2. Action will be taken and the next level up informed. If the conclusion is 3, the next level up must be informed first, because doing so will have implications there as well.

Between these review dates are meetings designed to address specific issues such as customer reactions to changes, people's performance, and internal motivation, and to discuss ways of maintaining energy and reinforcing direction. All are geared to the specific situation. The focus is not simply on understanding what has happened so far, but on what to do next, even if nothing has changed. This serves not just to adjust but to affirm and re-energize.

Budgets were originally designed as a control mechanism. As such they are traps, leading us into the jaws of the effects gap by allowing us to use them to exert more detailed control (see Chapter 2). It is time to use them in a more enlightened way, and many companies are already doing so.[41] The budget is, however, merely an example of a set of performance metrics. It measures financial performance, but that is just one aspect of business performance. In recognition of the need for nonfinancial measures, metrics of all kinds have proliferated. That is to be welcomed. We need them. They are seductive. And accordingly, we must also beware.

KEEPING SCORE

Organizations like processes, but they adore metrics. The knowledge gap acts like a vacuum which sucks metrics in. Their precision creates the satisfying illusion that they lack ambiguity, and our ability to collect and collate them creates an equally seductive feeling of control. As advances in technology over the last 15 years or so have allowed the collection and dissemination of ever more measures, adoration has turned into infatuation. Infatuation leads to perversity. Metrics become an end in themselves, and get separated from what it was they were intended to measure in the first place. They become a fetish.

This danger is particularly pronounced if the metrics are not simply monitored to see whether things are on track, but are turned into targets which define performance and hence individuals' success. If they are furthermore linked to compensation, the danger becomes acute. For then, if faced with a choice between optimizing targets and optimizing what really matters, people optimize the targets.

It is very common to link performance to pay. Whether all human beings are driven by financial rewards is controversial, and whether linking performance to pay increases performance is even more questionable. However, there is an industry devoted to linking performance to pay, so until the more grotesque side effects of this practice have become unacceptable, it will probably continue.[42] It may be that the financial crisis of 2008 has brought us to that point, but at the time of writing this is still unclear.

From the point of view of making strategy happen, we must grasp that linking performance to pay raises the stakes. If we first turn measures into targets and then link targets to incentives, we have created a very powerful force for good or for ill. We have also made it very hard to change our minds about the measures. And we have also invited the creation of a fetish.

This phenomenon was experienced by a sales director in a global pharmaceutical company at the year end, when everybody turned up to demand their bonuses. The sales results were in and they were flat. However, according to the measures the organization had set up, everyone had done very well. "We hit all our targets," he observed. "Pity we did not sell anything." He seemed to be the only one who cared.

Target setting is not inherently bad; far from it. But the practice leaves a lot to be desired. It is precisely because measurable targets are so powerful that we need to treat them with great care. What gets measured gets done. That is the beauty of it. The Beauty can turn into a Beast. What gets measured gets done – and nothing else. If we are not careful, we may get exactly what we have asked for, and regret it.

In the 1990s the British Government started to introduce targets in the public sector. Everybody liked them at first, but as time went on there were signs of discontent. A feeling grew that maybe the relationship between the number of targets and effectiveness was nonlinear. There were stories about doctors and nurses caring more about their targets than about their patients. How could that be? So in 2002 the British Government set up a Select Committee to assess the use of targets in the UK public sector.

In November of that year, the Select Committee interviewed Lord Browne, then Group CEO of BP, to see what it could learn from the practices of an acknowledged master of the art of target setting in the private sector. In his submission, Lord Browne opined:

It is important to acknowledge that performance targets are but one of many levers at management's disposal to direct attention towards crucial areas of the company's activity. They are not a substitute for good management, and should be assessed within the context of a company's panoply of standards and values. This means, in particular, that it is necessary to avoid an obsessive preoccupation with any single target if it leads to a distorted sense of priorities, or to undue concentration upon certain activities at the expense of others.

He went on to explain:

With the exception of some of the financial targets, BP's targets are often indicative, rather than absolute. They should not be viewed as alternatives to, or substitutes for, "good management" and they must be regarded within a company's total context. They comprise a very useful element in an experimental process to search constantly for better ways of measuring performance, testing limits and assessing possible "trade-offs" between various objectives.

In the private sector, a target does not carry the political sensitivity and significance of some of those in the public services. As a consequence, private-sector targets can be more easily regarded as "means" rather than "ends." "However," Browne went on, "in both sectors it is in essence the credibility of the target which ought to determine its importance... it is in the interests of neither that targets should become detached from reality."[43] If targets do become ends in themselves, he told the Committee, "you can get very strange behaviour."[44]

As Browne repeatedly observed, targets should be approached "in a spirit of humility." If they become ends rather than means, they will assert the dominance of the organization's processes over its people. And that will be the end of "independent thinking obedience" and the beginning of "ours is not to reason why."[45]

Browne's spirit of humility is needed in the face of metrics, not least because we have to have them. If we are to know whether or not we are making a strategy happen, we need a strategic control system: financial and nonfinancial measures which tell us what the effects of our actions are and whether or not we are on track.[46] Otherwise, it is hard to adjust.

However, replacing direction setting with control would be like asking a compass to tell us our destination, rather than using it to help us get there. As Larry Bossidy quizzically observes:

> *Your boss has asked you to drive from Chicago to Oskaloosa, Iowa, a journey of 317 miles. He's prepared a budget for you with clear metrics. You can spend no more than $16 on gas, you must arrive in 5 hours and 37 minutes and you can't drive over 60 miles an hour. But no one has a map with a route to Oskaloosa, and you don't know whether you'll run into a snowstorm on the way.*
>
> *Ludicrous? No more so than the way many companies translated their strategic plans into operations.*[47]

The reason many companies do this sort of thing is that they fall prey to the temptation of replacing clarity with detail.[48] Careless of this hazard, Robert Kaplan and David Norton suggest that if it is sophisticated enough, a balanced set of financial and nonfinancial metrics can in fact be used to do the work of strategy. "The Balanced Scorecard," they aver, "should be used as a communication, informing and learning system, not a controlling system."[49] They go further, describing it as "an integrated strategic-management system," in which every measure is "an element in a chain of cause and effect relationships that communicates the meaning of a business unit's strategy to an organization."[50]

In their later publication, *The Strategy Focused Organization*, they go further still, recommending the creation of a "strategy map," which lays out the causal relationships between all the measures in their four categories (financial, customer, internal, and learning) so as to produce a one-page "map" of the strategy itself.[51]

Balanced scorecards have become very widely used, for they do indeed fulfill a real need in execution. However, there are signs that humility may in some cases have become hubris. There are some dark sides to the balanced scorecard.[52]

The first thing is that – all protestations to the contrary apart – a scorecard is fundamentally a control system, whereas the prime purpose of strategy is command; that is, setting direction. Unless the "what" and the "why" are clear, the fetishization of the metrics is a near certainty. Metrics provide a means of making strategic thinking more precise, a set of milestones, and a means of identifying the destination. They help us to navigate. If we follow a satellite navigation system slavishly we can end up in traffic jams, roadworks, and one-way systems we would rather avoid.[53] If we hit our targets and don't fulfill the purpose, we should not congratulate ourselves and relax, but *change the targets.*

For example, in one organization which was trying to follow the principles of leading through intent, a regional sales organization set itself a KPI (key performance indicator) of making 120 client calls in the next six months to present a new product. The purpose, of course, was to increase sales of the product. Nothing happened. That prompted an investigation of the metric, which revealed that the sales people had not seen the real decision makers. So they changed the metric, visited a smaller number of decision makers, and the sales followed. Had the targets been the only thing they had, they would have collected their bonuses and gone home after a night in the bar.

In the language of business, "command and control" has come to mean "micromanagement" with an authoritarian bent.

In military thinking it is the means of setting direction and achieving specific outcomes.[54] Authoritarian micromanagement is just one – particularly bad – way of doing it. Now, we could claim, like Humpty Dumpty, that when we use words they mean exactly what we choose them to mean. Conceptually, however, by choosing "command and control" to mean what we do, we are confusing "rotten apples" with "fruit." That may have the adverse consequence of leading us to turn up our noses at many tasty apples, not to mention oranges and pears, that are ripe for the picking.

It is ironic that of the two concepts of "command" and "control," we feel far more comfortable with control than with command. Perhaps we have the feeling that command has the rather undemocratic ring of telling people what to do, whereas control is just about acting responsibly. Whatever the reason, it has taken us down a path which has led us to widespread acceptance of the principle that it is a good idea to use a control system like the balanced scorecard to exercise command.

Let us consider the difference between command and control by thinking of a purely mechanical system such as central heating. Based on our aim of having a comfortable ambient temperature around the house, we set the thermostat. We have thereby exercised command. We then need to monitor the results to see if we are achieving our aim. The bottom line is whether or not we feel comfortable. But if we are to get the system to reach the temperature we want, we need to be able to adjust it, and it helps to have some metrics. We need some means of control. So we use controls to read the actual temperature and allow us to take action to adjust the amount of heat in each radiator. While the temperature read-outs are useful, they do not determine the actions we take. The amount of heat pumped out by the system may be dependent on only one central thermostat. The data could mislead us. If the temperature around the central thermostat is high, it may shut down the whole system, leaving other rooms cold. Reliance on the measure alone could lead us astray. We need specific, local observation as well.

If the temperature is not as we wish, we can take a range of actions. The obvious thing to do is to pump out more heat, but we might also increase insulation in the house, or indeed put on a pullover. If some rooms are hot and others cold, we could take a variety of local actions depending on our diagnosis of the cause. It could be a broken window pane or a draught coming down a chimney. We maintain our aim, set the system to behave in a way that we believe will fulfill the aim, use controls to monitor the results by measuring them, and then take action to alter the behavior of the system, or act on things outside it which affect the outcome (such as draughty windows). This is not very complicated; it is merely common sense.[55]

Command is an act of will, based on considerations outside the system it is commanding. We decide what we think is comfortable. We may believe it is a temperature of 18°C. If we achieve that, we may decide it is actually too cold and set the target to 20°C. The system will not tell us what is right. Control is the ability to adjust, which means knowing what is actually happening and having some means of affecting it. Deciding what to do to affect it is another act of command. Without the original act of command, control is helpless because it does not know what it is trying to do. And no act of command can be derived from *any* act of control even in principle, no matter how sophisticated the system. Nobody in their right mind who is feeling cold would look at a thermostat reading 20°C and conclude that they were mistaken to feel cold. They might conclude that the temperature was too low and put it up. They might conclude that they were ill and needed to go to the doctor. But they would not conclude that they were actually feeling warm. Not a lot of science is needed here.

To exercise command is to articulate an intention to achieve a desired outcome and align a system to behave in such a way that the outcome can be expected to be achieved. To exercise control is to monitor the actual effects resulting from the behavior, assess the information, and report on the system's performance with respect to the desired outcome. It is then the function of command to decide what to do: to adjust the behavior of the system, take some other action outside the system, or indeed to abandon the original intention and change the desired outcome.

The second observation about the balanced scorecard is that, despite Kaplan and Norton's distinction between the need to monitor a large number of diagnostic measures and to set only a few strategic measures as targets, in practice they elide this critical difference, even recommending the general rules that *all* good targets should involve stretch and be tied to compensation systems.[56] Lord Browne, who made great use of stretch goals and sometimes linked them to compensation, would have baulked at that as a universal principle, for it turns measures into ends rather than means. Sometimes it is right to do so, but that depends on the situation.

The third aspect follows from the critical difference between monitoring and targeting. Monitoring should be balanced. The instrument panel of a car or aeroplane should provide a range of information. Most of the time we are not very interested in how much fuel we have, but if it runs out the journey is at an end, so when the fuel is low we become very interested in it. At any point in time, *the scorecard is actually unbalanced.* In operations, everything matters all the time because we are as strong as our weakest link. In strategy, we are focused, and our focus shifts over time. In Reuters' "main effort map," which reflected its strategic staircase, defending market share had primacy over developing the new product suite, then developing the new product suite had primacy over revenue, and so on. The instrument panel was the same, but the significance of the metrics changed. Reuters used a balanced scorecard and monitored a wide range of things in each of the four categories. But it managed itself according to the needs of the strategic situation, not the dictates of an instrument.

The fourth thing is that while no driver would undertake a journey in a car with no instrument panel, when they're actually driving good drivers spend most of their time looking through the windscreen at the road and the other traffic, and react fast to what they see. Similarly, no company should neglect the need for a scorecard, but sophisticated measuring systems can encourage bad driving habits. If there is a problem with a major customer it may not be a good idea to wait for the monthly customer satisfaction indices to come in, even if they are a target you are trying to optimize. Better to get out there and find out what is wrong. You will learn a lot more that way anyway. There is no substitute for direct observation, which is why von Moltke had a telescope, talked to people all the time, and had his own staff officers visit units and report back to him what they saw. He was not going to rely on reports. An executive needs an up-to-date mental picture of what is going on in and around the business; a scorecard is only one source of information from which that picture can be formed.

The fifth concern is that a scorecard does not explain causality. This is where Kaplan and Norton go seriously awry. In *The Balanced Scorecard*, they explicitly define strategy as "a set of hypotheses about cause and effect," and in *The Strategy Focused Organization*, this belief underpins the whole notion of the strategy map.[57] This is to step from humility to hubris.

They would like the strategy map, which links up the different measures into a causal pyramid, to be the strategic equivalent of the seminal DuPont pyramid of financial ratios. The DuPont pyramid is rigorous – it breaks down financial ratios into their component parts, and the rigor is mathematical. Kaplan and Norton know that the strategy map is not rigorous, which is why they say that the causal relationships it shows are hypotheses which have to be continually tested and adapted.[58] The error is not in claiming unwarranted rigor. It is in assuming that linear causality is at work here at all. At root, this is a pre-Clausewitzian, mechanical view of business, organizations, and the economy. Kaplan and Norton are the intellectual heirs of von Bülow. We could get by with balanced scorecards and strategy maps alone if business organizations were frictionless machines. But in fact they are complex adaptive systems trying to survive and prosper in a fitness landscape full of diverse organisms with different agendas in which their interaction produces unpredictable first-, second-, and third-order effects. Every cause is itself an effect and every effect a cause, linked by feedback loops, some dampening, some reinforcing. Changing an organization involves careful judgment about how and where to intervene in the system.

Suppose we set up a simple and plausible hypothesis about the effects actions have on outcomes. Supported by generations of economists, let us suppose that if we cut price we will sell more product. Suppose then that our scorecard shows us that revenues and margins have fallen. It will not tell us why. Common sense, however, may lead us to suspect that our competitors have matched our price cuts and that we have started a price war. We are surrounded by independent wills, and some of them are actually hostile. When thinking strategically, we must bring them into our equation from the first, and when acting strategically, we need an organization which will adapt to what they do.

Furthermore, the causal nexus that the balanced scorecard is supposed to illuminate cannot be complete, even in theory, for it is not based on a systematic view of stakeholders, let alone all the other actors who can affect outcomes. It has no "competitor" perspective, no "government" or "regulator" perspective, no "social" or "environmental" perspective, any more than the instrument panel of a car monitors the traffic conditions, road surfaces, or roadworks. It merely tells you some useful things about how you are doing. In an adaptive organization, everyone is looking at the measures and beyond them, and always asking why. From the first, the proselytizers of the balanced scorecard claimed that it "establishes goals but assumes that people will adopt whatever behaviors and take whatever actions are necessary to arrive at those goals."[59] Making such an assumption is unwise, particularly as balancing on the high wire of the scorecard can itself discourage such behavior. A wise commander will take a look through his telescope.

In the final analysis it is behavior that counts. If we close the knowledge and the alignment gaps in the ways suggested so far, we will be able to gain traction, focus effort, and deliver a strategy – until something unexpected happens, which sooner or later it will. At that point everything depends on people. Metrics give us information. Interpreting the information can impart understanding. Taking the right action requires wisdom. Only people can have that.

QUICK RECAP

❑ There is a general requirement for individuals in a leadership position to adapt what they do in line with the organization's intent, and to take responsibility for their decisions. Not everybody will be willing to do this. Equally, there will be others with an authoritarian personality who will be unwilling to give subordinates the space they require to be adaptive. Both groups are minorities in the management population, but they need to be detected in the recruitment and development process.

❑ The bulk of the management population do not fall into either of these problem groups, but they need to be developed so that they master the appropriate briefing and decision-making skills. A common development program covering the behaviors which go along with these skills can begin to shape the culture, as long as it is reflected in day-to-day practice.

❏ Even if they understand what part they are to play in executing a company's strategy, people do not always behave in the way required. However, they usually do behave rationally from the point of view of the subsystem of the organization to which they belong. If we examine the goals, resources, and constraints of the subsystem, we can understand why they behave as they do and can take steps to change the subsystem itself in order to produce the behavior we want.

❏ Day-to-day practice is in part determined by organizational processes, most importantly budgeting and performance management. They should themselves be aligned with the strategy, and using a briefing cascade to link them all together is a practical way of achieving this. They should also enable rather than inhibit adaptation. A good first step toward making them flexible is to create an operating rhythm with quarterly reviews of progress, in which adjustment is expected and the budget is a treated as a rolling forecast.

❏ In order to know if the intent is being realized, we need a system of metrics. However, we should not allow metrics to be separated from what they are supposed to measure and substitute for it, or they become a fetish. A scorecard should be used to support strategy execution by monitoring the effects actions are realizing, not to supplant strategy. Business leaders should supplement internal scorecards by taking a look outside through the commander's telescope.

CHAPTER SEVEN

LEADERSHIP THAT WORKS

From Common Sense to Common Practice

The director is detached, calculating, and flexible;
the manager is engaged, realistic, and pragmatic;
the leader is committed, passionate, and determined

THE THREE LEVELS

Business has inherited from the military the distinction between strategy and tactics. Strategy was the art of the general and tactics the craft of the soldier. For centuries, tactics were based on routines that were turned into drills and practiced on the parade ground to make sure that soldiers could and would carry them out in the heat of battle. Generals were the planners and soldiers were the implementers. The main role of regimental officers, the middle managers of their day, was to control the implementers to see that they did what they were told, and to lead them into battle – the act of execution in every sense.

By the time of Napoleon and Clausewitz, this two-tier distinction had become problematic. In the course of the nineteenth century, the difficulties it posed increased, but most armies still clung to it. The difficulties a twentieth-century army could face in trying to execute a strategic plan in the belief that execution meant translating strategy into tactics are graphically illustrated by the British Army on the Somme on 1 July 1916.

The British Fourth Army, which was tasked with carrying out the attack on the Somme, had spent five months working out a plan. It was detailed, and it had to be, because to make it work it had to be translated into tactics. Most of the planning was carried out by the corps, one level of hierarchy below the Fourth Army. Great care was taken to prepare accurate maps of the German positions to be attacked and to give specific objectives to every unit down to battalions, three levels below the corps. These included phase lines which specified when troops were supposed to reach certain points. This was necessary in order to avoid "friendly fire" casualties from artillery which was coordinated at corps level in order to produce the necessary level of concentration. In addition, the Fourth Army issued a set of extensive notes designed to pass on "best practice." These went into such matters as how to organize a battalion attack on a trench, and what equipment men needed to carry to ensure that they could consolidate the positions they captured. The notes also explained that as the Army consisted mainly of new recruits, it was not skilled enough to carry out complex maneuvers such as outflanking enemy positions, and because the men lacked the discipline of regular soldiers, they had to be tightly managed. They should walk across no-man's land to make sure that they stuck together under the control of their officers. It was important to maintain order.[1]

One result of this was to create a plan so rigid that all three of the execution gaps were yawning wide open, waiting for friction to enter them, which it did in the first minutes of the attack. It had been preceded by an unprecedented week-long artillery bombardment. Because it was unprecedented, nobody knew what effects it would have. Most people expected it to destroy the German dugouts and cut the barbed wire in front of them so that the attacking infantry could advance across open ground to take their objectives. It did neither. Because middle-ranking officers had no decision-making authority, they became messengers who relayed information upward to the corps commanders, and asked them what to do. Because the corps had multiple objectives and the overall intention was unclear because of an unresolved disagreement at the top – Rawlinson of the Fourth Army wanted a "bite and hold" operation, but his boss Haig wanted a

STRATEGY

TACTICS

Figure 20 Three levels

breakthrough – they were unable to help very much either, so everybody followed the ultimate authority: the plan. The end result was indeed execution. The 60,000 casualties suffered by the Fourth Army make 1 July 1916 the bloodiest day in the entire history of the British Army. It had little to show for it.

Fifty years before the Battle of the Somme, von Moltke had realized that thinking in terms of strategy and tactics was not going to work. He was the first to conceptualize a third level situated between strategy and tactics which he called "operations" (Figure 20).[2] This was the realm of free thinking that translated strategy into action, requiring strategic thinking and operational direction on the part of the entire officer corps. The three levels co-determine each other. Von Moltke saw the relationship between them as reciprocal.[3]

In von Moltke's mind, "operations" was an area of problem solving. The binding strategic objective was the war aim, which specified "why." The operational objective specified "what." Operational decision making meant thinking through how to do what was needed to achieve the strategic aim, considering alternative solutions to the problems raised by the specific situation, and evaluating possible courses of action.[4] It was the realm of one-off, nonroutine decisions in which von Moltke demanded free, creative thinking of himself and others, for even the operational objective could change. Tactics, on the other hand, was the realm of routine day-to-day activities which could be learned on the parade ground, and some general rules embodying best practice about how to carry out nonroutine but recurrent tasks.

Routine tasks such as forming up a column of march or deploying a skirmishing line were standardized and everybody was trained in how to do them. Today, they include things such as forming a road block, and are called standard operating procedures or SOPs. They are very useful because they create uniformity and therefore predictability where that has high value. They enhance *efficiency* by enabling these tasks to be carried out at speed with little supervision.

The three levels tend to correspond naturally to levels in the organization. Strategy is about winning wars and involves armies; operations is about winning campaigns and involves corps and divisions; tactics is about winning battles and involves brigades, battalions, and companies. We might say (very broadly) that strategy involves business units, operations involves departments and functions, and tactics involves subunits, whether in support roles or with direct customer contact.

The three levels are distinct but linked together. Strategic thinking penetrates operational activity. Operational decisions are made within the framework of strategy, so that they make sense within the whole. Because strategy is unitary, it allows these decisions to be consistent, even when taken by different people at different times under different circumstances. Everybody follows tactics, and managers do not have to waste their time thinking about how they should be carried out. They can concentrate instead on the more important task of directing operations.

With three conceptual levels, von Moltke was able to reconcile two apparently conflicting requirements: flexibility and efficiency. As one writer has put it: "productivity is highest when most of the activity necessary to win is highly routinized, but specialized work is most valuable when there is uncertainty about how to achieve this goal."[5] Formulating strategy is "specialized work" whereby top management makes a commitment on behalf of the organization about how it is going to try to shape the future. Creating a realm of operational direction allows middle managers to do the "specialized work" of making commitments about how they are going to contribute toward that without reengineering well-oiled processes.[6]

Introducing the concept of an operational level was an innovation. However, by placing it between strategy and tactics, it is given limits. Not everything the army did required creativity, and no officer was free to do everything exactly as he pleased. Extending the operational level down too far would sacrifice efficiency, reliability, and speed. At worst, it could create confusion. The tactical level imposes a deliberate constraint on independent thinking obedience. Tactics specify how to do things and are binding on everyone. Good tactics are important.

Von Moltke took a hand in creating tactical guidelines. For example, he recommended that infantry use firepower rather than shock tactics (charging), that artillery be used for close support, and cavalry mainly for scouting and pursuit.[7] This guidance was based on his assessment of the technology of the time, and represented the default practice, which could be departed from if circumstances called for it. Good tactics were a matter of competence and the result of good doctrine and good training. Officers could rely on their troops and NCOs to know how to do things. They concentrated their minds on the nonstandard realm of operations where they had to exercise professional judgment.

So the realm of standardized tactics was just as important as the realm of flexible operations. Moreover, occasions arise even within the operational realm when leading with directives will not work.

During the Franco-Prussian War of 1870–71, von Moltke generally ran the campaign by issuing directives. Under circumstances, however, when major decisions were pending, "we considered it to be right and necessary to control the movements of large formations through specific orders from the center, even though this temporarily restricted the independence of the Army commanders."[8]

Von Moltke himself mentions such an occasion. After the first battles at the frontier in August 1870, he wanted to move his forces to the right through difficult terrain without losing contact with the retreating French. There were only two good roads, and nine corps in three separate armies to move along them, so von Moltke took direct control. "This necessitated bringing the First and Second Armies into very close proximity. The time had come when it was no longer enough for Central Headquarters to issue general directions to the Armies; First and Second Armies had to be precisely controlled by issuing instructions to their individual corps to ensure their movements were properly coordinated."[9] So for several days the center managed the whole operation by controlling two levels down and bypassing the two Army headquarters. This violated von Moltke's general principle of always following the chain of command and never bypassing levels. But then, "the man stands above the principle."

The reasons for this departure from normal practice are clear enough. The task was one of detailed organization which required little creativity; the staff in the center had at least as much experience of this kind of work as the staff in the Army Headquarters; and because coordination was critical to avoiding a vast traffic jam, the plans could only be drawn up in the knowledge of what each of the armies was intending to do. Everything argued for one central plan. It was difficult, but it was done and it worked.

Von Moltke makes the point more generally, and adds: "At the same time, it was recognized how important it was to ensure that the Army Commands had an overview of the motives behind the orders issued to them by the Supreme Commander and properly understood them."[10] Even when assuming direct control, von Moltke explained himself, and he relinquished control again as soon as he felt able to do so.

To help do the explaining, von Moltke despatched one of his three senior General Staff officers, the so-called Demigods, to each of the armies. They also made sure that his wishes were carried out and reported back to him. He used them in this way as a control mechanism, but also on other occasions to give advice and to bring him back fresh news about what was happening. Apart from these three, there were about nine other fully trained General Staff officers at von Moltke's headquarters, supported by a staff of about 70 to deal with operational matters such as processing incoming messages, finding lodgings, requisitions, and so on.[11] In effect, the Prussian Army was run at the top by a dozen or so people.

STRATEGY, TACTICS, AND EXECUTION

It is hard to talk about something if it does not even have a name, and unfortunately in business we do not make the distinction between strategy, operations, and tactics. When we try to execute a strategy we therefore run the risk of behaving rather like the British Army on the first day of the Somme. Strategy is unitary and binding, and tactics are standardized and binding. So unless we create a third level, we have tied everybody's hands. Unless we place limits around that level, we invite chaos into the organization instead of keeping it outside, where it belongs.

We are further hampered by our language because we often refer to "tactics" and "operations" interchangeably. The suggestion here is that we therefore depart from the military terminology and refer to the operational level as the level of "execution."

Business thinking about these three levels is fuzzy and in practice we try to plug the chasm between strategy and tactics by

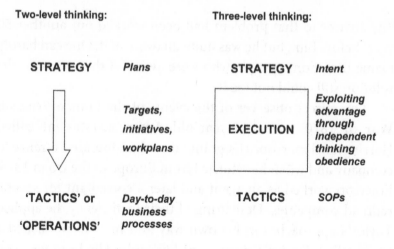

Figure 21 Freedom and its boundaries

using targets and initiatives which get layered on top of day-to-day activity, as in Figure 21.

At its worst, we have managers suffering from overload, who see strategy as stress-inducing interference from the center in their attempts to run the "real business." It constrains them, as do tactics. These repetitive processes, such as sending out invoices or making payments, carrying out performance evaluations or submitting expenses, are standardized in the interests of efficiency and consistency. SOPs are often embedded in systems courtesy of SAP; that is as it should be. But if there is no level of "operations" blocking them, they will tend to rise inexorably upward, removing more and more discretion from managers in the field until the slaves become our masters.

Three-level thinking helps us to understand the legacy we have inherited from scientific management. Taylor had insights, and they endure. The prize is efficiency and no business can afford to be inefficient. Taylor's error was to universalize his approach and apply it to all business activity instead of restricting it to the realm of tactics. He thereby created a problem for businesses trying to follow his edicts 50 years later when the world had changed.

The answer to that problem had been worked out another 50 years before him, but he was quite unaware of it. One can hardly blame him. Some people who were aware of the source of the solution still could not see it.

One direct observer of the events of the Franco-Prussian War of 1870 was a 17-year-old American student called Harrington Emerson. His grandfather had founded a railroad company and when he returned from Europe to the US in 1876, Emerson worked as an agent and later a consultant for several railroad companies. Despairing of their inefficiency, he applied Taylor's approaches in his own way and in 1913 published a book called *Twelve Principles of Efficiency*. His hero was von Moltke, who, he wrote, had based his approach on "natural laws," implemented through his staff, which is what made his "stupendous achievements" possible.[12] The achievement Emerson singles out is not the campaign, but the mobilization, the despatching of a million men because of "perfect preparation": "the German army had no track, no perfect locomotives, no built and tested signal towers, but it had a perfectly working organization that had not omitted to give attention to every little detail." Emerson believed that this enabled "the great despatcher" to fight "empire-making and destroying battles" at "a predetermined time and place."[13] The latter is, of course, precisely wrong, and all the more interesting for that.

While Woide, a Russian general, marveled at the Prussians' effectiveness in conducting unplanned battles, Emerson, an American railroad engineer, marveled at the efficiency of their pre-planned mobilization. The different backgrounds of the observers drew their attention to different things. Emerson jumped to the erroneous conclusion that everything von Moltke did was planned, and thereby confirmed Taylor's prejudice that all business activity must be standardized to maximize efficiency. Only von Moltke had realized that he needed – and could get – alignment *and* autonomy, efficiency *and* effectiveness.

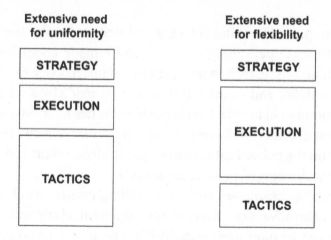

Figure 22 Shaping the business model

The three levels give us choices about where to draw the lines between them. There are no rules: we can draw them according to the needs of the business, as in Figure 22.

In some businesses tactics are very important. A tactical advantage over a competitor could turn into a strategic one. For example, running a chain of pub restaurants involves deploying large numbers of people in valuable assets every day. Inefficiencies in things such as weekly staff scheduling can have a significant cost impact, and slipping service standards can have a rapid effect on revenue. Large numbers of people are employed to carry out fairly mundane, repetitive tasks. To keep costs under control, you need to keep wages under control, so it is better to pay a school leaver to work in the kitchen chopping vegetables and tell them exactly how to do it than to employ a PhD who might have an outside chance of coming up with a better way of chopping. The consistency of the product and service is vital to sustaining the brand. Achieving this requires tight control of details, and the organization as a whole, benefiting from massive cumulative experience, has a lot of wisdom to impart to any new restaurant manager responsible for that control. So it makes sense to prescribe uniform tactics and write manuals. There are nevertheless operational decisions to be made about how to refresh brands, launch marketing campaigns, manage the property portfolio, and so on, but these can be made by a relatively small number of people. Businesses like this need a strong, highly competent center, well-supplied with fresh data, which keeps its finger on the pulse. That is where clear strategic intent and independent thinking obedience are needed.

In other businesses, such as consulting, tactics do not confer much of an advantage. Every client is different, every project has a different solution, and creativity is at a premium. Almost all the staff are highly paid professionals who are self-motivated and recruited for their talent. If they are told to follow a standard procedure, the first thing they will do is to question it and tell you why it won't work in their case, and the second thing they will do is to invent a better one. There is still a need for SOPs (like slide formats, payment terms, or boilerplating on proposals) and room for some guidance on best practice (like how to write proposals, how to work with clients, or how to use the firm's resources to the best advantage). But most of the business of a consulting firm is about the art of execution. The difference with hospitality retailing is the percentage of staff who fall within each realm, and therefore how large a part of the operating model it should make up. All consultants need a high degree of flexibility within the broad direction (covering things such as target clients and the type of work offered) set by the partners.

There are periods in most businesses when things are fairly predictable both in the short and long term. Such times should be exploited by honing tactical efficiency. The danger is in believing that those times will last. Large changes often creep up unnoticed as the cumulative effect of small increments. Sometimes, those changes are clearly seen, but there is no response, or the response is inadequate. The reason is that the executional realm has become squeezed to near extinction by tactical processes and procedures. Guarding against this is only possible if you have a concept of execution in the first place.[14]

THE EXECUTIVE'S TRINITY

The volume of business literature devoted to leadership is vast. The avalanche of publications was in part prompted by some influential thinking about how it differs from management, which concluded that we need less management and more leadership.[15]

In the military domain, there is a third concept: command. As we have already noted, this word has an unpleasant ring to most civilians. However, not using the word will not make the activity referred to as "command" go away. NATO defines command as "the authority invested in an individual for the direction, coordination and control of military forces."[16]

Command is something granted to someone by an external party. The external party confers rights of authority and along with them go responsibilities, duties, and accountability. Responsibilities may be delegated or shared, but the commander remains accountable for what is done with them.[17] In the British Armed Forces, command is ultimately granted by the Sovereign; in the United States, by the President. In businesses it is granted by the owners of the business, who are most commonly the shareholders. The duties encompass direction, decision making, and control, and are exercised in the context of direction from the external party.[18] The organization is not the property of the commander. It is entrusted to the commander for a time, during which he or she is its steward.

Command is as unavoidable in the business world as it is in the military one. Because it is a real requirement, somebody has got to do it, and because of its central importance in business we have to talk about it. So we do. We include it under "leadership." As a result, we cause confusion.

Figure 23 The trinity

Military literature has similar numbers of publications about leadership and command, though few on management.[19] Business literature used to be about management, is now all about leadership, and has never mentioned command. This is an unsatisfactory situation for both domains, for officers and executives alike need to understand and practice all three. Business thinking suffers from offering the simple duality of management and leadership, and the leadership literature contains futile debates because of a failure to distinguish leadership from command. There is a trinity, illustrated in Figure 23. The three types of activity encompassed in this trinity overlap, which is why it is easy to confuse them. Indeed, at any point in time, a single individual might be doing all three.

Accounts of the nature of the three differ, but I would suggest that their relationship could be understood as in Figure 24. The duties and responsibilities of command involve setting direction. The skills required are primarily intellectual. Commanders develop strategic direction considering the aims they have been given, the environment they are in, and the capabilities of their organization. They also further build the capabilities the organization needs to realize the

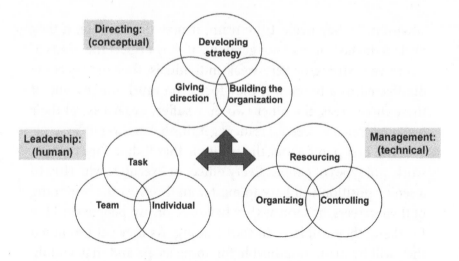

Figure 24 The elements of the trinity

strategy. They then have to actually give direction by communicating their intent in ways on which the organization can act.

Management is about providing and controlling the means of following the direction. It requires brainwork, but is less conceptual than the work of command, and more a matter of physical direction: marshalling resources, organizing and controlling them. Managing means understanding objectives, solving problems so that they can be achieved, and creating processes so that the work of others can be organized efficiently. Good management means making the maximum use of resources, including money and people.

Leading is a human activity that is moral and emotional. The work of a leader is to motivate and, if possible, inspire followers so that they are willing to go in the required direction and perform their own tasks better than they would have done had the leader not been there. Leaders have to balance their attention between defining and achieving the specific task of their group, building and maintaining the team as a team, and meeting the needs of and developing the individuals within it. They will shift their attention across each of these over time depending on the situation. If they neglect the team, it may disintegrate; if they neglect the task, it may not get done; if they neglect the needs of either very strong or very weak individuals, they may become disaffected or a burden. If they focus too much on any one of these three areas, the other two may suffer. Regardless of their personal traits, successful leaders get this balance right.[20]

The first point about the trinity is that it describes types of work, not types of people. Every officer or executive who rises to a senior position will have to master all three. At the beginning of their careers, as soon as they have one or two people working for them, they will have to start leading. As they get promoted they will be made responsible for some assets and may end up running a department, which will have to be not only led but managed. Finally, as they rise through the ranks of middle management, they will have to learn how to exercise command.[21]

The second point is that although the trinity does not define different people, it does define different skills, and people's ability to master them varies. Some inspiring leaders are poor managers, some brilliant commanders are ineffectual leaders, and some very efficient managers can neither command nor lead. In most organizations, all three sets of skills are equally important. This has two consequences. It means that although the circles overlap, each of us must be aware of what mode we are primarily operating in at any point in time; and it means that we must beware of how we select our commanders.

In leading, we cast doubts aside and encourage people by focusing on the positive. If things are difficult, we try to overcome the difficulties. We persuade and cajole. Even if a strategy is not watertight, energetic leadership can make it work.

In commanding we step back, appraise the facts, and do our utmost to grasp reality. We develop hypotheses and test them. We generate ideas about possible direction and then probe them for weaknesses. We make sober assessments of what our organization is capable of doing. We strive to sort out the essentials and hone our messages until they are clear and simple.

If we continue in command mode when we are called on to lead, we are liable to come across as cold and calculating, and sow doubts in people's minds. If we approach the work of command in the belief that it is about leadership, we are liable to ignore warning signs, produce biased appraisals of what is possible, and come up with a gung-ho strategy that will send the organization down a path to ruin.

If we as individuals have a balance of leadership and command skills, we can guard against this by being self-aware. The danger is charismatic leaders who neither understand nor have the intellect to carry out the tasks of command. They can wreak havoc.

Great commanders who are not great leaders are not so much of a problem. In fact in the right role, which is often the very top, they can be outstandingly effective. Because of their integrity, dedication to the task, and technical competence, they inspire confidence and people will follow them. The taciturn and retiring von Moltke was like this. The humble and unassuming "Level 5 Leader" described by Jim Collins is also made of this stuff.[22] Collins identifies 11 such characters, prompting Tom Peters to express some skepticism by trenchantly observing "More Collins, more claptrap," and listing other leaders who were not like this, but did have a great impact in their diverse domains.[23] Neither Collins nor Peters can explain how these uncharismatic people were able to be so effective, however, because they lump leadership and command together.

Of course, occasionally some folk emerge who are outstanding at leadership, command, and management, but they are rare, and usually become celebrated, as Welch is in our day and Nelson was in his. The fact remains that most companies looking for people to fill their top jobs will have to choose from among people with varying strengths in the different realms, and at the very top making the trade-off in favor of command skills will generally be well advised.

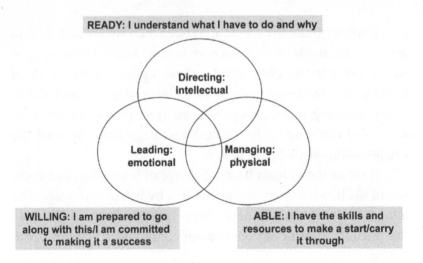

Figure 25 Directing as "command in business"

The way in which leadership, management, and command are exercised should be attuned to the needs of the situation rather than the habits of the person exercising them. Even if the default method of exercising command is to issue directives, as we have seen occasions can always occur, even with highly competent subordinates, when closer direction is needed.

The trinity defines the work of the executive as much as the work of the officer. If we are to use it though, we will no doubt meet resistance to the dreaded word "command." To make it acceptable in business, we need to change the word. My suggestion is to use the word "directing."

Executives who master the disciplines of formulating and giving good direction can explain to people what they have to achieve and why, and so make them *ready* to act. By mastering management they can put people into a position in which they are *able* to act. And by leading them effectively they can sustain people's *willingness* to carry on until the job is done.

It is notoriously hard to learn the skills of leadership. However, people of the right intellectual caliber can be taught how to give good direction. There is a rich literature on strategy development and courses are on offer at every business school. Organizational development is a discipline in its own right. Sadly, however, the third core skill of directing, that of actually giving direction – the formulating and communicating of guidance and instructions – is neglected. Unlike von Moltke's staff officers, business executives are not generally required to practice the writing of orders so that they are succinct and unambiguous. This deficit needs to be made good. Readers wishing to make a start may benefit from the approach described in Chapter 5.

No single element of the trinity is more important than the others. Management is unfashionable, but it has lost none of its relevance. Few need convincing that leadership matters. However, I have placed "directing" at the top of the trinity pyramid because it is not properly recognized, because it is in practice where significant deficits are found, and because if it is poorly done, excellence in the other two cannot compensate. It is here that the answer to the question "What do you want me to do?" must ultimately be found.

So it is that in practice, when addressing some of the problems described in Chapter 1, it is often most worthwhile to start with setting clear direction. The pieces are usually there and merely need to be brought together. Once people have grasped that the essence of the task is to master and simplify complexity, progress can be rapid.

IMPACT

Examples of companies which have made a systematic attempt to do just that suggest what the effects can be.

One of them was the technology company whose starting point was described in Chapter 1. Some two years into the turnaround, I conducted a survey of middle and senior managers in

	"I have observed an increase in"	% of interviewees mentioning
1st-order effects	Clarity & alignment	90
	Focus	86
	Accountability	76
	Motivation/sense of purpose	57
2nd-order effects	Speed	43
	Cross-functional working	33
3rd-order effects	Commonality	81
	Use of initiative	52
	Revealing weaknesses	33
	Imposing structure/ discipline	24

key positions who had been involved in introducing the principles of leading through intent.

The table above gives the spontaneous replies to an open question about the main effects directly observed by the interviewee. They are divided into immediate first-order, less immediate second-order, and longer-term third-order effects.

The sequencing has two causes. First, gaining familiarity with the techniques and learning within a unit leads to further effects after a little elapsed time. For example, once people are clear and focused, they can make decisions faster. Evidently, some actually do so, others do not. Secondly, the rollout across the company over time has an additional impact beyond a local one. In the early stages, effects are restricted to isolated examples. As the new practices become more common, there is less concern with technique and more concern with behavior. But there is also a bonus to be had which is realized when critical mass is reached and the practices become a universal operating model.

All these effects were internal. The ultimate test was to achieve the outcomes. The year after this survey, revenue began to rise and profits jumped by nearly 30 percent. By the middle of the following year, the share price had risen 70 percent above its low point when the change process began.

At the pharmaceutical company also described in Chapter 1, it was decided to work at the point where the pain was greatest and the potential value was highest: some late-stage drug-development teams. The main process involved defining intent through a program of workshops, clarifying accountabilities, agreeing working methods, and setting people free to use their initiative to solve problems. A group of senior executives at the site agreed to give the teams "top cover" by providing firm but broader sets of boundaries and to suspend some requirements imposed by the bureaucracy.

The intangible effects on alignment and motivation were very similar to the above. Internal surveys of team members consistently produced comments such as "It was very good in helping us to determine the critical path and for the entire team to understand their role." The approach was found to be "refreshing," "very different," and "spot on." The performance of all the teams began to rise, in part because they were more focused and wasted less time, and in part because they were more motivated. Interestingly, the briefing exercises revealed that a lot of the constraints they complained of were more imagined than real. When they started to do what they thought was right they were not punished – in fact, they began to be applauded.

In terms of tangible impact, the critical variable in value realization was time. Filing a drug early is worth millions in extra revenue. One team agreed to move its filing deadline forward by several months. Originally, the team leader had estimated that they had a 10–20 percent chance of meeting the new deadline. Not only did they meet it, such was the quality of the submission that the drug enjoyed one of the smoothest passages through regulatory approval in the company's history. What is more, 18 months later it was exceeding its budgeted sales revenue by 400 percent. Another team stopped their program on their own initiative three months before a review date because the commercial rationale did not hold up. The decision was later ratified and estimated to have saved $750,000 in costs that would otherwise have been incurred to no purpose. A third drug project was severely threatened by difficulties in recruiting patients for late-stage clinical trials. The team found an innovative solution to the problem, imposed on themselves a target of filing three months early, and succeeded. The value of doing so was estimated to be in the tens of millions of dollars.

Broader changes began. The powerful line functions were dismantled and replaced by therapeutic areas. They were less restrictive, but still made it hard to develop a compound used in one area for use in another. So they evolved into much broader divisions. Management layers were removed, structure simplified, and authority devolved. The complex metrics and the milestone targets have been replaced by a simple value metric and a clear intent. Strategy briefings are now routine at every level. Everyone gets a clear message: add value to the baseline you have been given. The path you follow is up to you, and we expect it to change. The increments are measured over a two- to three-year period so that people have space to make decisions, take action, and have an impact. Personal goals are the business goals.

Accountability is clear and delivery is nonnegotiable. Over the 12 months prior to the time of writing, the value of the R&D portfolio grew by 59 percent.

It is worth noting that these examples are from global companies. The principles are universal, independent of national cultures, and can be understood and practiced across Europe, the US, and Asia. Their combination of alignment and autonomy makes them particularly valuable as businesses globalize.[24]

These effects are consistent with other experiences in a wide range of businesses: high technology, consumer goods, healthcare, publishing, retailing, financial services, marketing services, manufacturing, and professional services.

Introducing von Moltke's management principles with rigor and consistency can even help to win races. A company which builds and races Formula 1 cars made the change in late 2006. In mid-2007, the impact was judged to be as follows:

1 Bigger return on engineering time because effort is focused. This is as a result of more reflection about what matters (enforced by the discipline of strategy briefing) and the shared understanding of the overall objective and the part everyone plays in it. People no longer just come up with ideas and pursue them in isolation.

2 Teamworking has improved significantly... at races, the entire team now meets on Friday, Saturday and Sunday. Skeptics who thought this was a waste of time are beginning to come round. Alignment around objectives, roles and support has improved significantly.

3 Autonomy has improved in line with alignment – we are heading for the top right of the matrix. People are demonstrating more trust, and trying (in most cases) to follow the discipline of "not commanding more than is necessary" and not interfering with subordinates. The trust is being repaid with higher performance and greater honesty.

Backbriefs are getting shorter and more focused. Information demands are going down and the reporting burden reducing.

4 There is more rigor in processes and more objectivity. Reports ("Field Memoranda") create a common map of the situation, collective progress to date, current priorities and everybody's part in the plan. Issues like reliability are being addressed more systematically.

5 The approach enables people to stop doing some things and as a result there is less waste.

6 We have a common language, which is simple and transparent. Concepts like "being on mission," "constraints" or "main effort" are easy to understand and apply, and invigorating. The military language has traction and releases energy.

This is a good summary of the generic effects any business can expect to observe. It would be naïve to claim that leading through intent is a passport to success. As von Moltke often observed, the race is not always to the swift, nor battle to the strong – but swiftness and strength shift the odds.

CONCLUSION

In many ways, leading through intent is management by objectives for the twenty-first century. If one goes back to his original thoughts, penned in the middle of the last century, one sees that Drucker's concern was to create a common effort which avoids the gaps, overlaps, and friction which result from optimizing subsystems. He suggested that every manager write a "manager's letter" to his boss twice a year (which is very similar in content to a strategy briefing) and include the measures he would use to exercise self-control. It was the manager who was to get the control reports, not his boss, let alone an audit committee. The manager would act "not because somebody wants him to but because he himself decides that he has to – he acts, in other words, as a free man."[25]

Leading through intent draws on a longer and richer experience base than Drucker was able to access in 1955. It is more comprehensive, and its techniques, though similar, are more refined. But the spirit of management by objectives and that of leading through intent are the same. Sadly, as management by objectives became "MBO," it all too often turned from a management practice into a corporate process. The "manager's letter" became an approval process rather than a backbrief, and measures have became an external control mechanism. Intentions became dominated by targets, and rigidity returned. While it has undoubtedly had a positive impact on the practice of management, MBO has been reduced to a mechanism for closing the alignment gap, which leaves the knowledge and effects gaps wide open. Perhaps we can recapture the spirit of Drucker's original thinking.

The alignment gap is the focus of attention of the literature on implementation and is the most obvious of the gaps to managers. Others have found ways of closing it by cascading objectives. P&G has what it calls an OGSM technique. This starts with the corporate center defining its Objectives and Goals (corresponding to our "why" and "what") and its Strategies (sets of actions corresponding to our "implied tasks") and Measures – hence OGSM. These are then translated down into business and functional levels. In accordance with current best practice, goals have to be SMART – specific, measurable, actionable, realistic, and time-bound. In Hewlett-Packard, Yoji Akao devised what he calls the Hoshin method for aligning managers up and down and across the hierarchy behind a single goal.[26] With its roots in the total quality and lean manufacturing movements, it is a systematic engineering approach toward executing complex projects, and has also been deployed outside HP. There is a growing literature, including handbooks.[27]

There is no disputing that such techniques can have value, but they also have a danger. Focusing on closing the alignment gap without addressing the other two will tend to create rigidity. Techniques like this, which are forms of MBO, originate in specific corporate environments. When they are transferred into others, the process gets adopted but the culture is left behind. The result is often a bit more clarity and alignment and a lot more bureaucracy.

Some of the principles of *Auftragstaktik* probably influenced German management practice after the war. In 1962 Professor Reinhard Höhn expounded a comprehensive management system called the *Harzburger Modell* which is still taught at the Akademie der Führungskräfte der Wirtschaft in Bad Harzburg. Some 680,000 German executives have visited the Academy since its inception in 1956, which is enough for it to have had some impact on the performance of the German economy as a whole. The principles of the model are based on a view of managers as independent thinking individuals, the delegation of objectives, and decentralized decision making.

That there was direct military influence is clear from Höhn's publications. In 1952, he published a book about von Scharnhorst. *Führungsbrevier der Wirtschaft*, first published in 1966, draws heavily on military practice, and in *Die Führing mit Stäben in der Wirtschaft* of 1970, Höhn describes in detail how the workings of the General Staff could be re-created in business.[28]

But Höhn was no von Moltke. The techniques of the *Harzburger Modell* emphasize job descriptions and formal rules for giving direction and exercising control. While it signaled a move away from authoritarian leadership, because of its formal character it also created bureaucracy. At one point it contained 315 rules.[29] On the positive side, it provided a framework within which a more cooperative form of leadership could develop, created more role transparency, emphasized rational rather than authoritarian decision making, and gave companies a way of creating space for junior and middle managers to think and act. On the negative side, it set out to achieve these things through order and regulation which was time-consuming and costly, and actually stifled initiative. While the declared objective was a more democratic form of organization, Höhn claimed universal validity for his method and would have agreed with Taylor that "there is but one right way." The mindset behind the model is in fact authoritarian. It recommended that any employee breaking one of the 315 rules be fired.[30] As one critic has observed: "You cannot change leadership style by administrative decree."[31]

The story of the Prussian Army related in Chapter 3 is, in contrast, one of piecemeal evolution. There was no system, just a series of developments that slowly coalesced. The developments began with culture and what emerged was a strong and very particular ethos. Habits were created and techniques evolved to refine them. Progress was not linear – there were periods of stasis and even backtracking. There was a lot of debate and some very lively arguments. It was all brought together by the thought and practice of an enlightenment figure who established immense personal authority, although his post initially granted him very little. If we want to achieve something similar we cannot take decades, but as businesses are not slowed down by periods when they are not in operation, and we already know the end-point we are aiming for, we do not have to. But we do have to do more than merely set up a process for cascading goals.

The principles point beyond our current forms of hierarchical organization. The intelligence of an organization is never equal to the sum of the intelligence of the people who work in it. It is always either more or less. Scientists who study complexity have shown how insects such as ants and bees can create complex adaptive organizations by following very simple rules. Ants have evolved to become extremely efficient foragers by following two rules: "Lay pheromone and follow the trails of others." In human organizations, tactical subsystems such as freight cargo or call routing can improve their efficiency dramatically by adopting the same technique. The way in which bees allocate labor has been used to optimize scheduling of paint booths in a truck factory. However, predicting the collective effect of setting such rules for human beings to follow is beyond the capabilities of the human mind and has to be modeled by a computer.[32] This suggests that although the approach has tactical value, it would be fateful to rely on it to direct strategy.

However, simple rules have long been used by commanders to influence tactics and operations. Both Napoleon and von Moltke impressed on their officers the rule "always march toward the sound of the guns" in order to operationalize the behavioral principle of mutual support. Napoleon was famously shocked when his subordinate Grouchy failed to do so at Waterloo. Within a specific context, rules such as "allocate manufacturing capacity on the basis of gross margin" can work well in business too.[33] To make them work, humans, unlike ants, still need an understanding of intent. But intent does not need to be set by one person or indeed any single, central body.

Leading-edge business thinker Philip Evans has pointed out that organizations like Linux and Toyota are self-organizing networks in which the overall intent is shared without being laid down. Linux has no single leader. Self-organizing networks have all the characteristics we have observed to be cornerstones of leading through intent: a lot of people taking independent decisions on the basis of a shared intent and high mutual trust. The strong connection between the top and bottom of a hierarchy created by a briefing cascade is replaced by a strong network with widely dispersed knowledge and myriad dense interconnections.[34] This may not be a solution to everybody's problems, nor would it be practical for most organizations to transform themselves overnight into self-organizing networks. It may, however, reinforce the attractions of the compass heading I have been advocating.

As I observed at the outset, what I am advocating is no more than common sense, but common sense is not so common in practice. This observation is well captured in one of the more piquant acronyms sometimes used in military circles: GBO, standing for Glimpse of the Blindingly Obvious. The implications of the term GBO are worth a moment's reflection.

If the obvious only comes in glimpses, it is easy to miss it if we are not paying attention. If it is blinding, our natural reaction if we do glimpse it is to shield our eyes and look away. When we turn back, it is gone. GBOs can be disturbing, for they challenge the way we have always done things. Just as well that they pass so quickly, for then we can dismiss them as illusions and get back to our old ways of getting by. Winston Churchill is said to have observed:

> *Most people, sometimes in their lives, stumble across truth. And most jump up, brush themselves off, and hurry on about their business as if nothing had happened.*

Here, then, is a summary of the argument of this book in the form of 10 GBOs:

1 We are finite beings with limited knowledge and independent wills.
2 The business environment is unpredictable and uncertain, so we should expect the unexpected and should not plan beyond the circumstances we can foresee.
3 Within the constraints of our limited knowledge we should strive to identify the essentials of a situation and make choices about what it is most important to achieve.
4 To allow people to take effective action, we must make sure they understand what they are to achieve and why.
5 They should then explain what they are going to do as a result, define the implied tasks, and check back with us.

6   They should then assign the tasks they have defined to individuals who are accountable for achieving them, and specify boundaries within which they are free to act.

7   Everyone must have the skills and resources to do what is needed and the space to take independent decisions and actions when the unexpected occurs, as it will.

8   As the situation changes, everyone should be expected to adapt their actions according to their best judgment in order to achieve the intended outcomes.

9   People will only show the level of initiative required if they believe that the organization will support them.

10   What has not been made simple cannot be made clear and what is not clear will not get done.

Most of us spend most of our waking hours working for an organization. How we spend that time matters to the organization and it also matters to us. We spend it engaged in activity. Leading through intent is the art of turning activity into thoughtful, purposive action. Doing so does not only help organizations. It also alleviates the misery of the maligned middle manager and lightens the burden of the resented senior executive. It shows respect for individuals and allows them to grow. It enriches people's lives.

That is why I have written this book.

ON STRATEGY, 1871

Politics makes use of war to achieve its aims. It has a decisive influence on the beginning and the end of a war, and indeed reserves the right to raise its aspirations during the war's course, or to content itself with a more modest outcome.

As things are not fully determined, the aspiration of strategy can only ever be to achieve the highest end it can with the means available. It is therefore best if strategy works hand in hand with politics, working toward its goals, but free to act quite independently of it.

The first task of strategy is the assembly of forces, the initial deployment of the army. This involves the consideration of a whole range of disparate political, geographical, and national factors. A mistake in the initial disposition of armies is almost impossible to make good during the course of a campaign. However, there is plenty of time to consider these arrangements, and – assuming that the troops are prepared for war and the transportation system has been organized – they have to lead unfailingly to the intended result.

Things are different, however, in the next main task of strategy: the military use of the available resources, in other words operations.

Here, our will very soon encounters the independent will of an opponent. If we are ready and willing to take the initiative we can constrain the enemy's will, but the only way we can break it is through means of tactics, through battle.

However, the material and moral consequences of every major battle are so far-reaching that they almost invariably create a completely different situation, a new basis for new measures. No plan of operations can extend with any degree of certainty beyond the first encounter with the enemy's main body. Only a

General der Infanterie v. Moltke.

layman could imagine that in following the course of a campaign he is watching the logical unfolding of an initial idea conceived in advance, thought out in every detail, and pursued through to its conclusion.

Whatever the vicissitudes of events, a commander will need to keep his mind fixed unwaveringly on his main objectives, but he can never be certain beforehand which paths offer the best hopes of realizing them. Throughout the campaign he will find himself forced to make a whole series of decisions as situations arise which no one was able to predict. This means that the successive acts of a war do not follow a premeditated design but are acts of spontaneity guided by military judgment. Every case is unique. It is all a matter of seeing through the fog of uncertainty in which every situation is shrouded, making an accurate assessment of what you do know, guessing what you do not know, reaching a conclusion rapidly, and then vigorously and unwaveringly following it through.

While trying to calculate on the basis of one known and one unknown factor – your own will and that of your enemy – you have to take into account a third set of factors which are completely unpredictable. They include the weather, outbreaks of illness and railway accidents, misunderstandings and errors of perception; in short, all those influences on events that we ascribe to chance, fate, or divine providence, but which human beings neither create nor master.

Even so, this does not mean that the conduct of war is completely blind and arbitrary. The balance of probabilities is that the sum of all those chance events is as much to the detriment or advantage of one side as the other, and that a commander who in each case issues directions which are at least sensible, even if not optimal, stands a good chance of success.

It hardly needs saying that to do this, theoretical knowledge is not enough. Mastering this free, practical art means developing qualities of mind and character which are shaped by military training and guided by experience drawn from military history or from life itself.

When all is said and done, the reputation of a commander rests on his success. How much of it is in fact down to his own efforts is very hard to say. In the face of the irresistible power of circumstances even the best man can fail, and by the same token it can shield mediocrity. That said, in the long run, those who enjoy good luck usually deserve it.

Given that in war, once operations begin, everything is uncertain other than the will and dynamism of the commander himself, there is absolutely no practical value in rules of strategy and systems based on generalized doctrines.

Archduke Carl[1] considers strategy to be a science, and tactics an art. He believes that the "science of high command" can "determine the course of military affairs," and that the only place for art is in executing strategic designs.

General v. Clausewitz on the other hand says: "Strategy is the use of battle for the purposes of war." Indeed, strategy provides tactics with the means of beating the enemy, and can increase the chances of victory through the way in which it directs armies and brings them together on the battlefield. On the other hand, strategy builds on every successful engagement to exploit it further. In the face of tactical victory the demands of strategy are silent – it must adapt to the newly created situation.

Strategy is a system of heuristics. It is more than science, it is the application of knowledge to practical life, the evolution of an original guiding idea under constantly changing circumstances, the art of taking action under the pressure of the most difficult conditions.

STRATEGY BRIEFING

1 CONTEXT

What is the situation?

2 HIGHER INTENT

One level up (my boss)

Two levels up (my boss's boss)

3 MY INTENT

What are we trying to achieve and why?

What:

in order to

Why:

Measures

o
o
o

4 IMPLIED TASKS

Main Tasks	Responsibility	Timing

(Which task is the main effort? Highlight in bold or color)

5 BOUNDARIES

Freedoms

Constraints

6 BACKBRIEF: HAS THE SITUATION CHANGED?

- No – our brief is valid

- Yes – we have to change some tasks, but what we are trying to achieve is still valid

- Yes – and we have to change what we are trying to achieve

NOTES

PREFACE

1   Books that I am aware of that cite *The Art of Action*, some quite extensively, are *Lean Enterprise* by Jez Humble, Joanne Molesky and Barry O'Reilly, O'Reilly Media (2014); *The Business of Excellence* by Justin Hughes, Bloomsbury Business (2016); *Mission Mastery* by Brian Dive, Springer (2016); *Moltke Meets Confucius* by Dominik Thoma, Tectum (2016); *Sense and Respond* by Jeff Gothelf and Josh Seiden, HBR Press (2017); *Escaping the Build Trap* by Melissa Perri, O'Reilly Media (2018); and *Shipshape* by Nick Bashford, Biddles Books (2021). Other books have appeared that recommend applying the principles of mission command in business without having been influenced by this one. Outstanding amongst them are *Turn the Ship Around*, Penguin (2015) and *Leadership is Language*, Penguin (2020), both by L. David Marquet.

2   Having spent 23 years in the RAF, Brian Howieson is now professor of Business and Management at Edinburgh Napier University. Howard Kahn teaches at Edinburgh University Business School.

CHAPTER ONE

1   Gary L. Neilson, Karla L. Martin, & Elizabeth Powers, The Secrets to Successful Strategy Execution, *Harvard Business Review*, June 2008, p. 60.

2   Laurence G. Hrebiniak, *Making Strategy Work*, Wharton School Publishing 2005, p. 4. I might add that when I ask groups of managers today what in their experience are the biggest problems in executing strategy the lists, which usually include "the strategy is unclear," "getting buy-in," "translating goals into actions," "communication" and "resistance to change" are just the same as they were ten years ago. I do not expect that to change any time soon.

3   Frederick Winslow Taylor, *The Principles of Scientific Management*, New York 1911, p. 13.

4   Peter F. Drucker, *The Practice of Management*, Heinemann 1989 (original 1955), pp. 273 & 275.

5   *Ibid.*, p. 279.

6   Douglas McGregor, *The Human Side of Enterprise*, Penguin 1987, p. 47.

7   Henry Mintzberg, *The Rise and Fall of Strategic Planning*, Prentice Hall 1994, pp. 21–3 & 225–7.

8   *Ibid.*, p. 4.

9   Larry Bossidy & Ram Charan, *Execution*, Random House 2002, p. 7.

10 I begin the story then because it traces a direct line to the present. At the level of principle, the basic operating model is timeless. It was practiced by the eighteenth-century English Royal Navy and the Roman Army, two of the most successful organizations in history.

11 It comes from *stratos*, meaning "army," and *agein*, meaning "to lead." A *strategos* was an army leader, who in ancient Athens was also a Member of the Council of War with responsibilities as a civilian administrator. The word took on its modern meaning in the eighteenth century. See *Clausewitz on Strategy*, edited by Tiha von Ghyczy, Bolko von Oetinger, & Christopher Bassford, John Wiley 2001, pp. 30–31.

12 Lt Col J. P. Storr, The Nature of Military Thought, PhD thesis, University of Cranfield, May 2002, p. 77.

CHAPTER TWO

1   He and many other Prussian officers decided that their own conscience, bound up with a sense of honor, had to govern their actions. Technically at least, it was an act of treason. Von Scharnhorst wrote to another of them at the time: "I cannot condemn your decision, because everyone must first see that he remains true to himself" (Peter Paret, *Clausewitz and the State*, Oxford University Press 1976, p. 219). This view of personal integrity is a significant factor in light of the values which form the soil on which mission command can grow. It is a theme which can be traced through the plots against Hitler and which ended in Plötzensee prison.

2   The most authoritative biography of this remarkable thinker remains Peter Paret's *Clausewitz and the State*, which provides some analysis as well as a genesis of his ideas. The following is indebted to it, *passim*.

3   Clausewitz, *Vom Kriege*, ed. Hahlweg, 19. Auflage, Dümmler 1980.

4   See Martin van Creveld, The Eternal Clausewitz, in *Clausewitz and Modern Strategy*, ed. Handel, Frank Cass 1986, pp. 35–50.

5   Peter Paret, Clausewitz, in *Makers of Modern Strategy*, ed. Paret, Clarendon Press 2000, p. 190.

6   The method is Kantian. Given that he wishes to give an account of how experience is possible, Kant opens his *Critique of Pure Reason* with an analytical description of space and time which he calls *eine Erörterung* – a translation of the Latin *expositio* – as the dimensions within which experience takes place. Clausewitz was familiar with Kant from lectures given by one of his disciples Johann Gottfried Kiesewetter at the Berlin Institute for Young Officers in 1801–4. See Michael Howard, *The Franco-Prussian War*, Rupert Hart-Davis 1961, pp. 13–14 and Paret, Clausewitz, p. 194.

7   *Vom Kriege*, p. 261. All translations are the author's.

8   *Ibid.*, pp. 252 & 260.

9   *Ibid.*, p. 350.

10 *Ibid.*, p. 239.

11 *Ibid.*, pp. 261 & 263.

12 *Ibid.*, p. 262.

13 Paret, Clausewitz, p. 202.

14 They included the expatriate Welshman General Lloyd who greatly influenced von Bülow, and the Swiss Antoine-Henri Jomini who exercised a baleful influence long after his death. Napoleon read Lloyd and annotated his copy with damning marginalia such as "ignorance… absurd… impossible… very bad." However, he admired Jomini's writings, perhaps because Jomini served in his army as a staff officer from 1805 to 1813. See John Shy, Jomini, in *Makers of Modern Strategy*, ed. Paret, pp. 143–85.

15 Barry D. Watts, *Clausewitzian Friction and Future War*, McNair Paper 52, Institute for National Strategic Studies, National Defense University, Washington DC, revised edition 2000, pp. 22–3.

16 *Vom Kriege*, p. 261.

17 *Ibid.*, p. 262.

18 Watts, *op. cit.*, pp. 7–8.

19 *Ibid.*, p. 9.

20 *Ibid.*, pp. 9–10.

21 I am indebted to an unpublished paper by Aidan Walsh for his insights into the cognitive and informational essence of friction.

22 *Vom Kriege*, p. 213 (author's translation).

23 Alan D. Beyerchen, Clausewitz, Nonlinearity and the Unpredictability of War, *International Security*, Winter 1992, Harvard College and MIT, p. 6.

24 Watts, *op. cit.*, pp. 115–16.

25 Beyerchen, *op. cit.*, p. 2.

26 Watts, *op. cit.*, pp. 110–11.

27 *Vom Kriege*, p. 191.

28 *Ibid.*, pp. 193–5.

29 *Ibid.*, pp. 196–7.

30 *Ibid.*, pp. 209–10.

31 See, for example, Ralph Stacey, *Managing Chaos*, Kogan Page 1992.

32 See James Gleick, *Chaos*, Vintage 1998, pp. 83–6 & 92–3.

33 This makes execution an ever more important issue, as it can no longer be taken for granted. See Larry Bossidy & Ram Charan, *Execution*, Random House 2002, p. 69.

34 God does not experience friction because He is omniscient and has a single will. The corollary is that ignoring friction is playing at being God.

35 Bossidy and Charan, *op. cit.*, p. 19. It turns out, however, that when they come to cover the "core processes of execution" there are three of them. This is not coincidence.

36 Susan Miller, David Wilson, & David Hickson, Beyond Planning: Strategies for Successfully Implementing Strategic Decisions, *Long Range Planning* 37, 2004, p. 211.

37 Michael C. Mankins & Richard Steele, *Closing the Strategy-to-Performance Gap – Techniques for Turning Great Strategy into Great Performance*, Marakon Associates 2005.

38 Dr. Theresa M. Welbourne, *Leaders Talk about Executing Strategy*, Leadership Pulse Survey, Ross School of Business, University of Michigan, March 2005.

39 *Ibid.*, p. 7.

40 *Ibid.*

41 Laurence G. Hrebiniak, *Making Strategy Work*, Wharton School Publishing 2005, pp. 4–9.

42 *Ibid.*, p. 22.

43 Jeffrey Pfeffer & Robert I. Sutton, *The Knowing–Doing Gap*, Harvard Business School Press 2000.

CHAPTER THREE

1   An account of the genesis of mission command drawing on some of
     the same material as this chapter, but written for a military reader-
     ship, was published under the title The Road to Mission Command
     in the *British Army Review*, Number 137, summer 2005, pp. 22–9.
2   Significantly, none of them was from the old Prussian Junker class
     which dominated the Army. Von Scharnhorst himself was a
     Hanoverian. See Walter Görlitz, *Der Deutsche Generalstab*, Frankfurt
     1953, pp. 23–4.
3   On what follows see Dirk Oetting's superb *Auftragstaktik – Geschichte
     und Gegenwart einer Führungskonzeption*, Report Verlag 1993. All
     translations are the author's.
4   Douglas McGregor, *The Human Side of Enterprise*, Penguin 1987
     (first published by McGraw-Hill 1960).
5   Oetting, *op. cit.*, p. 32.
6   *Ibid.*, pp. 33–4.
7   They remained dominated by the Junker class, but the rules of con-
     scription in Prussia differed from those in other European coun-
     tries in that no one could buy themselves out of it or pay for a
     substitute. To that extent, Prussia drew on the full range of talent
     available to it more effectively than its rivals. See Hajo Holborn,
     The Prusso-German School: Moltke and the Rise of the General
     Staff, in *Makers of Modern Strategy*, ed. Paret, Clarendon 2000, p.
     282. In Britain there was no conscription, with the result that offi-
     cers came from a narrow group of aristocrats. The purchasing of
     commissions, which allowed any wealthy nobleman, regardless of
     his qualifications, to assume command of a regiment, was not
     abolished until 1873.
8   Görlitz, *op. cit.*, pp. 42–3.
9   *Ibid.*, pp. 97–103.
10   *Ibid.*, p. 100. The essay can be found in translation in Karl Demeter's
     classic *The German Officer-Corps in Society and State 1650–1945*,
     Weidenfeld & Nicolson 1965, pp. 257–77.
11   Michael Howard, *The Franco-Prussian War*, Rupert Hart-Davis
     1961, pp. 27–9. The original source of the story is the memoirs of
     General Count Wartensleben-Carow. There is still some confusion
     about who von Moltke is because his nephew and namesake also

became Chief of the General Staff in 1906. He is therefore sometimes referred to as "von Moltke the Elder."

12   A selection of his writings is available in English under the title *Moltke on the Art of War*, ed. Daniel J. Hughes, Ballantine Books, New York, 1993.

13   Oetting, *op. cit.*, p. 112.

14   *Ibid.*, p. 105. The *Memoire* is interesting not just because of its content but because it represents a rare example of determining that major reforms were needed in the wake of a success, thus bucking the trend noted at the beginning of this chapter.

15   Martin van Creveld, *Command in War*, Harvard University Press 1987, p. 121.

16   *Verordnungen für die Höheren Truppenführer.* A translation is included in the volume by Daniel Hughes, pp. 171–224. While I have rendered *Verordnungen* as "guidance," it was meant to be binding. A *Verordnung* is a prescription or decree.

17   As an example, Hughes compares a section from a related essay which found its way into the *Guidance for Large Unit Commanders* with a passage from the US Army's *Field Manual 100-5* of 1939 (*op. cit.*, p. 234, n. 9). It is important to note, however, that such similarities in wording do not necessarily translate into similarities in effect. Organizational behavior is not determined by manuals, nor does the existence of similar statements in those manuals necessarily reflect common beliefs. Despite lifting passages from German documents inspired by von Moltke, the US Army of 1939 had quite a different view of the nature of war, a view derived from scientific management with the emphasis on planning and control. The point is forcibly made by Martin van Creveld in his brilliant comparison of the US and German Armies in the Second World War, *Fighting Power*, Greenwood Press 1982, pp. 28–34.

18   Translations are the author's. They are based on the text reproduced in *General Feldmarshall Graf von Moltke, Ausgewählte Werke, Erster Band*, Reimar Hobbing Verlag, Berlin 1925, pp. 160–66. The passages cited can be found in Hughes' translation of the text on pp. 173, 176–7 and 184–6.

19   General Hans von Seekt, head of the German Army from 1918 to 1933, explicitly and repeatedly defined the job of the General Staff as

developing the average rather than producing geniuses. See Görlitz, *op. cit.*, p. 95.

20 One of the first analysts of the reasons for the excellence of the modern German Army, Colonel T. N. Dupuy, emphasizes that it institutionalized military excellence, and was therefore able to sustain it regardless of changes in top leadership, because it consistently produced high-quality leaders at all levels. See *A Genius for War – The German Army and General Staff, 1807–1945*, MacDonald & Janes, London 1977, *passim*, but especially pp. 44–53. Compare Collins and Porras's notion of "clock building, not telling the time," by which they mean "building a company that can prosper far beyond the presence of any single leader and through multiple product cycles," the first pillar of being "a visionary company" (James C. Collins & Jerry I. Porras, *Built to Last*, Century, London 1994, p. 23).

21 Oetting, *op. cit.*, p. 13.

22 Oetting, *op. cit.*, p. 116.

23 See Lothar Burchardt, Helmuth von Moltke, Wilhelm I. und der Aufstieg des preußischen Generalstabes in *Generalfeldmarschall von Moltke: Bedeutung und Wirkung*, ed. Roland G. Foerster, Oldenburg Verlag, Munich 1991, pp. 19–38.

24 Stephan Leistenschneider, *Auftragstaktik im preußisch-deutschen Heer 1871 bis 1914*, Mittler Verlag 2002, pp. 46–55.

25 Von Moltke, *Geschichte des Deutsch-Französischen Krieges von 1870–1871*, Mittler und Sohn, Berlin 1895, p. 5.

26 Quintin Barry, *The Franco-Prussian War 1870–71, Volume 1*, Helion & Co. 2007, pp. 108–9.

27 *Ibid.*, p. 110.

28 *Ibid.*, p. 109.

29 Von Moltke, *Geschichte des Deutsch-Französischen Krieges von 1870–1871*, p. 26.

30 Oetting, *op. cit.*, p. 126. For an account of the incident see pp. 113–14, and more broadly the one in Michael Howard's classic work, *op. cit.*, pp. 139–44. Though tactically a French victory, the strategic consequences were to impose a vital delay on the French. Howard tellingly observes that "no officer in the French Army had, or was supposed to have, any insight into the intentions of the commander-in-chief" (p. 145). It marched blindly to disaster.

31 Though they themselves and their followers presumably did not, as some German units employed these methods, with predictable results, in 1914.

32 In ordinary usage, *Auftrag* means "task" or "assignment." The military generally use the word "mission" to refer to a set of actions to be carried out by a unit with a particular end in mind, and have refined their lexicon so as to distinguish a "mission" from a "task." Thus we read: "Mission command derives its strength and value from the intention to tell subordinates what to achieve and why, rather than what to do and how. Most essentially, commanders do this by issuing missions rather than tasks (a mission is a task + a purpose)" (*Design for Military Operations – the British Military Doctrine*, Army Code 71451, D/CGS/50.8, 1996, p. 4–17). A task is something which has to be done. A mission is something which has to be done in order to achieve a set of effects or outcome. It is the purpose behind it which turns a task into a mission.

33 Leistenschneider, *op. cit.*, pp. 65–7.

34 *Ibid.*, pp. 95–6.

35 Anglophone that he was, he uses *Direktive* rather than the German word *Weisung*. See *Ausgewählte Werke, op. cit.*, pp. 162–3.

36 Oetting, *op. cit.*, p. 125.

37 Leistenschneider, *op. cit.*, pp. 72–92.

38 Leistenschneider, *op. cit.*, pp. 100–6. It was not officially defined until 1977. See Oetting, *op. cit.*, p. 14.

39 Oetting, *op. cit.*, pp. 16–19.

40 Leistenschneider, *op. cit.*, pp.123–37.

41 See Robert T. Foley, Institutionalised Innovation: The German Army and the Changing Nature of War 1871–1914, *RUSI Journal*, April 2002, pp. 84–90.

42 He confusingly shared his uncle's name and is accordingly known as Helmuth von Moltke the Younger. Schlieffen was a skeptic when it came to *Auftragstaktik* and true followers of von Moltke like von Schlichting had continual difficulties with him.

43 For an example of this see Martin Samuels' analysis of the German defense of Thiepval and the Schwaben Redoubt on the Somme in *Command or Control – Command, Training and Tactics in the British and German Armies 1888–1918*, Frank Cass 1995, pp. 149–57. The communications problem faced by the attackers was more severe still than that of the defenders. See Gary Sheffield, *Forgotten Victory*,

Headline 2001, pp. 120–23. The inherent balance of advantage was nevertheless compounded by each side's approach to command and control, and doctrine.

44 In a workshop conducted under the auspices of the US Army in 1980, two distinguished German Panzer generals who fought throughout the Second World War, Balck and von Mellenthin, continually commented on the importance of *Auftragstaktik* in determining the performance of the German Army. At one point von Mellenthin observed: "The following-through of an order requires that the person to whom it was given think at least one level above the one at which the order was given… The mission requires one to be able to think, or to penetrate by thought the functions of higher command. *Auftragstaktik* is not limited to any levels. It applies to the division commander and his chief-of-staff just as much as to the tank commander and his gunner" (Col William DePuy, *Generals Balck and von Mellenthin on Tactics: Implications for NATO Military Doctrine*, BDM Corporation 1980, ed. Reiner K. Huber, Universität der Bundeswehr 2004, p. 19). Perhaps the most striking thing about this comment is that von Mellenthin takes it as read that it applies to a tank crew, but explains that it applies to divisional commanders as well.

45 *Truppenführung*, §§ 36–7 (author's translation).

46 John Erickson, *The Road to Berlin*, Weidenfeld & Nicolson 1983, p. 622.

47 Hitler's perversion of the Army's leadership philosophy is charted by Oberstleutnant Dr. Hans-Peter Stein in Führen durch Auftrag, *Truppenpraxis*, Beiheft 1/85. The *Führerprinzip* was alien to Prussian traditions. The German General Staff's opposition to Hitler is charted by Görlitz, *op. cit.*, pp. 226–76. The then Chief of the General Staff, Ludwig Beck, the main author of the 1933 *Truppenführung*, resigned in 1938. In a letter to the head of the Army, von Brauchitsch, he wrote: "Your obedience as a soldier reaches its limits when your knowledge, your conscience and your responsibilities forbid you to carry out an order." His successor, Halder, had a plan for a coup which was only abandoned when war was averted by the Munich agreement. Beck was one of the first victims of the failure of von Stauffenberg's assassination attempt of July 1944. Outside the Army, resistance centered on Count James von Moltke, the great-grandnephew of Helmuth the elder. He was executed in January 1945.

48 Belton E. Cooper, *Death Traps*, Presidio Press 1998, p. 242.

49 Colonel Trevor Dupuy, *A Genius for War*, pp. 253–4. Dupuy bases his claims on an analysis of data from actual engagements in North Africa, Italy, and northwest Europe. This analysis has predictably been challenged, in particular its methodology, but the broad conclusions are generally accepted. See David French, *Raising Churchill's Army*, Oxford University Press 2000, pp. 8–10.

50 As argued by Martin van Creveld in his *Fighting Power*. Dupuy argues that the main reason was the creation of the General Staff. However, he concludes that *Auftragstaktik* was "very close to the heart of what the General Staff was all about" (*op. cit.*, p. 307. See also pp. 116 & 304).

51 Some have followed Richard Simpkin in preferring the term "directive control." Simpkin ably argues his case for rejecting the rendering "mission command" as "disastrous" in *Race to the Swift*, Brassey 1985, pp. 227–40. He seems nevertheless to have lost the battle over terminology.

52 Van Creveld, *Command in War*, pp. 258–60.

53 This is explained in an unpublished paper, Bagnall and the "Ginger" Group in Retrospect by Brian Holden-Reid, an academic who was himself intimately involved in the reform process.

54 Frederick Winslow Taylor, *The Principles of Scientific Management*, Dover 1998, p. 16.

55 *Ibid.*, p. 17.

56 *Ibid.*, pp. 20–21.

57 One landmark was the publication of *In Search of Excellence* by Thomas Peters and Robert Waterman, Harper & Row 1982, the first business book to hit the bestseller lists. It explicitly attacks what it calls the "rational model" of business, which it traces back to Taylor (pp. 42–4). The authors note with some curiosity that all their "excellent" companies showed numerous incidents of "extraordinary effort on the part of apparently ordinary employees" (p. xvii). Ironically, they quote Karl Weick's view that the military metaphor is the problem because it leads people to "overlook a different kind of organization, one that values improvisation rather than forecasting, dwells on opportunities rather than constraints, discovers new actions rather than defends past actions, values arguments more highly than serenity, and encourages doubt and contradiction rather than belief" (p. 7).

Some military practitioners had got to this point more than 100 years earlier. By and large, however, they were not American ones, which may be why these prejudices were plausible to an American audience.

58 Field Marshal List, quoted by Hans-Peter Stein in Führen durch Auftrag, *Truppenpraxis*, Beiheft I/85, p. 6.

59 This is the general tenor of Franz Uhle-Wettler's essay Auftragstaktik – Was ist das? Können wir sie wiederbeleben?, *Truppenpraxis*, Beiheft 2/1992, pp. 131–5.

60 The case against a purely cultural explanation is ably put by Leistenschneider, *op. cit.*, *passim*, especially pp. 98 ff.

61 The command philosophy of its greatest general, Wellington, was at the other extreme to that of von Moltke.

62 Interview with the Israeli Defence Attaché to Britain, Colonel Yizhar Sahar, 8 October 2002.

63 The Myth of Mission Command – The Impact of Risk Aversion and Cultural Dissonance on Current and Future Operational Effectiveness, unpublished MA dissertation by Major Colin Cape, pp. 49 & 50.

64 Even here it got lost for a time. See Andrew Gordon, *The Rules of the Game – Jutland and British Naval Command*, John Murray 1996, especially the chapter entitled The Long Calm Lee of Trafalgar, pp. 155–92.

65 For a succinct demonstration of how Nelson used the principles of mission command see Edgar Vincent, Nelson and Mission Command, *History Today*, June 2003. While they are commonly identified with Nelson as an individual, they were in fact the methods of the Royal Navy as an organization. He was their greatest practitioner.

66 Martin van Creveld, *Command in War*, p. 270. American historian Victor Davis Hanson provocatively attributes the 2,500-year dominance of western powers on the world's battlefields to the readiness of free citizens to combine the discipline implied by achieving alignment with the individualism and initiative which go along with a sense of personal responsibility for achieving a collective goal (*Carnage and Culture*, Anchor Books 2001). If he is right, mission command is a modern manifestation of successful principles which are far older.

67 As a reading of *Built to Last*, James C. Collins & Jerry I. Porras, London 1994, and *From Good to Great*, Jim Collins, Random House 2001 will suggest.

68 *Fortune* magazine, November 30 1981, p. 17.

69 This is referred to by Collins and Porras, who themselves quote Tichy and Sherman's rather unscholarly *Control Your Own Destiny or Somebody Else Will* as follows: "Planful opportunism crystallized in his own mind... after he read Johannes (sic) von Moltke, a nineteenth century Prussian general influenced by the renowned military theorist Karl (sic) von Clausewitz who argued that plans usually fail, because circumstances inevitably change" (*Built to Last*, p. 148).

70 See Appendix A of *Jack*, Jack Welch & John Byrne, Headline 2001, p. 448.

71 *Ibid.*, pp. 106–8.

72 Learning by doing is the most important single precept of Pfeffer and Sutton's solution to closing the knowing–doing gap (*op. cit.*, pp. 249 –51). Lieutenant Colonel Roger Noble argues that the German Army was a learning organization capable of sustaining performance through several generations of technology because of the culture it inculcated in order to sustain *Auftragstaktik*: "Through this focus on quality people, knowledge and output the organisation was able to deal with uncertainty by building an environment in which effective innovations could emerge and continuously evolve. This organisational skill in learning and adapting enabled the German Army to deal with complexity and chaos in peace and war." See The German Army 1914–45: The Imperfect Military Learning Organisation, *Australian Defence Force Journal* No. 162, Sep/Oct 2003, pp. 39–52, p. 48.

73 Its potential value in business has also been outlined by Ivan Yardsley and Andrew Kakabadse in Understanding Mission Command: A Model for Developing Competitive Advantage in a Business Context, *Strategic Change*, January–April 2007, pp. 69–78.

74 *Fighting Power*, p. 165.

CHAPTER FOUR

1 This statement occurs in various places in his writings. It is usually cited as "No plan survives first contact with the enemy," which does not occur anywhere.

2 Some readers may like to note that 1871 falls into that dark period of history pre-dating feminism, political correctness, and diversity initiatives. The original text clearly designates an adult male.

3   *Über Strategie*, 1871 in *Moltkes Militärische Werke*, ed. the Großer Generalstab, Kriegsgeschichtliche Abteilung I, Berlin 1892–1912, Band II, 2, pp. 291–3. Cf. Hughes' translation, *op. cit.*, pp. 45–7. A translation of the whole essay can be found in the Appendix. Its authenticity has been disputed, as it has been claimed that its editors, the General Staff, made alterations to it. The Prussian Military Archives were destroyed during the Second World War, so we will never know for sure. However that may be, the text is entirely consistent with von Moltke's other work and his practice, and it is remarkable in its concision, incisiveness, and insight.

4   Horace Greeley, the founder editor of the *New York Tribune*, wrote in 1850: "Go West, young man, and grow up with the country." It articulated American aspirations of the time so powerfully that another journalist, John Soule, used it in an editorial in an Indiana journal a year later and made it more memorable by simplifying it even further into "Go West, young man, go West!". Journalists know a good elevator speech when they find one.

5   Jim Storr argues that this is a general characteristic of military decision making. See Lt Col J. P. Storr, The Nature of Military Thought, unpublished PhD thesis, Cranfield University, May 2002, pp. 92 ff.

6   See Bucholz, *op. cit.*, pp. 56–7. He was, for example, surprised when the French Army of Châlons took a route which enabled him to eventually surround it. He feared, and expected, that it would move away to the west. Once he had convinced himself that they were making a mistake, he exploited it to the full.

7   A military example of the difference between strategy and planning is offered by the preparations made by the RAF and the Luftwaffe for what was to become known as the Battle of Britain. The curious reader may care to look at the author's account of this given in Chapters 9 and 10 of *The Most Dangerous Enemy*, Aurum Press 2000, pp. 116–38. It might be summarized by saying that the Luftwaffe had a plan but no strategy and the RAF had a strategy but no plan. From the first day, things did not go according to the Luftwaffe's plan, and it never worked out what its real intent was. Being thoroughly prepared and with a clear intent, the RAF adapted its actions to every move the Luftwaffe made and, unconstrained by any plan, thwarted every one of them. See also Stephen Bungay, Command or Control? – Leadership in the Battle of Britain, *Air*

Force Leadership – Beyond Command?, Royal Air Force Leadership Centre 2005, pp. 115–28.

8   Henry Mintzberg, *The Rise and Fall of Strategic Planning*, Pearson 2000, p. 393. They amount to supporting the process of strategy development and providing a means of communication and control.

9   *Ibid.*, pp. 330–31.

10   Henry Mintzberg, Crafting Strategy, *Harvard Business Review*, July/ August 1987, pp. 66–75.

11   Kathleen M. Eisenhardt & Donald N. Sull, Strategy as Simple Rules, *Harvard Business Review*, January 2001, pp. 107–16. Unfortunately, they also cite Enron in a sidebar, presciently noting: "Like the outlaw Willie Sutton, who robbed banks because that's where the money was, Enron managers embraced uncertainty because that's where the juicy opportunities lay" (p. 114). There is an unintended warning here, to do with the bedrock of values and culture, the nature of the "codes of honor" I noted in Chapter 3. While the form of *Auftragstaktik* guards against tyranny, only its content can guard against moral hazard or corruption. The warning is in the original story, for it was adopted not only by the Wehrmacht but also by the Waffen-SS.

12   Daniel G. Simpson, Why Most Strategic Planning Is a Waste of Time and What You Can Do about It, *Long Range Planning* Vol. 31, No. 3, pp. 476–80 and Vol. 31, No. 4, pp. 623–7.

13   See Mintzberg, *The Rise and Fall of Strategic Planning*, pp. 101–4.

14   Simpson, *op. cit.*, p. 477.

15   Mathew L. A. Hayward, Violina P. Rindova, & Timothy G. Pollock, Believing One's Own Press: The Causes and Consequences of CEO Celebrity, *Strategic Management Journal* 25, 2004, pp. 637–53.

16   Clausewitz, *op. cit.*, p. 810.

17   *Ibid*. The German word he uses meaning "center of gravity" is *Schwerpunkt*.

18   The third chapter of Book I, pp. 231–52 of the Hahlweg edition.

19   Kant, *Kritik der Urteilskraft* (Critique of Judgment) § 46: "Genius is the talent (gift of nature) which gives art its rulebook."

20   Clausewitz, p. 234. The word I have translated as "conviction" is *Entschlossenheit*. It is more usually rendered as "decisive" or "reso-lute." It conveys the sense of "reaching a decision and sticking to it," with an undertone of determination to see things through.

21 *Ibid.*, p. 236.

22 See Gary Klein, *Sources of Power*, MIT Press 1998 and *The Power of Intuition*, Doubleday 2003. Yves Doz and Mikko Kosonen likewise suggest that achieving strategic agility involves "a shift from foresight-based strategic planning to insight-based strategic sensitivity" (*Fast Strategy: How Strategic Agility Will Help You Stay Ahead of the Game*, Wharton School Publishing 2008, p. 33.

23 Witness the sad end to the career of Lord Browne in 2007, a man who possessed the highest degree of strategic insight into the oil business he ran with outstanding success for a long time.

24 Peter Williamson & Michael Hay, Strategic Staircases: Planning the Capabilities Required for Success, *Long Range Planning* Vol. 24, No. 4, pp. 36–43 (1991).

25 See Jeffrey Pfeffer & Robert I. Sutton, *The Knowing–Doing Gap*, Harvard Business School Press 2000, pp. 51–65.

26 It has since been reprinted in the series Best of HBR, *Harvard Business Review*, July–August 2005.

27 *Ibid.*, p. 2.

28 *Ibid.*, p. 2. Compare Woide's comments about Prussian behavior on the battlefield in 1870. See Chapter 3 above.

29 *Ibid.*, pp. 3–4.

30 *Ibid.*, p. 6.

31 *Ibid.*, p. 3.

32 *Ibid.*, p. 5.

33 *Ibid.*, pp. 7–10.

34 *Ibid.*, p. 14.

35 *Ibid.*, p. 10.

36 At the top level, Allied strategy in both World Wars involved doing precisely this. Operationally disadvantaged, the Allies gradually built up massive advantages in resources and simultaneously built capability to narrow the operational gap.

37 The neglect was being pointed out at the time. See, for example, Robert M. Grant, The Resource-Based Theory of Competitive Advantage: Implications for Strategy Formulation, *California Management Review* Vol. 33, No. 3, Spring 1991, pp. 114–35; or David J. Collis & Cynthia Montgomery, Competing on Resources: Strategy in the 1990s, *Harvard Business Review* July–August 1995, pp. 118–28.

38 Stephen Bungay, Mission Impossible: BP's Project Andrew, unpublished case study, 2003.

39 Gary Hamel & C. K. Prahalad, *Competing for the Future*, Harvard Business School Press 1994, pp. 37 ff. This approach has recently resurfaced, as things do, with a catchy new name. See W. Chan Kim & Renée Mauborgne, *Blue Ocean Strategy*, Harvard Business School Press 2005.

40 Hamel & Prahalad, *op. cit.*, pp. 73–126.

41 *Ibid.*, p. 129.

42 *Ibid.*, *passim* but especially pp. 127–47 & pp. 196–220.

43 *Ibid.*, pp. 155–6.

44 *Ibid.*, p. 132.

45 Strategic Intent, p. 4.

46 This is reflected in publications which show the continuing search for an appropriate model. For example, one recent suggestion is to adopt the methods of software development. See Keith R. McFarland, Should You Build Strategy Like You Build Software?, Sloan Management Review Spring 2008, pp. 67–74.

CHAPTER FIVE

1 See von Moltke, *Ausgewählte Werke, Erster Band*, Feldherr und Kriegslehrmeister, Berlin 1925, pp. 79, 94, & 104. Prussia's political war aim was to force the French to accept a peace treaty ceding Alsace and Lorraine to what they hoped by then would be a united Germany. The military objective was to force a surrender by capturing Paris, and the operational objective was to render Paris defenseless by destroying the French Army.

2 Von Moltke, *Geschichte des Deutsch-Französischen Krieges von 1870–71*, Berlin 1895, reprinted by Melchior Verlag, Wolfenbüttel, p. 49 (author's translation).

3 *Ibid.*, pp. 65 ff.

4 Howard, *op. cit.*, p. 191.

5 See Geoffrey Wawro, *The Franco-Prussian War*, Cambridge University Press 2003, p. 203.

6 Von Moltke, *Geschichte des Deutsch-Französischen Krieges von 1870–71*, pp. 53–4.

7 Eberhard Kessel, *Moltke*, Stuttgart 1957, pp. 563–4.

8   Wawro, *op. cit.*, pp. 202 & 203.

9   Von Moltke, *Ausgewählte Werke, Erster Band*, p. 289.

10   Von Moltke, *Ausgewählte Werke, Erster Band*, p. 290.

11   Wawro, *op. cit.*, p. 212.

12   Bucholz, *op. cit.*, p. 120.

13   Peter Mandelson, *The Third Man: Life at the Heart of New Labour*, Harper Press 2010, pp. 384–5.

14   Steven E. Prokesch, Competing on Service: An Interview with British Airways' Sir Colin Marshall, *Harvard Business Review* November–December 1995, p. 105.

15   *Ibid.*, pp. 106 & 108.

16   *Ibid.*, pp. 108–9.

17   *Ibid.*, p. 109–10.

18   They are included by Gary Klein in his article A Script for the Commander's Intent Statement, *Science of Command and Control: Part III – Coping with Change*, ed. Alexander H. Lewis & Ilze S. Lewis, AFCEA International Press 1994, pp. 75–85. The article is based on an analysis of 97 statements of intent written by middle and senior officers on exercises at the US Army's National Training Center. The form used varied a great deal. In part this was appropriate, but in part it was due to a lack of skill in formulating intent. NTC instructors' average rating of the 97 statements was "mediocre."

19   A point affirmed by David J. Collis and Michael G. Rukstad in Can You Say What Your Strategy Is?, *Harvard Business Review*, April 2008.

20   This is taken from a submission written by John Reid-Dodick which resulted in Reuters being awarded the Human Resources 2005 Excellence in Change Management award.

21   Most notably perhaps in recent years by Michael Goold and Andrew Campbell in *Designing Effective Organizations*, Jossey-Bass 2002.

22   Van Creveld, *Command in War*, p. 269.

23   The three questions relate to several of the tests of "fit drivers" and "good design principles" developed by Goold and Campbell. See particularly Chapters 2 & 3 and Chapter 8.

24   See James P. Kahan, D. Robert Worley, & Cathleen Sasz, *Understanding Commanders' Information Needs*, RAND 1989.

25   The exact origins of this dictum are obscure, but it is generally attributed to Lorenz. Many versions are quoted. They usually run

more or less as follows: "Gesagt ist nicht gehört; gehört ist nicht verstanden; verstanden ist lange nicht einverstanden, einverstanden ist nicht durchgeführt, durchgeführt ist nicht beibehalten." My version is "frei nach Konrad Lorenz," as they say in Germany.

26　In *Execution Plain and Simple*, McGraw Hill 2004, Robert A. Neiman also recommends defining your assignment in writing in order to understand what it really is about and avoiding ambiguity. The book contains worksheets and tables to accompany each of the 12 steps the author identifies as necessary to "achieving any goal on time and on budget." While the intention is laudable, one wonders how clear the core message will be at the end. In contrast, Michael Beer and Russell A. Eisenstat recommend having "honest conversations" about business strategy in a process they describe as a "fishbowl discussion" (How to Have an Honest Conversation, *Harvard Business Review*, February 2004, pp. 82–9), which is an elaborate form of backbrief. Clearly, if the content of a backbrief is dishonest, it is worthless or worse. But the point remains that a conversation is not enough.

27　Interview with Col Andy Salmon, Ministry of Defence, 28 May 2003.

28　"Independent thinking obedience" is an accurate translation of the original phrase so I use it throughout the text. When conveying the idea in the business world today I replace the word "obedience" with "commitment."

CHAPTER SIX

1　Collins, *From Good to Great*, pp. 17–40. Collins calls them "level 5 leaders." After his victory over Austria in 1866, von Moltke became a celebrity. He was rewarded with honors and a royal grant, became an intimate of the king and leading members of the court, and was ogled by the public in the streets. It was water off a duck's back. To the end of his life, he traveled about by train in civilian dress, always second class, and carried his own bag. He was not seduced by his own legend. See Bucholz, *op. cit.*, pp. 140–1 & 185.

2　He succeeded. By 1913, the figure had doubled to 70 percent. See Herbert Rosinski, *The German Army*, ed. Gordon Craig, Praeger 1966, pp. 98–9.

3　When it was noticed that a disproportionate number of Guards officers were winning places, von Moltke had the papers marked anonymously, with candidates identified only by a code number, to avoid favoritism. Oddly enough, the number of Guards officers accepted went up.

4   On all the above see Samuels, *op. cit.*, pp. 18–27.

5   The color of the pieces was standardized so that blue indicated friendly forces and red the enemy, a practice which has survived to this day, giving rise to incidents of "friendly fire" being referred to as "blue on blue."

6   See Andrew Wilson, *War Gaming*, Penguin 1970, pp. 15–19. On staff rides see David Ian Hall, The Modern Model for the Battlefield Tour and Staff Rides: Post 1815 Prussian and German Traditions, *Connections: The Quarterly Journal of the Partnership for Peace Consortium of Defence Academies and Security Studies Institutes*, Vol. 1, No. 3, September 2002, pp. 93–101.

7   The Allies regarded the General Staff as so formidable that they abolished it in 1919 and forbad its recreation in the Treaty of Versailles. Some historians have attributed the battlefield performance of the German Army almost entirely to the existence of the General Staff, which "can be said to have institutionalised military genius." See Dupuy, *A Genius for War*, p. 299.

8   *Ibid.*, p. 304.

9   Rosinski, *op. cit.*, p. 311. This exercise was abolished in 1914.

10   Samuels, *op. cit.*, p. 18.

11   Bucholz, *op. cit.*, p. 9. The influential "double-loop" model of organizational learning is expounded by Chris Argyris and Donald A. Schon in *Organizational Learning: A Theory of Action Perspective*, Addison-Wesley 1978.

12   Oetting, *op. cit.*, p. 112.

13   Part II, section 121, quoted by Leistenschneider, *op. cit.*, p.74, italics in the original.

14   Leistenschneider, pp. 96 & 90.

15   Steven E. Prokesch, Competing on Service: An Interview with British Airways' Sir Colin Marshall, Harvard Business Review, November–December 1995, p. 110.

16   *Ibid.*, p. 108.

17   Ed Michaels, Helen Handfield-Jones, & Beth Axelrod, *The War for Talent*, Harbard Business School Press 2001. A first indication that their message may not encompass the whole truth is the authors' often expressed admiration for Enron.

18   Jeffrey Pfeffer argues that even engaging in the "war for talent" is harmful because it overemphasizes individuals, produces a tendency to glorify outside talent, degrades those labeled as less able, de-emphasizes the more important systemic issues, and encourages arrogance. See Fighting the War for Talent Is Hazardous to Your Organization's Health, *Organizational Dynamics*, Vol. 29, Issue 4, Spring 2001, pp. 248–59.

19   One should beware of generalizations, but David Keirsey has identified four "temperaments" based on the most widely used theory of personality types, the Myers Briggs. He suggests that the SJ type is most likely to prefer following precise rules rather than exercising initiative. As a very rough indicator, they make up 40 percent of the overall population. See Keirsey, *Please Understand Me II: Temperament, Character and Intelligence*, Del Mar 1998 and the discussion in J. P. Storr, The Nature of Military Thought, PhD thesis, Cranfield University 2002, p. 242. In general, however, certain types select themselves out of uncongenial roles and this type is almost certainly a smaller percentage of the management population. For example, a survey of 8,000 managers attending courses at Ashridge Business School between 2000 and 2003 found that only 5–6 percent were SFs, compared to 25 percent in the population at large. See Melissa Carr, Judy Curd, and Fiona Dent, *MBTI Research into Distribution of Type*, Ashridge Business School 2004.

20   See Leistenschneider, *op. cit.*, p. 91.

21   T. W. Adorno, E. Frenkel-Brunswik, D. J. Levinson, & R. N. Sanford, *The Authoritarian Personality*, Harper 1950. Their model has been challenged, but was broadly supported in a review of it conducted nearly 50 years later. See M. Brewster-Smith, The Authoritarian Personality: A Re-Review 46 Years Later, *Political Psychology* Vol. 18, No. 1, pp. 159–63.

22   Norman Dixon, *On the Psychology of Military Incompetence*, Pimlico 1994. I have been told that it is consistently the most requested book at the library of the UK Defence Academy, the Joint Services Command and Staff College at Shrivenham.

23   See *ibid.*, pp. 257–79 and Storr, *op. cit.*, pp. 240–46. Translating this into Myers-Briggs terms, Storr suggests that there is some correlation between authoritarianism and extreme SJ behavior, especially ESTJ. One should not, of course, condemn all ESTJs, let alone all SJs, as authoritarians. After all, SJs make up about 40 percent of the population.

24 This was precisely what happened in the British Army in both World Wars.

25 Dixon, *op. cit.*, p. 287.

26 Dixon, *op. cit.*, pp. 324–6. Storr suggests that in Myers-Briggs terms they are typically NTs, particularly ENTJs, a type characterized in MBTI terms as "the field marshal" (*ibid.*, p. 256).

27 Storr offers some evidence to this effect on pp. 246–55.

28 Von Moltke opens the *Verordnungen für die Höheren Truppenführer* by pointing out the difficulty an army faces in creating effective training in peace when its real business is war.

29 Collins & Porras, *Built to Last*, p. 117. For other examples of "cult-like cultures" see pp. 116–39.

30 See *ibid.*, pp. 117–21.

31 See Pfeffer & Sutton, *The Knowing–Doing Gap*, pp. 109 ff.

32 See Yves Morieux & Robert Howard, *Strategic Workforce Engagement: Designing the Behaviour of Organizations for Competitive Advantage*, The Boston Consulting Group, August 2000.

33 *Ibid.*, pp. 6–8.

34 *Ibid.*, pp. 19–24.

35 Taiichi Ohno, *Toyota Production System – Beyond Large Scale Production*, Productivity Press 1988, p. xiii.

36 See Felix Barber, Phil Catchings, & Yves Morieux, *Rules of the Game for People Businesses*, The Boston Consulting Group, April 2005.

37 Kaplan and Norton claim that "most organizations have separate processes and separate organizational units for strategic planning and for operational budgeting" (*The Balanced Scorecard*, p. 247). They wrote that in 1996. In the author's experience linking them up is becoming more common, but it is still far from universal.

38 *The Strategy Focused Organization*, p. 274.

39 Jeremy Hope and Robin Fraser have suggested that companies abandon budgeting, make no budget-based commitments to financial markets, and replace budgets with a new performance contract based on a broader set of measures, and a rolling financial forecast. They cite examples of companies which are already doing so. See Who Needs Budgets?, *Harvard Business Review* February 2003, pp. 108–15.

40 Conversation with the author, 28 November 2005.

41 See Hope & Fraser above. They and others have set up the Beyond Budgeting Round Table to help investigate practical ways in which

the limitations of traditional budgeting can be overcome. See www.bbrt.org.

42   The author's view is that not everybody is motivated by money and that financial incentives do not always increase performance. However, it serves many interests to believe otherwise, and the practice of linking performance to pay is almost universal. Thus one of the most experienced academic experts in strategy execution can write: "Execution will fail if no one has skin in the game." See Lawrence G Hrebiniak, *Making Strategy Work*, Wharton School Publishing 2005, p. 186.

43   Minutes of Select Committee Hearing, 28 November 2002, Memorandum by Lord Browne of Madingley, Public Sector Performance Targets and League Tables.

44   *Ibid.*, Interrogation of Witness, p. 6. It may well be that after Browne left BP his own company fell victim to the very thing he was warning against. Whatever happened in the Gulf of Mexico in 2010, there was clearly a failure of direction, and it could well have been connected to target setting.

45   What this means for individuals, and the public, is illustrated by an article written by a doctor in London for the *Daily Mail*. She wanted to prescribe statins to reduce a patient's cholesterol to a level that, based on her judgment, would be safe. She could not get the drugs needed because the National Institute for Clinical Excellence (known, with due irony, as NICE) has set guideline targets for "safe" cholesterol levels which in her view were out of date and wrong. Everyone knew the NICE guidelines were out of date, but she had to follow them (Dr. Sarah Jarvis, Sentenced to Death by NICE, *Daily Mail*, November 28 2006, pp. 46–7).

46   As Michael Goold and the present author advocated a long time ago in Creating a Strategic Control System, *Long Range Planning* Vol. 24, No 3, 1991, which was written at a time when financial controls were ubiquitous but nonfinancial measures were just emerging. The full case for measuring the execution of strategy is made by Michael Goold and John J. Quinn in *Strategic Control – Milestones for Long-Term Performance*, Economist Books 1990.

47   Bossidy, *op. cit.*, p. 226.

48   See Figure 5 in Chapter 2.

49   Robert S. Kaplan & David P. Norton, *The Balanced Scorecard*,

Harvard Business School Press 1996, p. 25. An article, The Balanced Scorecard – Measures that Drive Performance, appeared in *Harvard Business Review*, January–February 1992, pp. 71–9.

50   *Ibid.*, pp. 43 & 149.

51   Robert S. Kaplan & David P. Norton, *The Strategy Focused Organization*, HBS Press 2001, pp. 69–105.

52   Compare what follows with Pfeffer & Sutton, *op. cit.*, pp. 147–60, and for some advice about good practice pp. 173–4.

53   One scholarly assessment of the effects of using a balanced scorecard concluded that it indeed had positive effects when used to align company strategy, but when used as a comprehensive performance measurement system its effects were actually negative. See Geert J. M. Braam & Edwin J. Nijssen, Performance Effects of Using the Balanced Scorecard: A Note on the Dutch Experience, *Long Range Planning* 37, pp. 335–49 (2004).

54   Compare David S. Alberts & Richard E. Hayes, *Understanding Command and Control*, Command and Control Programme Research Publications 2006, Chapter IV.

55   Albert and Hayes use this example to illustrate the principles, deriving from it a system model which they also express as a mathematical equation. See *ibid.*, Chapter III.

56   See *The Balanced Scorecard*, pp. 163 ff for the warning and pp. 226 ff and 283 ff for the recommended practice.

57   See *The Balanced Scorecard*, pp. 30 and pp. 149 ff and *The Strategy Focused Organization*, pp. 69 ff.

58   For example *The Strategy Focused Organization*, p. 76.

59   Kaplan & Norton, *Harvard Business Review* January–February 1992, p. 79.

Chapter Seven

1   The documentation is extensive. See, for example, Samuels, *op. cit.*, pp. 140–43.

2   See Bucholz, *op. cit.*, p. 131 and Michael D. Krause, Moltke and the Origins of the Operational Level of War, *Generalfeldmarschall von Moltke, Bedeutung und Wirkung*, ed. Roland G. Foerster, R. Oldenburg Verlag 1991, p. 142. Napoleon had practiced operational art before him but did not conceptualise it.

3   See Wilhelm Meier-Dörnberg, Moltke und die taktisch-operative Ausbildung im preußisch-deutschen Heer, in Foerster, *op. cit.*, p. 39.

4   See Krause, *op. cit.*, pp. 145 & 147.

5   Arden Bucholz, *Moltke and the German Wars 1864–1871*, Palgrave 2001, p. 191.

6   The nature of the operational realm is implicitly described by Donald N. Sull and Charles Spinosa in Promise-Based Management, *Harvard Business Review*, April 2007, pp. 79–86. The authors refer to the USMC's use of mission-based orders, but do not mention that they also use large numbers of tactical level SOPs which, far from constraining operational direction, actually facilitate it.

7   Meier-Dörnberg, *op. cit.*, pp. 42–3.

8   Von Moltke, Ausgewählte Werke, Erster Band, p. 65.

9   *Ibid.*, pp. 67–8.

10 *Ibid.*, p. 65.

11 Bucholz, *op. cit.*, p. 164.

12 Harrington Emerson, *Twelve Principles of Efficiency*, New York 1913, p. 46.

13 *Ibid.*, p. 245.

14 Donald Sull has suggested that the pursuit of a formula to the point of "rigid devotion to the status quo" is the main reason successful companies fail. Alongside business examples such as Firestone, Laura Ashley, or Xerox, he cites the French Army between the wars. At the time, the French had no concept of operational art. See Why Good Companies Go Bad, *Harvard Business Review*, July–August 1999.

15 Abraham Zaleznik, Managers and Leaders: Are They Different?, *Harvard Business Review*, March–April 1992.

16 Army Doctrine Publication Volume 2: Command, Army Code 71564, Chapter 1, § 0103.

17 *Ibid.*, § 0105.

18 *Ibid.*, § 0104.

19 Brian Howieson & Howard Kahn, Leadership, Management and Command: The Officer's Trinity, *Air Power Leadership: Theory and Practice*, eds. Peter W. Gray & Sebastian Cox, The Stationery Office 2002, p. 15. The concept of the trinity and the thinking behind it, which the author has been able to deepen in conversations with Brian Howieson, informs what follows. The Royal Navy has now accepted a

model of competencies which run across the three areas. Command is described a "exercising the authority," leadership as "influencing the people," and management as "using the resources." See Mike Young & Victor Dulewicz, A Model of Command, Leadership and Management Competency in the British Royal Navy, *Leadership and Organization Development Journal* Vol. 26, No. 3, 2005, Table VII, p. 239.

20   This model of leadership was developed in the 1970s by John Adair, and is the standard model taught in the British Army among others. Adair has expounded it for the business community as well in many seminars and books such as *The Skills of Leadership*, Gower, 1984.

21   Unfortunately, Zaleznik writes about managers and leaders as if he were discussing different individuals. As he also regards leadership as good and management as at best rather dull, the stage was set to turn business leaders into heroes. This is particularly nefarious because he does not mention command, but assumes it is part of leadership and requires the same qualities.

22   Jim Collins, *Good to Great*, pp. 17–40.

23   Tom Peters, *Re-Imagine!*, Dorling Kindersley 2003, p. 44.

24   In the same way, the US military are finding it particularly useful when fighting as part of a coalition, which they are increasingly doing. See David M. Keithly & Stephen P. Ferris, *Auftragstaktik* – or Directive Control – in Joint and Combined Operations, *Parameters*, Autumn 1999, pp. 118–33.

25   Peter Drucker, *The Practice of Management*, Heinemann 1989 (original 1955), p. 133. For his succinct account of management by objectives, see Chapter 11, pp. 119–34.

26   Yoji Akao, *Hoshin Kanri: Policy Deployment for Successful TQM*, Productivity Press 2004. *Hoshin* means compass.

27   For example, Michael Cowley & Ellen Domb, *Beyond Strategic Vision*, Heinemann 1997; Pete Babich, *Hoshin Handbook*, 3rd edition, Total Quality Engineering 2006.

28   Reinhard Höhn, *Scharnhorsts Vermächtnis*, Bernhard und Graefe 1972 (original 1952); *Führungsbrevier der Wirtschaft*, 12th edition, Bad Harzburg 1986; *Die Führing mit Stäben in der Wirtschaft*, Bad Harzburg 1970.

29   Richard Gruserl, *Das Harzburger Modell: Idee und Wirklichkeit*, Verlag Dr Gabler 1973, p. 159. This book offers a detailed critical appraisal of the model covering both theory and practice.

30 *Ibid.*, p. 160.

31 *Ibid.*, p. 246 (author's translation). There is a reason for this mismatch between content and form. Professor Höhn had a dark past. Educated as a lawyer, he joined the Nazi party and the SS in 1933. He subsequently worked for a time for Reinhard Heydrich, one of the most chilling and sinister characters in a singularly malevolent regime. From 1941 to 1943 he worked on a publication which propagated legal justifications for Nazi policy. Höhn was officially de-Nazified in 1955. He may have changed his mind about a number of things, but old habits of mind and values die hard.

32 Eric Bonabeau & Christopher Meyer, Swarm Intelligence, *Harvard Business Review* May 2001.

33 See Eisenhardt & Sull, Strategy as Simple Rules, p. 112.

34 Philip B. Evans & Bob Wolff, Collaboration Rules, *Harvard Business Review* July–August 2005.

APPENDIX I

1   Archduke Charles of Austria (1771–1847) was a highly accomplished commander who led Austrian forces in several campaigns against France. He achieved considerable success during the revolutionary wars in the 1790s before becoming one of Napoleon's most formidable opponents. In 1809 he managed to check Napoleon at Aspern–Essling before suffering a major defeat at Wagram. In his writings, he raises the benefits of maintaining security and holding strategic points to the level of absolute principles, which he in fact departed from in practice.

BIBLIOGRAPHY

Adair, John. *The Skills of Leadership*, Gower 1984.

Argyris, Chris & Donald A. Schon, *Organizational Learning: A Theory of Action Perspective*, Addison-Wesley 1978.

Barry, Quintin, *The Franco-Prussian War 1870–71, Volume 1*, Helion & Co. 2007.

Beer, Michael & Russell A. Eisenstat, How to Have an Honest Conversation, *Harvard Business Review*, February 2004, pp. 82–9.

Bonabeau, Eric & Christopher Meyer, Swarm Intelligence, *Harvard Business Review*, May 2001.

Bossidy, Larry & Ram Charan, *Execution*, Random House 2002.

Bucholz, Arden, *Moltke and the German Wars 1864–1871*, Palgrave 2001.

Collins, James C. & Jerry I. Porras, *Built to Last*, London 1994.

Collins, Jim, *From Good to Great*, Random House 2001.

Collis, David J. & Cynthia Montgomery, Competing on Resources: Strategy in the 1990s, *Harvard Business Review*, July–August 1995, pp. 118–28.

Collis, David J. & Michael G. Rukstad, Can You Say What Your Strategy Is?, *Harvard Business Review*, April 2008.

Cooper, Belton E., *Death Traps*, Presidio Press 1998.

Demeter, Karl, *The German Officer-Corps in Society and State 1650–1945*, Weidenfeld & Nicolson 1965.

Dixon, Norman, *On the Psychology of Military Incompetence*, Pimlico 1994.

Doz, Yves & Mikko Kosonen, *Fast Strategy: How Strategic Agility Will Help You Stay Ahead of the Game*, Wharton School Publishing 2008.

Drucker, Peter, *The Practice of Management*, Heinemann 1989.

Eisenhardt, Kathleen M. & Donald N. Sull, Strategy as Simple Rules, *Harvard Business Review*, January 2001, pp. 107–16.

Erickson, John, *The Road to Berlin*, Weidenfeld & Nicolson 1983.

Evans, Philip B. & Bob Wolff, Collaboration Rules, *Harvard Business Review*, July–August 2005.

French, David, *Raising Churchill's Army*, Oxford University Press 2000.

Gleick, James, *Chaos*, Vintage 1998.

Goold, Michael & Andrew Campbell, *Designing Effective Organizations*, Jossey-Bass 2002.

Goold, Michael & John J. Quinn, *Strategic Control – Milestones for Long-Term Performance*, Economist Books 1990.

Goold, Michael & Stephen Bungay, Creating a Strategic Control System, *Long Range Planning*, Vol. 24, No 3, 1991.

Gordon, Andrew, *The Rules of the Game – Jutland and British Naval Command*, John Murray 1996.

Grant, Robert M., The Resource-Based Theory of Competitive Advantage: Implications for Strategy Formulation, *California Management Review*, Vol. 33, No. 3, Spring 1991, pp. 114–35.

Hamel, Gary & C. K. Prahalad, *Competing for the Future*, Harvard Business School Press 1994.

Hayward, Mathew L. A., Violina P. Rindova, & Timothy G. Pollock, Believing One's Own Press: The Causes and Consequences of CEO Celebrity, *Strategic Management Journal*, 25, 2004, pp. 637–53.

Howard, Michael, *The Franco-Prussian War*, Rupert Hart-Davis 1961.

Hrebiniak, Laurence G., *Making Strategy Work*, Wharton School Publishing 2005.

Hughes, Daniel J. (ed.) *Moltke on the Art of War*, Ballantine Books, New York, 1993.

Kahan, James P., D. Robert Worley, & Cathleen Sasz, *Understanding Commanders' Information Needs*, RAND 1989.

Kaplan, Robert S. & David P. Norton, *The Balanced Scorecard*, Harvard Business School Press 1996.

Kaplan, Robert S. & David P. Norton, *The Strategy Focused Organization*, HBS Press 2001.

Klein, Gary, *Sources of Power*, MIT Press 1998.

Klein, Gary, *The Power of Intuition*, Doubleday 2003.

Mankins, Michael C. & Richard Steele, *Closing the Strategy-to-Performance Gap – Techniques for Turning Great Strategy into Great Performance*, Marakon Associates 2005.

McGregor, Douglas, *The Human Side of Enterprise*, Penguin 1987.

Michaels, Ed, Helen Handfield-Jones, & Beth Axelrod, *The War for Talent*, Harvard Business School Press 2001.

Miller, Susan, David Wilson, & David Hickson, Beyond Planning: Strategies for Successfully Implementing Strategic Decisions, *Long Range Planning*, 37, 2004.

Mintzberg, Henry, Crafting Strategy, *Harvard Business Review*, July/August 1987, pp. 66–75.

Mintzberg, Henry, *The Rise and Fall of Strategic Planning*, Prentice Hall 1994.

Neilson, Gary L., Karla L. Martin, & Elizabeth Powers, The Secrets to Successful Strategy Execution, *Harvard Business Review*, June 2008.

Neiman, Robert A., *Execution Plain and Simple*, McGraw-Hill 2004.

Paret, Peter, *Clausewitz and the State*, Oxford University Press 1976.

Pfeffer, Jeffrey & Robert I. Sutton, *The Knowing–Doing Gap*, Harvard Business School Press 2000.

Samuels, Martin, *Command or Control – Command: Training and Tactics in the British and German Armies 1888–1918*, Frank Cass 1995.

Simpson, Daniel G., Why Most Strategic Planning Is a Waste of Time and What You Can Do about It, *Long Range Planning*, Vol. 31, No. 3, pp. 476–80 and Vol. 31, No. 4, pp. 623–7.

Stacey, Ralph, *Managing Chaos*, Kogan Page 1992.

Sull, Donald N. & Charles Spinosa, Promise-Based Management, *Harvard Business Review*, April 2007, pp. 79–86.

Vincent, Edgar, Nelson and Mission Command, *History Today*, June 2003.

Wawro, Geoffrey, *The Franco-Prussian War*, Cambridge University Press 2003.

Welch, Jack & John Byrne, *Jack*, Headline 2001.

Williamson, Peter & Michael Hay, Strategic Staircases: Planning the Capabilities Required for Success, *Long Range Planning*, Vol. 24, No. 4, 1991, pp. 36–43.

Wilson, Andrew, *War Gaming*, Penguin 1970.

Yardsley, Ivan & Andrew Kakabadse, Understanding Mission Command: A Model for Developing Competitive Advantage in a Business Context, *Strategic Change*, January–April 2007.

Young, Desmond, *Rommel*, Collins 1950.

Young, Mike & Victor Dulewicz, A Model of Command, Leadership and Management Competency in the British Royal Navy, *Leadership and Organization Development Journal*, Vol. 26, No. 3, 2005.

Zaleznik, Abraham, Managers and Leaders: Are They Different?, *Harvard Business Review*, March–April 1992.

INDEX

ACKNOWLEDGMENTS

Winston Churchill once described writing a book as an adventure with four phases. "To begin with it was a toy, an amusement," he observed, "then it became a mistress, and then a master, and then a tyrant." As in so many things, he was right. Many have accompanied me on the adventure, offering encouragement, complicity, advice, and consolation, through each of its phases.

Early encouragement was offered by Damian McKinney, who provided the first accomplices. They included Andy Williams, Graham Smith, and Mark Bouch, but I owe a particular debt to Iain Dixon with whom I spent many hours in workshops playing with the new toy and on long walks as the amusing dalliance turned into a serious affair.

Further walks ensued with David Slavin, who arranged assignations with the mistress. Our many hours of conversation helped concepts to mature, but above all we were able to test and refine practices and techniques. We mustered further accomplices in the form of the Mission Command Dining Group, which included David Benest, Simon Chapman, Eitan Shamir, Jim Storr, Richard Sullivan, Aidan Walsh, and Stephen White. Aidan's own insightful analyses of Taylorism, the Austrian economists, and rule-based behaviour added rigour to some emerging thinking.

I was now in the power of the mistress and sure enough, she turned into a master. My colleagues at the Ashridge Strategic Management Centre – Marcus Alexander, Felix Barber, Andrew Campbell, Anthony Freeling, Michael Goold, and Joe Whitehead – helped me to deal with the master's demands. A common challenge was: "That's all very well in practice, but how does it work in theory?" Sessions with flipcharts and whiteboards tightened up the conceptual frameworks and teaching together helped to hone the messages.

As the ideas matured, Felix helped me to turn the approaches described in the book into the open programme "Making Strategy

Happen", which we deliver together at Ashridge Business School twice a year. We would be unable to do that without the constant support and endless patience of Melinda Pooley and Angela Munro at ASMC. Andrew has helped me to work through various versions of "strategy briefing" so that it can be done in a short workshop, and through his work on evolutionary marketing Anthony has helped to clarify some of the conceptual links to evolution and OODA loops.

My old friend Peter Williamson, the co-inventor of the strategic staircase, helped to work through the implications of uncertainty in strategy, a theme we have by no means exhausted.

Sometimes the master can demand exclusive attention which can only be given in extended periods free from disturbance. Dominic Houlder offered more conversational walks in Skye, and Karen Thomson and Gavin Strachan provided me with quiet sojourns in their cottage in the Oxford countryside, without which the manuscript would never have been written.

It is as a manuscript that the master becomes a tyrant, rather in the way a teenager does. As far as you are concerned it is ready to go out into the world and be read, but it still hangs around at home whinging at you that it wants to be written a bit more. At this point you need moral encouragement as well as practical help, and Poul Bukh has provided plenty of both. Importantly, and very practically, he understands the intimate relationship between good writing and good wine. Among his inspirations was a visit to the Moltke House in Copenhagen. By some happy chance it turned out to house a rather fine restaurant.

My indefatigably enthusiastic agent David Grossman found a publisher in the form of Nicholas Brealey, who finally freed me from the tyrant's grip. He has sent it on its way dressed in a jacket far more striking than I had thought possible. My editor Sally Lansdell has made the proofreading process far less painful than it usually is.

Kai Peters of Ashridge has been a constant source of encouragement over the years, provided platforms for me to write and talk about what he calls "cool Prussian stuff," and has shown the patience of Job as I struggled with the tyrant. Without Ashridge it could never have been done, and Toby Roe and his team have helped greatly in getting the tyrant out of the door. Poul Bukh has provided a platform to send it off to Scandinavia and, thanks to Patrick Forth of BCG, it has even headed towards Australia.

So I was free at last.

Along the course of the whole adventure I have benefited enormously from clients and course participants. It is through working with clients that I have learned how to make the ideas work in practice, and it is through teaching courses that I have learned how to put the messages across. Neither task is yet complete, but things have come a long way. Some who played a significant part are John Reid-Dodick, David Roblin, Eliot Forster, Colin Ewen, Anne-Sophie Curet, Paddy Lowe, and Paul Hauff. Paul serendipitously managed to get me introduced to the descendants of the Moltke family living in London. They are as talented, as charming, and as self-effacing as one might expect.

As the tyrant finally leaves home, one forgives the tyranny and thinks back to the good times. It is on its own now and I am not sure what it will get up to. I hope it finds some indulgent readers, but I know it is not perfect. I accept responsibility for that. The final result is all my fault.

And finally I must thank Kam for putting up with it all.

AGILE STRATEGY

How to flourish in an *uncertain world*

The business environment is uncertain and constantly changing. Dealing with it requires organisational agility, and by implication, agile strategy. But what is agile strategy and how do you achieve it?

Any business needs to provide a direction of travel, focus efforts, and make better decisions. It needs to be able to adapt to unforeseen circumstances and move faster than the competition without disrupting operations.

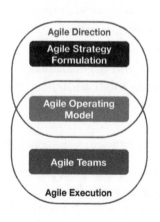

Agile direction is about formulating strategy in a way that creates both focus and flexibility, an approach we call directional strategy.

Agile execution is about using leading through intent as an organizational operating model which can translate that directional strategy into focused flexible action.

Agile execution relies on enabling and supporting agile teams to adapt and make decisions as the situation changes.

Find out more by visiting agilestrategy.co.uk, where you will find insight, content, and debate about how to develop winning strategies in an uncertain world.

Agile Strategy is a collaboration between
Stephen Bungay (Author of *The Art of Action*)
and Mark Bouch (Leading Change Limited)

Would you like your people to read this book?

If you would like to discuss how you could bring these ideas to your team, we would love to hear from you. Our titles are available at competitive discounts when purchased in bulk across both physical and digital formats. We can offer bespoke editions featuring corporate logos, customized covers, or letters from company directors in the front matter can also be created in line with your special requirements.

We work closely with leading experts and organizations to bring forward-thinking ideas to a global audience. Our books are designed to help you be more successful in work and life.

For further information, or to request a catalogue, please contact: **business@johnmurrays.co.uk** **sales-US@nicholasbrealey.com** (North America only)

Nicholas Brealey Publishing is an imprint of John Murray Press.